CO-AYH-216

Developmental Tasks
Resource Guide For
Elementary School Children

by

Charles M. Harris

and

Nancy D. Gardenhour

The Scarecrow Press, Inc.

Metuchen, N.J.   1976

55686

Library of Congress Cataloging in Publication Data

Harris, Charles M   1936-
  Developmental tasks resource guide for elementary
school children.

    Includes indexes.
    1. Child development--Audio-visual aids--Catalogs.
2. Child development--Bibliography. 3. Socialization--
Audio-visual aids--Catalogs. 4. Audio-visual materials
--Catalogs. I. Gardenhour, Nancy D., joint author.
II. Title.
LB1117.H32 1976   016.3721   75-21740
ISBN 0-8108-0877-3

Copyright © 1976 by Charles M. Harris
and Nancy D. Gardenhour

Manufactured in the United States of America

PREFACE

The Developmental Tasks Resource Guide for Elementary School Children is an annotated guide to books, filmstrips, films, records, transparencies, audio-tapes and video-tapes, focusing on the major developmental tasks of childhood. In compiling this Guide, the authors acknowledge the significant challenges confronting children in their socialization. Beginning with the transition from home to school, each child must individually engage those major tasks which are common to all children within the culture. In this context, the elementary school child's facility in the language arts makes bibliotherapy an appropriate technique for facilitating task achievement. The identification of relevant media presented in this Guide is intended to assist teachers, counselors, school psychologists, librarians, parents, and the many others who contribute to the personal and social development of children.

Any work focusing on developmental tasks should acknowledge the contributions of former writers, especially Tryon, Lilienthal, and Havighurst. Tryon and Lilienthal effectively conceptualized developmental tasks within a comprehensive, coherent framework. Havighurst popularized developmental tasks and related them to educational practice. In this Guide, we propose to operationalize developmental tasks through the identification of relevant media. Acknowledgment is also due our colleagues, students, and families for their encouragement and support.

This Guide is dedicated to Kevin and Dana who, like all children, must successfully accomplish the major developmental tasks of childhood.

Charles M. Harris
Madison College

Nancy D. Gardenhour
Frederick County Public Schools
Frederick County, Virginia

CONTENTS

55686

55686

HOW TO USE THE GUIDE

Bibliotherapy: Bibliotherapy, which involves providing individuals with appropriate audio and/or visual material, is a strategy which is available to nearly all persons interested in assisting children toward socialization. Since a variety of current publications describe the process of bibliotherapy, a detailed discussion will not be included in this Guide. It should be noted, however, that bibliotherapy is a therapeutic process. Accordingly, it involves considerably more than simply making materials available to a person with a problem or a task to achieve. One should be knowledgeable concerning the strengths and limitations of the therapeutic process. Such knowledge can increase the possibility of contributing to the personal and social development of children.

Task Definitions: In the process of achieving personal and social development, each child must successfully integrate certain key experiences and relationships. As Tryon and Lilienthal have stated,

> Developmental tasks are those major common tasks that face all individuals within a given society or sub-culture of society.... There are two major areas of force which interact to set these tasks. The first are the expectancies and pressures of society.... The second are the changes that take place in the physical organism through the processes of maturation.[1]

Eight major developmental tasks confronting elementary school children have been organized in two categories: self development and social development. The following task definitions are intended to assist users in the efficient selection of appropriate media.

Tasks for Self Development

DEVELOPING PERSONAL INDEPENDENCE: Establishing a pattern of self-reliant behavior evidencing a growing independence from parental and adult support.

---

1. Tryon, C. and Lilienthal III, J. W. "Developmental Tasks: I. The Concept and Its Importance," Fostering Mental Health in Our Schools, 1950 Yearbook, ASCD, Washington, D. C.: National Education Association, 1950, pp. 77 and 78.

DEVELOPING PERSONAL VALUES: Developing an understanding of formal and informal rules of fairness in work and play. Value orientations vary according to social setting (home, school, community) and participants (peers, adults).

ACCEPTING AND VALUING ONESELF AS A DEVELOPING ORGANISM: Developing a sense of one's worth, including one's ideas, feelings, and physical characteristics.

DEVELOPING PHYSICAL SKILLS: Becoming competent in the common physical games and activities of childhood.

Tasks for Social Development

DEVELOPING SYMBOL SYSTEMS: Achieving competency in the use and meaning of communication concepts, including reading, writing, and calculating.

DEVELOPING PEER RELATIONS: Developing skills in initiating and maintaining associations with age-mates.

LEARNING ONE'S SOCIAL ROLE: Becoming aware of and adopting patterns of behavior considered to be socially appropriate for persons of the same sex.

ESTABLISHING RELATIONS WITH SOCIAL GROUPS AND INSTITUTIONS: Becoming a functioning member of common social groups and institutions, including ethnic groups, school, community, and nation.

Organization: The Developmental Tasks Resource Guide for Elementary School Children is organized in three parts. Part I, Tasks for Self Development, includes four chapters of annotated media entries related to independence, values, self-esteem, and physical skills. Part II, Tasks for Social Development, includes four chapters of annotated media entries related to communication concepts, peer relations, social role, and social groups. Within each of the eight chapters in Parts I and II, annotated entries are organized according to primary and intermediate levels. Primary Level entries are generally appropriate for children in Kindergarten through grade three. Intermediate Level entries are generally appropriate for children in grades four through six. Part III, Indexes, includes author, subject, title indexes and a publishers' list.

Using the Guide: Systematic use of the Guide involves the indexes and the Alpha-Numeric code assigned to each entry in Parts I and II. Indexes designate the location of each entry by an Alpha-Numeric code not by page number. Within each Alpha-Numeric code, the ALPHA component is a two-letter abbreviation derived from the chapter title. Alpha codes for each chapter follow:

Chapter title	Alpha Code
Developing Personal Independence	In
Developing Personal Values	Va
Accepting and Valuing Oneself as a Developing Organism	Ac
Developing Physical Skills	Ps
Developing Symbol Systems	Sy
Developing Peer Relations	Pr
Learning One's Social Role	Sr
Establishing Relations With Social Groups and Institutions	Sg

The NUMERIC component is the serially ordered number of each entry within a chapter. For example, within Chapter One, the Alpha-Numeric code for the first entry is In 1; the second entry, In 2, etc. Within Chapter Two, the Alpha-Numeric code for the first entry is Va 1; the second entry, Va 2, etc.

In Parts I, Tasks for Self Development, and II, Tasks for Social Development, users will find basic information for each entry.

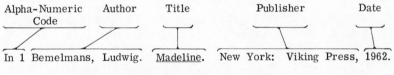

Alpha-Numeric Code — Author — Title — Publisher — Date

In 1 Bemelmans, Ludwig. Madeline. New York: Viking Press, 1962.

Madeline is the smallest, bravest and....

Annotation

The citations for audio-visual media will include specific information such as color or black-and-white for films, the number of frames for filmstrips, rpms for records, etc.

While users may benefit from a random perusal of chapters and topics, systematic use of the indexes and Alpha-Numeric codes is recommended. A Publishers' List is provided to assist in the acquisition of specific media.

PART I

TASKS FOR SELF DEVELOPMENT

Chapter 1

DEVELOPING PERSONAL INDEPENDENCE

Primary

COURAGE

In 1   Bemelmans, Ludwig. Madeline. New York: Viking, 1962.
Madeline is the smallest, bravest and most adventurous
of twelve little girls in a Parisian boarding school.

In 2   Brave little duck and cold north wind. Glenview, Ill.: Educational Projections Corporation, n.d.
Stresses the importance of independence by telling the Indian fable of Shingebiss and the Great North Wind. (series
--35mm film)

In 3   Brenner, Anita. A hero by mistake. New York: Scott,
1953.
A frightened Indian overcomes his fears and finally becomes a hero.

In 4   Napoli, Guillier. Adventure at Mont-Saint-Michel. New
York: McGraw-Hill, 1966.
The changing tide and the mysteries of the sea are sources
of wonder for Yan and Centauree, the children of fisherman
on the coast of Normandy. One day Centauree sets out to
find for herself where the sea goes while the tide is out.
Bold illustrations help tell of her narrow escape when she is
marooned on a lonely, rocky island in the shadows of Mont-
Saint-Michel.

In 5   Sometimes I feel. (filmstrips/records) New York: Learn-
Corporation of America, n.d.
At the heart of self-expression is the ability to recognize
and accept one's own emotions and the reactions they sometimes provoke. These sensitive and often humorous stories
explain how people deal with fear, anger, loneliness, the
need for friendship. While learning about their own feelings,
children will discover that others often have the same feelings, too. Included are "Giants Are Very Brave People,"
"Boy, Was I Mad!" "Maxie," "The Blah" and "Did You
Ever?"

3

DECISION MAKING

In 6   Beginning responsibility - Being on time. Chicago: Coronet
        Instructional Films, 1956.
        Explains the importance of being prompt by using firemen
        and train engineers as examples. Presents Jimmy who learns
        to be on time by proper planning and estimating how long it
        takes to get things done.

In 7   Beginning responsibility - Getting ready for school. Chicago:
        Coronet Instructional Films, 1969. (16mm film, 11 min-
        utes)
        Presents Ricky with the problem of oversleeping. Reveals
        that after a night with his friend Pete, he understands that
        he can use his time wisely and become better organized.

In 8   Clark, Ann Holan. This for that. San Carlos, Cal.: Gold-
        en Gate Junior Books, 1965.
        Wise Grandfather helps the desert Indian boy learn to
        make the right choices.

In 9   Hoban, Russell. Nothing to do. New York: Harper, 1964.
        Walter can never think of anything to do until his father
        gives him a magic "something to do" stone, providing a use-
        ful lesson for children that they can think for themselves.

In 10   Johnson, Crockett. Harold and the purple crayon. New York:
        Harper, 1955.
        Fantasy of a small boy who decides to go for a walk one
        night. He uses his purple crayon to draw all the things
        necessary for a successful walk--a moon, a path, houses,
        the ocean, a boat, a mountain, a balloon, and finally his own
        room again. Stimulates children in planning their own imag-
        inative adventures. Also available in a film.

In 11   Leaf, Munro. Wee Gillis. New York: Viking, 1938.
        Wee Gillis has to decide whether to call cows or stalk
        stags. This story tells how he decides.

In 12   Ward, Lynd. The biggest bear. Boston: Houghton, 1952.
        All the other barns in the valley had a bearskin and Johnny
        didn't want his to be different. He decided to shoot a bear.
        He met one, but did not shoot it. Instead he brought it home.
        When it grew too big, he took it out into the woods, but the
        bear came back. It was up to Johnny to find a solution to
        his problem.

INITIATIVE

In 13   Arthur's world. New York: Sterling Educational Films, n.d.
        (16mm film, optical sound, color, 10 minutes)
        Delightful story of Arthur's yearning to see the world be-

yond his backyard fence. Features an imaginative view of
the world and its surprising landscapes in addition to a close
look at wonders to be found at home.

In 14   Beskow, Elsa. Pelle's new suit. New York: Harper, 1929.
A Swedish boy has to work at many different things before
he can earn his new suit.

In 15   Caudill, Rebecca. Did you carry the flag today, Charley?
New York: Holt, 1966.
A really delightful, tender story of curious, five-year-old
Charley who is just beginning to attend school in the Appala-
chian Mountains. No one expects it to happen, but somehow,
independent little Charley does manage to receive the highest
honor in school, being chosen to carry the flag for having
been the most helpful.

In 16   Developing responsibility. Chicago: Coronet Instructional
Films, n.d. (11 minutes, sound, color)
Tells the story of how Frank assumes his everyday responsibilities at home, at school, and on his paper route, and is
rewarded by being given a pedigreed dog by a man on his
paper route who has observed his acceptance of responsibility.

In 17   Fritz, Jean. Fish head. New York: Coward, 1972.
An independent cat finds himself at sea and has to cope
with many unusual experiences. He finally wins the respect
of his fellow sailors.

In 18   Keats, Ezra Jack. My dog is lost! New York: Harper,
1969.
Juanito was sad and lonely. Just arriving in New York
from Puerto Rico, he only knew Spanish and he'd lost his
dog. He found that sign language helped bridge the language
gap with other children he met when they couldn't understand
him. He not only found his dog, but got a good notion of the
neighborhood and a lot of new friends.

In 19   Lexau, Joan M. Benjie on his own. Los Angeles: Dial,
1970.
Benjie's grandmother always walks him to and from school,
even though Benjie is sure he is too big for that. One after-
noon, Granny doesn't appear. Benjie is worried, but decides
he will just prove he can go alone. It isn't so easy. He's
not sure which way to turn at the corners; a big dog chases
him; some bullies threaten him; and he's still worried about
Granny. He tries not to cry. At last, he gets home and
finds his grandmother is very sick. It's up to Benjie to get
help.

In 20   Udray, Janice May. Mary Jo's grandmother. Racine, Wis.:
Whitman, 1970.
Mary Joe keeps her head and helps to comfort her grand-

mother when she falls while they are alone. Mary Jo also
thinks of a way to get help for her grandmother.

RUNAWAYS

In 21   Hitte, Kathryn. Boy, was I mad. New York: Parents,
         1969.
         A little boy runs away from home only to wander in a
circle and wind up in front of his own home.

In 22   Lobel, Arnold. Small pig. New York: Harper, 1969.
         The small pig likes mud, but the farmer's wife does not,
so the small pig gets out to find a nice, muddy place to live.
After trying a swamp and a junkyard, small pig finds what
he thinks is mud in the city, but just as he begins to wallow,
it becomes apparent that the mud is really cement.

In 23   Shortall, Leonard. Andy the dog walker. New York: Mor-
         row, 1968.
         When Andy becomes acquainted with a professional dog
walker, he longs for the job himself so he can walk Charlie,
a neighbor's dog.   How can be prove that he's responsible
enough?   His chance comes when Charlie runs away, and
Andy's search for the dog turns into an exploration of New
York City.   In this lively story young readers encounter a
joy which is peculiar to large cities.

SELF-RELIANCE: ADULTS

In 24   Beginning responsibility: doing things for yourself. Chicago:
         Coronet Instructional Films, 1969. (color, 49 frames,
         sound, 11 minutes)
         Shows a small boy as he learns to do things for himself
at home and at school and develops the idea that the satisfaction of self-reliance and of learning will motivate children to
assume responsibility.   Stresses the need to learn by watching others by trial and error, by asking for help, and by
practice.   Pictures and discusses both individual and cooperative efforts in schools.

In 25   Bennett, Rainy. The secret hiding place. Cleveland: World,
         1960.
         Small children who are themselves "pet of the herd" will
understand Little Hippo, who wanted to be alone, but not too
alone.   How he finds a secret hiding place makes an entertaining tale.

In 26   Cole, William. Frances face-maker. Cleveland: World,
         1963.
         When a little girl refuses to go to bed, her father devises
a scheme where she will go to sleep by her own free will.

In 27 Doing things yourself. Los Angeles: Churchill Films, 1969.
       (filmstrip, color, 49 frames)
       Teaches children to become independent by performing for
       themselves without the help from others.

In 28 Ets, Marie Hall. Nine days to Christmas. New York: Vik-
       ing, 1959.
       Ceci, a little Mexican girl, is excited because now she is
       old enough to buy a piñata for her first Christmas party.

In 29 Getting along in school--doing things for yourself. Series.
       Chicago: Coronet Instructional Films, 1969. (color, 49
       frs. sound filmstrip)
       Uses a picture story about a lazy prince to motivate chil-
       dren to become more self-reliant and to learn the satisfac-
       tion that self-reliance can bring.

In 30 Guilfoile, Elizabeth. Have you seen my brother? Chicago:
       Follett, 1962.
       Andrew asks this question of everyone, but it is really
       Andrew who is lost--he doesn't want to feel dependent upon
       anyone.

In 31 Leaf, Monroe. Gordon a goat. New York: Scholastic, 1971.
       Gordon decides not to be like all the other goats and fol-
       low the leader.

In 32 Steiner, Charlotte. I'd rather stay with you. New York:
       Seabury, 1965.
       A baby kangaroo is afraid to make his appearance outside
       his mother's pouch. He has to be coaxed, wheedled, and
       finally becomes persuaded to leave the pouch and take his
       place in the world.

                        SELF-RELIANCE: PEERS

In 33 Brown, Myra Berry. Benjy's blanket. New York: Watts,
       1962.
       Everywhere that Benjy went, his ragged baby blanket was
       sure to go--leaving him wide open to the teasing of others.
       This is the story of the generous act he performs to break
       with the past and prove that he can live without his security
       blanket.

In 34 Brown, Myra Berry. First night away from home. New
       York: Watts, 1960.
       Stevie was so excited at the prospect of spending the night
       away from home that he almost forgot his pajames. But he
       was not going to admit it to anyone. Happily, his mother
       came to the rescue finally, but he had not lost his standing
       of being independent.

In 35   Fiskey, Margaret.   Chicken little, count to ten.   Chicago:
            Children's Press, 1946.
            Not one of ten animals can tell Chicken Little how to
         drink, so he has to find out for himself.

In 36   Lionni, Leo.   Swimmy.   New York: Pantheon, 1963.
            When all his brothers and sisters have been swallowed by
         a hungry Tuna--Swimmy the only black fish of the entire
         school, is left alone in dangerous waters! He decides to ex-
         plore the unknown depths of the ocean, until at last he de-
         vises for himself and his newly adopted brothers and sisters
         a safer way to live in this world.

In 37   Won't you be my friend.   New York: Education Activities,
            n. d.   (record)
            These songs guide the child in emotional and social aware-
         ness; to help him better understand the concept of growing;
         help him feel good about what he is able to do by himself;
         reassure him he is not alone with his feelings of being little,
         afraid, angry or sad.   Included are rhythm games and songs
         to help children learn one another's names, to enrich dra-
         matic play, and to enjoy the experience of taking turns through
         rhythmic activities.   There is a variety of musical styles--
         calypso, rock, folk, pop and country.   The music provides
         both structured and creative ways to express feelings through
         songs and body movement.

Intermediate

COURAGE

In 38   Anderson, Lonzo.   Zeb.   Illustrated by Peter Burchard.
            Westminster, Md.:   Knopf, 1966.
            When Zeb's father and brother are drowned as they all
         attempt to ford the Delaware River in the 1680's, he over-
         comes near-panic and goes on westward with only his dog
         and an ax.   Without his guns or supplies, he manages to
         clear a place in the wilderness ready to receive the remain-
         der of his family and is rewarded with the satisfaction of
         the feeling of independence.

In 39   _____.   Zeb and his family.   New York: Viking, 1963.
            After the death of his father and brothers, Zeb must
         face the wild west and clear a place for the rest of his
         family.   From his advantures he learns responsibility and
         independence.

In 40   Annixter, Jane and Paul.   Wagon Scout.   New York: Holi-
            day House, 1965.
            A wagon train of Virginians on their way to California in
         the post-Civil War period encounters many dangers and hard-
         ships.   When their leader dies, his son, Eric, is forced to

learn how to assume responsibility and how to meet the
crises of the frontier.

In 41   Baastad, Babbis Friis. Kristy's courage. New York: Harcourt, 1965.
Seven-year-old Kristy, disfigured and with a speech de-
fect as a result of an accident is rejected by her classmates.
Her family, also is preoccupied with problems of a new baby.
When Kristy runs away, however, they are awakened to her
need for love and understanding and eventually she finds
courage.

In 42   Barth, Edna Day. Luis was lost. Boston: Little, Brown,
1971.
Luis, small for his age and newly come to New York City
from Puerto Rico, is determined to walk to school by himself. He is sure he knows the way, but he has not counted
on a broken water main, a friendly policeman who did not
speak Spanish, or the locked door when he finally got to
school late.

In 43   Bloch, Marie Halun. Aunt America. New York: Atheneum,
1963.
Lesya lives in a small town in the Ukraine, which is
thrown into great excitement when it is learned that her
Aunt is coming from America. Conflicting ideas of freedom
are finally resolved by a courageous act on Lesya's part.

In 44   Bosworth, J. Allen. White water, still water. Garden City,
N.Y.: Doubleday, 1966.
Thirteen-year-old Chris Holm, considered a disappointing
dreamer by his Norwegian father, accidentally launches his
raft and himself on a Canadian river. He rides the swift
current for a hundred miles before he is able to land. Then
he starts the long walk through the wilderness, racing time,
to reach home before winter. A fascinating story of endurance and adventure.

In 45   Brecht, Edith. Timothy's Hawk. New York: Viking, 1965.
Timothy and his mother are depressed when his job-hunt-
ing father moves the family to an abandoned farm. At first
Timothy feels utterly alone, but grows in his appreciation
for the country as friendly neighbors make the first overtures. When his pet rabbit is threatened by a hawk, Timothy
uses his head and does the best he can, demonstrating courage and confidence gained from his new environment.

In 46   Brink, Carol Ryrie. Caddie Woodlawn. Illustrated by Kate
Seredy. New York: Macmillan, 1935.
When the Woodlawn family moves from New England to
Wisconsin, they bring with them their New England customs.
Caddie, eleven years old and a spirited tomboy, makes
friends in the Indian village and initiates a Boston cousin

into the ways of the Wisconsin frontier. Life is not easy but
when the opportunity to leave comes in the form of an inheri-
tance in England the family decides to remain. The happiness
and satisfaction found by the Woodlawns in their new home is
the result of their complete adjustment to pioneer life.

In 47   . Magical Melons. New York: Macmillan, 1944.
        A pleasant atmosphere of family life pervades these new
adventures of Caddie Woodlawn and her brothers. Although
told as separate stories, and of somewhat uneven quality,
they read with enough continuity to give the impression of
one narrative. Caddie, who is about 10 in the first of them,
grows up slightly as they progress.

In 48   Catherall, Arthur. Prisoners in the snow. West Caldwell,
        N. J. : Lothrop, 1967.
        Trapped in their undamaged Austrian farmhouse by an ava-
lanche caused by a plane crash, two children and their lame
grandfather risk life and limb to rescue the pilot, who is
buried against the collapsing roof of their shed. Their clever
use of things at hand and their adventure story and lesson on
the value of clear thinking.

In 49   Clark, Billy C. The trail of the hunter's horn. New York:
        Putnam's, 1957.
        A sensitive, beautifully written story of a young boy in the
Kentucky mountains who is given a pup that is blind in one
eye. Bitterly ashamed of the dog at first, the boy comes to
awareness of his responsibility for helping it to overcome its
handicap, and in the process, he takes a long step toward
maturity. The story shows great understanding of a young
boy's reaction to a difficult situation.

In 50   Clymer, Eleanor. My brother, Stevie. New York: Holt,
        1967.
        If you live in a big city project with a poor grandmother
and an eight-year-old brother who seems to be becoming de-
linquent, life can seem terribly hard. That's how it is for
twelve-year-old Annie Jenner until a teacher, a dog and her
own courage help her change her life.

In 51   Corbett, Scott. Cop's kid. Boston: Little, Brown, 1968.
        Story of a policeman's son who was in the grocery store
at the time it was robbed. He decides to follow up the clues
himself and ends up face to face with the robber.

In 52   Corcoran, Barbara. The long journey. New York: Athene-
        um, 1970.
        Grandfather, with whom orphaned (13-year-old) Laurie has
lived from the age of three in an abandoned mining town, is
going blind and because he fears hospitals and orphanages,
Laurie must ride horseback across the state of Montana to
fetch Uncle Arthur. Since everything Laurie knows of the

outside world is second-hand, the things she sees and the people she meets on her eventual journey are new experiences-- some frightening, some astonishing, some rewarding. Though in retrospect the story as a whole strains credibility, Laurie is a believable character holding the reader's interest and concern from beginning to end of the enjoyable narrative.

In 53 Dalgliesh, Alice. The courage of Sarah Noble. New York: Scribner, 1954.
Here is a remarkable book for younger readers--a true pioneer adventure, written for easy reading but without any sacrifice of literary quality or depth of feeling. Sarah, though only eight, was her father's companion on a grueling and dangerous journey to build a new home in the Connecticut wilderness of 1707, and she succeeded well in following her mother's advice to "keep up your courage, Sarah Noble." When, however, the log cabin was finished and her father was leaving her with the Indians while he went back alone to get the rest of the family, Sarah, who had been very brave, confessed that she had lost her courage. To this her father made the discerning and heartening reply, "To be afraid and to be brave is the best courage of all."

In 54 Everyday courage and a common sense. Chicago: Coronet Instructional Films, 1969. (16mm)
Reminds the student of the experiences which require courage tempered by common sense. Illustrates physical courage by a boy going off a high diver and fire-fighters parachuting into a flaming forest. Recalls that courage is needed in everyday activities where social acceptance, self-esteem and morals and personal values are at stake.

In 55 Fante, John. Bravo, burro! New York: Hawthorn, 1970.
Juan Cabriz is the tender of the hacienda's bull, Montana Negro. He is also the village drunk. But to twelve-year-old Manuel, he is a beloved father. Long ago the patron, Don Francisco, would have gotten rid of Juan except for the motherless Manuel. Due to Juan's carelessness, a fire destroys the bull pens and Montana Negro escapes, just when he was to be sold to liberate the hacienda from debt. Manuel sets out to find the bull and bring him back.

In 56 Faulkner, Georgene and John Becker. Melindy's medal. New York: Messner, 1945.
Melindy receives the Carnegie Medal for heroism which leads to the recognition by her family and herself as a praiseworthy individual.

In 57 Fisher, Laura. Never try Nathaniel. New York: Holt, 1968.
Nathaniel is the youngest of five and the only one left at home, but his nephews and nieces. This is good, except that his oldest nephew, Little Joe, is braver and a better

worker than twelve-year-old Than.   Than tries hard but the
dog and one of the cows chase him and the horses take their
own lead when he tries to drive.   When Pa gets hurt, Joe's
scorn of Than increases, until Than resolves to show everybody his courage.   Well written account of a boy's battle with
himself.

In 58   Fox, Paula. How many miles to Babylon? Canfield, Ohio:
        White, 1967.
        Based on a nursery rhyme, this is a story of James who
        has a terrifying adventure while alone in a tenement flat in
        Brooklyn.   He lives with his mother, father and three old
        aunts in a slum area.   The story provides glimpses of slum
        life.   It provides insight into the need for a child to learn
        large city survival skills if the child is to live there.

In 59   Franklin, George Cory. Indian uprising. Boston: Houghton,
        1962.
        Trouble with the Ute tribe helps a young man grow up
        rapidly.

In 60   Fritz, Jean. Brady. New York: Coward, 1960.
        In 1836, after Brady, a Pennsylvania preacher's son, dis-
        covered an underground railroad station near his family's
        farm and knew his father did not trust him with that secret,
        he wished he had never heard of slavery because it had got
        him into such trouble; but in a time of great need he was
        able to prove that he was becoming a man.

In 61   Fry, Rosalie. September island. New York: Dutton, 1965.
        The story of three children who find themselves stranded
        on a deserted (sandbar) island.   Alex, Martin, and young
        Linda must learn to face danger and accept responsibility
        before they are rescued.   A story "with an English flavor
        ... (and) quiet manner. "

In 62   Gibson, Althea. I always wanted to be somebody. New York:
        Harper, 1958.
        Born in Harlem, deliberate truant and pool-hall habitué
        in her teens, Althea Gibson decided she wanted to make
        something of her life.   Tennis provided her with the means.
        Learning to play with just a wooden paddle, she progressed
        to win the Wimbledon and U. S. Lawn Tennis Association
        championships.   She was frustrated by the subtle pressures
        of prejudice practiced by the fans, other players, and even
        the black press, but she fought relentlessly to win them over.
        Getting a foothold in the all-white world of tennis was diffi-
        cult, but a tremendous triumph for her.   After winning the
        championship, she said, "I've already got the main thing I've
        always wanted, which is to be somebody, to have identity. "

In 63   Goldthwait, Priscilla. Night of the wall. New York: Put-
        nam, 1964.

On the night that the Berlin Wall is erected, Hans' mother fails to return from her accustomed visit to East Berlin. He eludes the sentries and crosses the barrier to find her. He learns to accept adult responsibility when he learns the real reason for his mother's trips.

In 64 Gripe, Maria. <u>Pappa Pellerin's daughter.</u> New York: Day, 1966.
Twelve-year-old Loella is a very brave and imaginative Swedish girl who is left alone by her mother, a ship's cook, to take care of her little twin brothers. Pappa Pellerin is the name she gives to a scarecrow which serves as her mail-box--and a kind of charm to bring her father home. The authorities finally step in, place Loella in an orphanage, and the twins in a family home--but all ends happily, thanks to Loella's spirit.

In 65 Jackson, Jesse. <u>Call me Charley</u>. New York: Harper, 1945.
Charley proves that he can meet the challenge of being the only Negro boy in his school. But this happens only after he learns that there are people hoping he can live up to the demands of daily life.

In 66 Lenski, Lois. <u>Corn farm boy.</u> Philadelphia: Lippincott, 1954.
Dick Hoffman lives on an Iowa corn farm where he enjoys driving a tractor. In addition, he cares for the animals, and always has several pets. With him constantly is the threat of an attack of rheumatic fever, which sometimes disables him or puts him on crutches for weeks at a time. After an accident caused by his chest pains and momentary blackout, Dick realizes that he does not have the physical stamina for farming, which requires the operation of powerful machines. He will, instead, follow up his interest in animals by becoming a veterinarian.... Readers may capture his courage in making a difficult decision.

In 67 Lipkind, William. <u>Boy with a harpoon</u>. New York: Harcourt, 1952.
Little Seal, a twelve-year-old Eskimo boy finally wins the right to go on a whale hunt with the men.

In 68 Little, Jean. <u>Take wing</u>. Boston: Little, Brown, 1968.
Burdened by her awareness that seven-year-old James (her younger brother) is retarded, a fact their parents can't face, Laurel is prodded by a bossy aunt and stuck-up cousin into accepting James' need for help; and into seeking a normal life for herself. The author has written an absorbing story that is a thoroughly realistic treatment of a too common situation in which parents ignore reality to the detriment of the whole family. Recommended reading for parents and teachers as well as for young people.

In 69   Merriam, Eve. Independent voices. New York: Atheneum,
        1968.
            In this book the author presents profiles in verse of seven
        people who had courage enough to be themselves; Benjamin
        Franklin, Elizabeth Blockwell, Frederick Douglass, Henry
        Thoreau, Lucretia Mott, Ida B. Wells, and Fiorello La
        Guardia. For some she has given a complete biography in
        verse; for others she has chosen significant moments to por-
        tray.

In 70   Morrow, Honoré. On to Oregon. New York: Morrow, 1946.
            The hero, John Sager, is a thirteen-year-old boy who with
        his parents and younger brothers and sisters left Missouri
        for Oregon in early pioneer days. At first John was a wist-
        ful, disobedient and selfish little boy. But with the death of
        his father and then of his mother, the lad wakes up and,
        taking charge of his six little dependents, actually succeeds
        in making the frightful journey across the Rockies.

In 71   O'Dell, Scott. Island of the blue dolphins. New York:
        Houghton, 1960.
            A young Indian girl sees her father and the strongest men
        of her island tribe killed by white hunters. The tribe is
        evacuated from the island except for Karana and her younger
        brother who is later killed by wild dogs. This book tells of
        Karana's independence in learning to survive on her island
        until she is rescued.

In 72   Pederson, Elsa. House upon a rock. New York: Atheneum,
        1968.
            A story of toughness and courage and how a world can be
        changed in a few minutes. An exciting tale of a recent ca-
        tastrophe, and its influence on Derrick's future life.

In 73   Potter, Beatrix. Antonio. New York: Atheneum, 1968.
            Twelve-year-old Antonio wished to go out with the men on
        the fishing boats rather than tend the oxen which launched and
        retrieved the boats, but a childhood injury to his hand made
        work on the boats dangerous for him ... or so the fishermen
        thought until the day of the great storm. On that day An-
        tonio proved his worth to the fishing fleet and discovered what
        he really wanted to do with his life.

In 74   Shecter, Ben. Someplace else. Illustrated. New York:
        Harper, 1971.
            Arnie Shiffman had many problems--moving to a new neigh-
        borhood and a new school, Gloria the original pest, and hav-
        ing to study for his Bar Mitzvah with cranky old Robbie
        Bleisch. A moving story of a boy's growing up and adjust-
        ing to family tragedy and his own small achievement.

In 75   Sperry, Armstrong. Call it courage. Riverside, N. J. :
        Macmillan, 1940.

Because he fears the ocean, a Polynesian boy is scorned by his people and must redeem himself by an act of courage. His lone journey to a sacred island and the dangers he faces there earn him the name Mafatu, "Stout Heart."

In 76   Taylor, Mark. Henry explores the jungle. New York: Atheneum, 1968.
Henry sets off into the jungle in search of a tiger. He meets one that has escaped from a circus. Henry captures him and earns for himself a free seat at the circus and the surprised admiration of his mother.

In 77   Thompson, Mary. Two in the wilderness. New York: McKay, 1967.
Tabby and her brother, Zeke, are left to spend a summer alone in the wilderness in the Hampshire Grants (later Vermont) while their father returns to the settlement to bring back their mother, the little children, and, of course, the cow. Fear and loneliness, adventures with wild animals, and finally a sudden visit by two Indians are among the experiences of these two brave children on the American frontier. Based on a true incident.

In 78   Ullman, James Ramsey. Banner in the sky. Philadelphia: Lippincott, 1954.
To a Swiss boy one of the most challenging adventures is that of mountain climbing. This boy had to struggle for his right to that tremendous opportunity.

In 79   Witheridge, Elizabeth. Dead end bluff. New York: Atheneum, 1966.
Guig, thirteen and blind from birth, proves his capabilities to himself and his overprotective father.

In 80   Wojciechowska, Maia. Shadow of a bull. New York: Atheneum, 1964.
In spare economical prose the author makes one feel, see, smell the heat, endure the hot Andalusian sun and shows one the sand and the glare of the bull ring. Above all, she lifts the veil and gives glimpses of the terrible loneliness in the soul of a boy. Perhaps the ending is ever so slightly contrived, but it does not detract from an eloquent, moving book of a boy's maturing.

In 81   Wooldridge, Rhoda. Hannah's brave year. Indianapolis: Bobbs-Merrill, 1964.
After their parents' death, the three oldest Harelson children stick together and work hard to prevent separation of the family. Twelve-year-old Hannah cares for the cholera-stricken parents and it is she who makes the plans on which they pin their hopes.

In 82   Yates, Elizabeth. Carolina's courage. New York: Dutton,

1964.

Carolina's family makes a long journey by ox-drawn cov-
ered wagon from New Hampshire to Nebraska. The last
stage of the trip is made in safety because Carolina is brave
enough to play with an Indian child and exchange dolls with
her.

DECISION MAKING

In 83   Alan, Delgado. The very hot water bottle. Chicago: Fol-
         lett, 1962.
         Mike is on his first trip away from home and he has to
make many decisions on his own.

In 84   Ayer, Jacqueline. A wish for little sister. New York: Har-
         court, 1966.
         A myna bird tells Little Sister on her birthday that a wish
will be granted her at twilight. All day long she seeks a
suitable, sensible, valuable wish, asking advice of her relatives and friends, who are all hard at work spinning and
weaving the precious silk of Bangkok, famous all over the
world. She receives only gay impracticable suggestions,
which she visualizes and discards.... Finally, all by herself she thinks of the perfect "little sister wish" and to her
delight her simple happy wish is granted.

In 85   Ball, Zachary. Swamp chief. New York: Holiday, 1952.
         Joe develops the ability to use his own best judgment
rather than depend upon the tribal distrust of white men.

In 86   Bawden, Nina. A handful of thieves. Philadelphia: Lippin-
         cott, 1967.
         Mrs. Blackadder's grandson, Fred, and his young friends
felt personally involved when the money that she had been
saving for a rainy day disappeared. Only two people knew
she had kept it in an old teapot--Fred and Gran's mysterious
lodger, Mr. Gribble.... The group decide to track down the
lodger by themselves. This seems the right thing to do.
All ways to recover the stolen money are closed but one: to
steal it back from the thief. Miss Bawden rightly makes no
concessions toward the argument that it is all right to do to
others what they did to you, and she keeps an even balance
between tough-minded independence and family warmth and
security.

In 87   Brown, Margaret W. The big decision. New York: Double-
         day, 1965.
         Debbie must decide between joining a group of girls or
just being herself.

In 88   Carlson, Natalie Savage. Ann Aurelia and Dorothy. New
         York: Harper, 1968.

Ann Aurelia, living in a foster home because her mother
has remarried and can't have her, makes friends with Dorothy, another fifth grader with whom she shares pranks and
good times.   When her mother reappears, Ann must decide
whether to stay with her foster mother or rejoin her real one.

In 89   Chonz, Selina.   Florina and the wild bird.   New York:
Walck, 1966.
Florina moves up to a mountain meadow with her parents
for the summer.   When a fox steals a woodfowl, Florina
adopts the lone chick and treasures it as her pet until she
must give the bird its freedom.

In 90   Cleaver, Bill and Vera.   Where the lillies bloom.   Philadelphia: Lippincott, 1969.
Fourteen-year-old Mary has to take over the responsibility
of her ten-year-old brother and her retarded older sister
after the death of her father.   She has to make many decisions in order to keep the family together.

In 91   Cone, Molly.   Annie, Annie.   New York: Houghton, 1969.
Annie's parents allow her to make all her own decisions.
She misunderstands their policy, feels that they don't really
care about her and rebels by taking a live-in job with the
Sigbys, where there are rules for everything.   All Annie has
to do is what she's told and she loves it--at first, that is.

In 92   Corcos, Lucille.   Joel spends his money.   New York: Abelard-Schuman, 1952.
Joel learns the value of money and thrift after being given
an allowance.

In 93   Fisher, Dorothy Canfield.   A fair world for all.   New York:
McGraw-Hill, 1952.
An interpretation based on a study of official records of
the debates concerning the Universal Declaration of Human
Rights, and on consultations with members of the United Na-
tions Department of Social Affairs, the Department of Public
Information and the Educational Scientific and Cultural Or-
ganization.   Subtitle--explains the need for the Universal
Declaration of Human Rights and its 30 articles, written to
promote human rights and fundamental freedoms.

In 94   Gipson, Fred.   Old Yeller.   New York: Harper, 1956.
At fourteen Travis is left "man of the family" at his Texas
ranch home while his father goes to Kansas to sell cattle.
Having recently lost a beloved dog, Travis does not at first
take kindly to the big yellow dog that shows up at the ranch
one morning, stealing a side of pork.   Little brother, Arliss,
immediately loves and adopts the dog, which the family names
Old Yeller.   Later, when the dog saves Arliss's life, as he
is threatened by an angered mother bear, Travis looks upon
him with growing affection.   When Old Yeller proves himself

valuable in countless ways, Travis realizes that he cannot
carry on as "man of the family" without him.   Finally,
while saving Travis's mother from a mad wolf, Old Yeller
is bitten by the wolf, and Travis is forced to shoot the beloved dog.

In 95   Gorsline, Douglas W.   Farm boy.   New York: Viking Press,
          1950.
              After failing at school, a 15-year-old boy is sent to his
          uncle's farm where he learns that self-control and self-
          discipline are prerequisites of freedom.

In 96   Ideas, thoughts and feelings.   Freeport, N.Y.:   Education
                  Activities, n.d.
              The emphasis in this album is on discovery, problem
          solving, and independent thinking.   Children are encouraged
          to think about the variety of ways a task can be executed or
          a question answered.   They are allowed flexibility of re-
          sponse and can create their own complexity; thus the less
          skilled, as well as the highly skilled, are challenged.   As
          the students gain confidence in their abilities to make choices
          and express themselves, their dependency on the teacher
          gradually diminishes.

In 97   James, Scott.   Trouble after school.   New York: Harcourt,
          1957.
              When Lee Emerson's mother decides to help with the
          family finances by taking a job, Lee begins spending more
          and more time with a tough boy and his gang.   His grades
          slip and eventually when the gang plans to wreck a new high
          school recreation center, Lee is faced with the biggest prob-
          lem of his life.

In 98   Keats, Ezra Jack.   Peter's chair.   New York: Harper,
          1967.
              Peter is no longer the only child.   His father asks if
          he'd like to help paint his new little sister's high chair.
          It's his chair, not hers, and his crib which is being painted
          pink.   Peter takes his chair and plans to run away.   He
          tires out after the walk down the stairs and starts to sit in
          the chair for a rest.   Then he finds he can't fit!   He re-
          alizes he has gotten bigger as well as older, and makes the
          decision to paint the chair pink.

In 99   Lewiton, Mina.   That bad Carlos.   New York: Viking, 1965.
              When the family moves to New York City from Puerto
          Rico, their son, Carlos, and a new friend persist in borrow-
          ing things without asking.   The story tells of how they came
          to an understanding of borrowing and of the difference be-
          tween right and wrong when doing things on their own.

In 100   Muechl, Lois.   The hidden year of Devlin Bates.   New York:
          Holiday, 1967.

A very convincing portrait of a "loner" whose noncon-
formity and poor achievement at school cause friction and
conflict between him and his parents. His gradual acceptance of responsibility and his decision to "make the first
move" toward mutual understanding are believable and satisfying.

In 101   Sayder, Zipha Kettly. The velvet room. New York:
          Atheneum, 1967.
          A story of a twelve-year-old, independent, resentful
Robin who must decide whether to go with her migratory
worker family or stay at the McCurdy Ranch as a companion
to young Gwen McCurdy.

In 102   Taylor, Sydney. A papa like everyone else. Chicago: Fol-
          lett, 1966.
          Young Grisella can't understand why her papa has left
them in Hungary before World War I to go to America, even
though her older sister, Szerena, tries to explain that papa
has gone to seek work. Meanwhile, mama is holding things
together as well as she can and Gisella isn't sure she wants
to leave even if her father sends for them. She enjoys her
Jewish customs and traditions, and doesn't want to change--
except that she does want a papa like everyone else.

INITIATIVE

In 103   Agle, Nan Hayden. Baney's lake. New York: Seabury,
          1972.
          Baney is an eleven-year-old inventor, very much ham-
pered by lack of privacy in his crowded home. Old Miss
Luke decides to sell him 1/16 of an acre of her land (for
$6.85) and give him an old chicken house. Overjoyed with
this windfall, he quickly discovers the trials of land owner-
ship when it develops that the Conservation Department is
planning to use the land for development of a lake and dam
to protect the people lower down the watershed from floods.
An excellent and amusing story on a current problem.

In 104   _____. Maple street. New York: Seabury, 1970.
          The story of a family living on a street rapidly going
"down hill" and the daughter's efforts to turn the vacant lot
into a playground and to get on with the new "poor white"
neighbors.

In 105   Ardizonne, Edward. Tim all alone. New York: Walck,
          1956.
          After a long holiday, Tim returns home by the sea, only
to find that his parents are no longer there; he sets out to
find them.

In 106   Baily, Carolyn Sherwin. Children of the handcrafts. New

York: Viking, 1935.

The stories of seventeen real children who learned to
work with their hands, and in most cases became famous in
their individual crafts; included are Lora Standish, who made
the first sampler; Paul Revere, the silversmith; Duncan
Phyfe, the joiner; Betsy Metcalf, who made the first straw
hat in the New World; Thoreau, the pencil maker; and Simon Ide, the printer. Based on general knowledge and
town records, early letters and stories, the book is well
written original historical material.

In 107   Beatty, Patricia.   The nickel plated beauty.   New York:
           Morrow, 1964.
           When the Kimball's old stove began to rust away, Whit,
the eldest of the seven Kimball kids, ordered a new one
C. O. D.   All the kids had to organize a campaign to secretly earn the price for the elegant new stove, even if it meant
working for their mean Aunt Rose.

In 108   Biem, Lorraine.   Alice's family.   New York: Harcourt,
           1948.
           Alice learns to assume the domestic responsibilities
when her mother becomes injured.

In 109   Brown, Pamela.   The other side of the street.   Chicago:
           Follett, 1965.
           Linda lives in a big old-fashioned apartment house on
the wrong side of the street in London.   Her ambition in
life is to gather enough money to give her mother one of
the little houses across the street.   She tries to get a
modeling job for her younger sister, she establishes a
"helping hands cleaning service," but nothing works out until she herself gets on a television show.   A story of life
in a big city with a really exciting ending.

In 110   Bulla, Clyde Robert.   Benito.   New York: Crowell, 1961.
           When Benito, an orphan of twelve, comes to live with
Uncle Pedro, he is admonished that he will have much to
do at his new home.   There will be no time for him to draw
pictures with the crayons he brought with him.   With Benito's strong urge to draw and carve, this is a severe ulti-
matum.   Later, when selling vegetables for Uncle Pedro in
a nearby town, Benito meets a professional artist who en-
courages his interest, giving him art materials with which
to work.   Secretly Benito carves the figure of a lady he
has seen, and when it wins professional approval he has the
courage to pursue his dream to learn more and perfect his
talent.

In 111   Cohen, Peter Z.   Morena.   New York: Atheneum, 1970.
           A survival story in which the life of a young boy, strand-
ed during a snow storm, "depends on his ability to outwit
and use a willful, stubborn old mare as his means to escape.

The characterization of the mare is done with great skill,
and her obstinacy is shown as simply another force of nature against which the boy must struggle. Told with consistency of viewpoint and rightness of detail, this is an unusual and original handling of a perennial theme."

In 112   Edwards, Julie. Mandy. New York: Harper, 1971.
          A story about a ten-year-old orphan who takes the inia-
tive to fix her a place all of her own.

In 113   Ervin, Janet. More than halfway there. Chicago: Follett,
          1970.
          Can you imagine a time when a boy had to use every way
he could think of to persuade his father to let him go to
school? Time--1829, when Albert Long met Abe Lincoln;
it was a very eventful day.

In 114   Flory, Jane. Mist on the mountain. New York: Houghton,
          1966.
          None of the eight fatherless Scoville girls wants to ac-
cept the charity of Uncle Bolivar. Therefore, they work
hard to keep themselves independent of it.

In 115   Freuchen, Pipaluk. Eskimo Boy. West Caldwell, N. J. :
          Lothrop, 1951.
          Young Ivic, who becomes head of his family when his
father is killed by a walrus, provides for his family with
determination.

In 116   Fry, Rosaline. September island. New York: Dutton, 1965.
          The story of three children who find themselves stranded
on a deserted (sandbar) island. Alex, Martin, and young
Linda must learn to face danger and accept responsibility
before they are rescued.

In 117   Hoff, Carol. Johnny Texas on the San Antonio Road. Chi-
          cago: Follett, 1953.
          Johnny must learn self reliance and initiative when he
has to go on an errand south into Mexico because of his
father's accident.

In 118   Krumgold, Joseph. ... And Now Miguel. New York:
          Crowell, 1953.
          A boy learns that responsibilities as well as privileges
go with growing up.

In 119   Ladd, Elizabeth. Night of the hurricane. Eau Claire,
          Wis. : E. M. Hale, 1956.
          When Judy experiences her first hurricane on the Marine
coast, she finds comfort in her Aunt Kate's loving arms.
She vows then she'll earn the money to be able to give her
aunt a Christmas present she really wants. This book tells
how she achieved this aim.

In 120   Marquis, H. <u>Longest day of the year</u>. Des Moines: Mere-
          dith, 1969.
              Thirteen-year-old Cissy is proud to be left in charge of
          her younger sister, eleven-year-old Marie, and brother,
          seven-year-old Tim, when her parents go to deliver Christ-
          mas gifts. When a blizzard strikes, the parents are forced
          to remain in town. Cissy then makes a good Christmas for
          Tim, who believes in Santa, and helps keep Margie and Tim
          occupied, warm, fed, and happy until her parents return.

In 121   Merrill, Jean. <u>Superlative Horse.</u> New York: Scott, 1961.
              In ancient China, the head groom of the Duke's stables
          is about to retire. Instead of a pompous official who wants
          the position, a young unknown lad is put to the test--and
          wins.

In 122   Nash, Mary. <u>While Mrs. Coverlet was away.</u> Boston:
          Little, Brown, 1958.
              With their father away on a trip and Mrs. Coverlet, the
          housekeeper called home, the Persever children manage
          everything and discover amazing ways to make money.

In 123   Neff, Priscilla Holton. <u>Tressa's dream.</u> New York: Mc-
          Kay, 1965.
              Tressa proves to be an enterprising and staunch child.
          She gradually learns to enjoy taking care of a goat and
          manages to earn enough money to buy a neglected-looking
          Shetland pony.

In 124   Perrine, Mary. <u>Salt boy.</u> Boston: Houghton, 1968.
              Salt Boy's deepest wish is for his father to teach him
          how to rope the black horse, but his father thinks he is too
          young. The Navajo boy earns his father's respect and his
          own wish in an unusual way.

In 125   Pertwee, Roland. <u>The islander.</u> Indianapolis: Bobbs-Mer-
          rill, 1957.
              Three young school boys are offered a summer vacation
          on a five-hundred acre estate, with the provisions that they
          stay within its boundaries, obeying all fish and game laws,
          and provide their own food and shelter. They have many
          problems but they manage to survive and in the end have a
          successful vacation. Young readers will appreciate the rela-
          tive freedom from adult supervision.

In 126   Potter, Marian. <u>Milepost 67.</u> Chicago: Follett, 1965.
              Ten-year-old Evaline is frail, but she works well during
          threshing time and helps her father capture a criminal on
          the railroad.

In 127   Prishvin, M. <u>Treasure trove of the sun.</u> New York: Vik-
          ing, 1952.
              After World War II, Anna and Peterkin, Russian war

orphans, go their separate ways to gather cranberries.
One meets a wolf, the other, a snake, but they demonstrate
their ability to take care of themselves and win the admiration of villagers.

In 128   Robertson, Keith. Henry Reed's baby sitting service. New
          York: Viking, 1966.
          Henry Reed records in his diary the devastating results
          of his and Midge's latest business endeavor--a babysitting
          service.

In 129   _____. The year of the jeep. New York: Viking, 1968.
          Fifteen-year-old Cloud Selby, who has long dreamed of
          owning a jeep, discovers an old abandoned jeep on a de-
          serted farm and, with his new neighbor, Wong Ling, an
          able ally, directs all his efforts toward salvaging the jeep
          and earning money to buy it if the owner can be found.
          Set in a rural community in New Jersey, the story of the
          boys' money-making projects and adventures, which range
          from catching bats to catching thieves, is lively, humorous,
          and altogether enjoyable.

In 130   Russ, Lavinia. Alec's sand castle. New York: Harper,
          1972.
          When Alec's parents and his aunt and uncle take over
          building his sand castle, Alec wanders off to build another
          of his own. He builds the biggest, most magnificent, and
          versatile castle his imagination can create.

In 131   Wilder, Laura Ingalls. Little town on the prairie. New
          York: Harper, 1953.
          Laura is growing up and her life is filled with the excite-
          ment of a job in town, school activities, socials, suppers,
          and a boy friend.

                              RUNAWAYS

In 132   Aaron, Chester. Better than laughter. New York: Har-
          court, 1972.
          Being wealthy means little to twelve-year-old Allan and
          ten-year-old Sam Collins. The boys want more than a bal-
          sawood boat and plane models and a father whom they fear.
          They make up their minds to run away but only get as far
          as the city dump where they meet Horace Butright, aged
          ninety. Horace had never had parents and a home but he
          shares what he has with the boys. He also tells them
          stories during their visit. Later, under a beating from his
          father, Sam tells where they had spent the day, which brings
          about the quick ousting of Horace as dumpkeeper. A story
          of maturing under hard circumstances.

In 133   Adventures of Giorgio. Pasadena, Cal.: Kleinberg Films,

1969.   (16mm film)
Dramatizes the story of an eleven-year-old Italian boy
who runs away from home and discovers the importance of
education.   Pictures Giorgio as a typical boy who tires of
school and runs away to go to sea.   At Genoa he gets
aboard a ship where an officer provides a guided tour and
suggests that he needs more education to be a good seaman.

In 134   Burn, Doris.   Andrew Henry's meadow.   New York: Cow-
          ard-McCann, 1965.
          A boy's family does not appreciate the odd contraptions
he builds, so he quietly leaves and goes to a meadow where
eight children with similar problems join him.

In 135   Christgau, Alice E.   Run away to glory.   New York: Young
          Scott Books, 1965.
          Grandpa and twelve-year-old Reuben feel inadequate in a
large Minnesota farm family until that day in 1905, while on
an errand in Stillwater, they prove their courage and resourcefulness by capturing bank robbers.

In 136   Corbett, Scott.   Pippa passes.   New York: Holt, 1966.
          Pippa, a young movie star, runs away from her uncle
and aunt.   She chances upon Meg and Lulie and enlists
their help.

In 137   Fleischman, Sid.   By the great horn spoon.   Boston: Lit-
          tle, Brown, 1963.
          Jack Flagg, an orphan, runs away from home accom-
panied by the butler, Praiseworthy, and becomes involved
in the Gold Rush of 1849.   The pompous and ubiquitous butler involves them in many hilarious adventures.

In 138   George, Jean C.   Julie of the wolves.   New York: Harper,
          1972.
          Julie is an eskimo girl who gets lost running away from
home.   She latches herself on to a pack of wolves to survive.   She remembers many things her father has taught
her and, by making decisions on her own, learns to survive
and be independent.

In 139   _____.   My side of the mountain.   New York: Dutton,
          1959.
          A New York City boy determines to run away from home
and to live alone and be completely self-sufficient.   This,
his diary, tells about his adventures during the year he
spent in the Catskills--his struggle for survival, his dependence on nature, his animal friends, and his ultimate
realization that he needs human companionship.

In 140   Harris, Marilyn.   Runaway's diary.   New York: Four
          Winds, 1971.
          Catherine Toven's search for happiness takes her away

at fifteen.   She takes $40.00 and a change of clothing and
sets out for nowhere and anywhere.   Eastern Canada is
where she finds herself.   Pain and general misery are other companions of the runaway.   A tale which does not con-
done running away but is an effective account of a girl's
protest against many of today's views toward life.

In 141   Held, Kurt.   The outsiders of Uskoken Castle.   New York:
           Doubleday, 1967.
           Here are the adventures of five Yugoslav children left
homeless by the Second World War.   The gang, led by a
red-haired girl named Zora, inhabits a ruined castle.   They
pattern their own lives after the courageous knights and
sailors who once lived there.

In 142   Konigsburg, E. L.   From the mixed-up files of Mrs. Basil
           E. Frankweiler.   New York: Atheneum, 1967.
           Claudia is bored, disturbed by injustice and wants to
teach her family a lesson in "Claudia appreciation."   She
plans to teach this lesson by running away from home and
having her family miss her and search for her.   She chooses
a runaway companion--her nine-year-old brother.   They use
the funds they have to get to the New York Metropolitan
Museum of Art where they hide for a week, eating just
enough to maintain life and dodging the guards.   Mrs. Frank-
weiler saves the children from an embarrassing return to
their home and community.

In 143   Morgan, Bryon.   Pepe's island.   New York: Criterion
           Books, 1966.
           Pepe's father is an innkeeper on the island of Ibiza off
the coast of Spain.   Long before she died, Pepe's mother
had taught him to play the guitar, which is a great joy to
the boy--so great that he stows away on a ship bound for
Barcelona so he can hear the great guitarist Miguel Leon
play.

In 144   Morris, Ruth.   Runaway girl.   Westminster, Md. : Ran-
           dom House, 1962.
           Orphaned Joanne is farmed out to live with an uncle and
aunt on a sheep ranch in the Australian outback.   Her life
there is one of hardship and work.   When she finds she is
to be sent to another relative, she runs away.   How she
works out her problems makes a satisfying story and a realistic picture of life on a faraway continent.

In 145   Muche, Lois.   The hidden year of Devlin Bates.   New York:
           Holiday, 1967.
           Devlin is a rebel--bored by school, preferring to roam
the hills rather than to play with the other children his age.
When he fails at the end of the year, he decides to save his
money to run away.   Only old Mrs. Thornton, who is also
"different," seems to understand.

55686

In 146   Robinson, Joan. Charley. New York: Coward, 1970.
          Charley thinks that she isn't wanted by her aunt, so she
          runs away and "makes it on her own."

In 147   Shotwell, Louisa R. Adam bookout. New York: Viking,
          1967.
          Grieving for parents killed in an air accident, Adam runs
          away from his aunt's home in Oklahoma and heads for Brook-
          lyn and unknown cousins. New companions come from varied
          economic and ethnic backgrounds, for his cousins live in a
          changing area where deteriorating older buildings, new hous-
          ing projects, and elegant apartments can all be found. A
          year in this complex environment helps him face his own
          problems with greater understanding, and he is ready to re-
          turn to Oklahoma and Aunt Meg's guardianship.

SELF-RELIANCE: ADULTS

In 148   Armer, Alberta. Troublemaker. Cleveland: World, 1966.
          Joe Fuller is sent by the judge and the court to spend
          the summer with foster parents in a small Indiana town.
          His broken home, his father in prison, his mother hospit-
          alized with a serious breakdown, all inflict on Joe more
          problems than he can cope with. His summer with the Mur-
          rays, his reactions to family life there, and his eventual
          improved understanding of his own problems are realistical-
          ly narrated.

In 149   Blume, Judy. It's not the end of the world. Scarsdale,
          N.Y.: Bradbury, 1972.
          Unwilling to adjust to her parents impending divorce,
          twelve-year-old Karen Newman attempts a last-ditch effort
          at arranging a reconciliation. Eventually, Karen comes to
          accept her parents' divorce and recognizes that it is not
          the end of the world for any of them. A believable story
          with good characterization, particularly of twelve-year-old
          Karen, and realistic treatment of the situation.

In 150   Burch, Robert. Queenie Peavy. New York: Viking, 1966.
          "Queenie's daddy's in the chain gang" echoes and re-
          echoes through the school year, but thirteen-year-old Queen-
          ie feels sure that her dad will make everything right when
          he gets out and comes home. As the only girl in the eighth
          grade who can chew and spit tobacco, Queenie finds that her
          bad reputation gets her into trouble, even when she isn't
          directly to blame for the events in question. When Mr.
          Peavy is paroled, Queenie discovers that he isn't interested
          in her and that she must be responsible for her own actions.

In 151   Burn, Doris. Andrew Henry's meadow. New York: Cow-
          ard-McCann, 1965.
          The story of a little boy, Andrew Henry, who didn't feel

55686

that he was an individual in the family. Nobody seemed to
see any worth in the things he did. So he found a way to
show his parents that he was an independent individual and
they began to recognize him more.

In 152   Cantly, Mary. The green gate. New York: McKay, 1965.
         Lonely, unhappy, and blind eight-year-old Emily finds
her way through a green gate into a garden which her Aunt
Alice brings alive. She learns independence from her aunt
who is also blind.

In 153   Cleaver, Vera. The whys and wherefores of Littabelle Lee.
         New York: Atheneum, 1973.
         Set in the 1920s or early 1930s in the Ozark Mountains,
this is the story of a sixteen-year-old girl whose only family
is her grandparents and her aunt. A series of tragedies
put Littabelle Lee at the head of the family. Relatives are
forced by law to help but Littabelle learns that only love can
make the arrangement work.

In 154   Cutting the apron strings. Los Angeles: Family Films,
         Inc., 1970. (filmstrip with record)
         Children speaking of many aspects of how to cut the
apron strings: showing parents they are dependable and
responsible, helping with family chores and learning to
handle and use money wisely. From Family Problems of
Young Teens Series.

In 155   Dobrin, Arnold. Scat. New York: Four Winds, 1971.
         Scat loved the music his father and the other men in the
jazz band played. He longed to make music his career
despite his grandmother's disapproval.

In 156   Edmonds, Walter. 2 Logs crossing. New York: Dodd,
         1943.
         John, oldest of four, becomes the head of the family
when his father dies and must overcome his father's bad
reputation and irresponsibility. He does this by paying back
a fake fine the judge claims he owes him. It takes some
time but he repays the judge--not only with money but also
with the knowledge that he has become an independent, responsible young man.

In 157   Ellis, Ella Thorp. Celebrate the morning. New York:
         Atheneum, 1972.
         A quiet, moving story told without self-pity by fourteen-
year-old (fatherless) April who lives with her mother on
welfare in a small California farming town. April gives
realistic accounts of their struggle for independence and
clearly conveys their constant fear of separation because of
her mother's not quite normal behavior. When her mother
is hospitalized for pneumonia and later is committed to a
mental institution, April finds life increasingly difficult.

Older readers will sympathize with April and appreciate
that solutions to problems are not presented in a tidy pack-
age, but will recognize the message of hope.

In 158   Fisher, Dorothy Canfield. Understood Betsy. New York:
          Holt, 1972.
          Elizabeth Ann, who has been too much understood and
          coddled by an over-conscientious aunt, is suddenly set down
          on a Vermont farm in a simple, wholesome environment
          which changes the nervous self-conscious child into a strong,
          self-reliant little individual.

In 159   Flory, Jane. One hundred and eight bells. Boston: Hough-
          ton, 1963.
          A good family story of present-day Japan; the protagonist
          is twelve-year-old Setsuko who lives in a small house in
          Tokyo with her parents, older brother, and a young widowed
          aunt. Setsuko's problem is forgetfulness. A budding artist,
          she loses track of time when she paints; and to her mother's
          dismay, neglects her household chores. The 108 bells of
          the title are used in the closing episode of the book when
          Setsuko vows at the New Year to change for the better. Re-
          lationships are excellent.

In 160   Gates, Doris. Sensible Kate. New York: Viking, 1943.
          Ten-year-old Kate, an orphan, wanted more than any-
          thing to be pretty and cute. Passed about among indifferent
          relatives, she was placed with a middle-aged couple as a
          family helper and life became full of pleasant surprises.
          When the two young people she loved most decided to adopt
          her, she knew that being sensible was more important than
          anything else.

In 161   Nash, Ogden. Parents keep out! Boston: Little, Brown,
          1951.
          Humorous poems for young people about parents.

In 162   Neville, Emily. It's like this, Cat. New York: Harper,
          1963.
          David gets a cat named Cat and begins taking it every-
          where. He meets Tom and helps him out of trouble. He
          also meets Mary who he likes because of her independence.
          Kate has a problem which his father helps solve and David
          gets closer to his father.

In 163   _____. The seventeenth-street gang. New York: Harp-
          er, 1969.
          Louise wants to stop telling lies and Minnow would like
          to stop plotting mischief but they can't seem to, especially
          when unexpected questions are asked or there is a situation
          begging for leadership. Minnow even persuades the local
          children to give Hollis, a new boy in the neighborhood, the
          cold shoulder. These are New York City children, but very

much like children everywhere in their struggle against
adults and authority.

In 164   Nordstrom, Ursula. The secret language. New York:
          Harper, 1960.
          A story about two eight-year-old girls at boarding school.
          None of the experiences that Vicky and Martha have are un-
          usual; none dramatic, yet all of the details of their year
          make absorbing reading. Vicky is homesick and Martha is
          a rebel; as they adjust to the pattern of school life, both
          girls find satisfaction and both grow up a little. The writ-
          ing style has a gentle humor, a warm understanding, and
          an easy narrative flow that seems effortless.

In 165   Pyle, Howard. Otto of the silver hand. New York: Scrib-
          ners, n. d.
          The story of Otto, the son of a German robber baron,
          and his adventures in a time of cruel war and deadly feuds.
          Howard Pyle has done some of his best work in this story
          of a gentle boy who held to his own ideals of right, although
          they were opposed to the spirit of the age.

In 166   Rose, Karen. Brooklyn girl. Chicago: Follett, 1963.
          Kay Ross, a seventh-grade tomboy, who lives near Eb-
          bets Field and Coney Island, really matures during a trip
          away from her urban home, the serious illness of a friend
          and her participation in a school election.

In 167   Talbot, Charles Joy. Tomas takes charge. West Caldwell,
          N. J. : Lothrop, 1966.
          The sights and sounds of the old Washington market come
          to life through the eyes of Thomas, an alert eleven-year-old
          Puerto Rican boy in New York City. When Papa fails to
          come home, Thomas and his sister, Fernanda, hide in an
          empty building to keep from being taken over by the welfare
          department and separated. That summer they manage to
          live without the help of any adults.

In 168   Thompson, Mary Wolfe. Two in the wilderness; before Ver-
          mont had a name. New York: McKay, 1967.
          Tabby and her brother, Zeke, are left to spend a sum-
          mer in the Hampshire Grants alone while their father re-
          turns to the settlement to bring back their mother, the lit-
          tle children, and, of course, the cow. Fear and loneliness,
          adventure with wild animals, and a sudden visit by two In-
          dians are among their experiences. Based on a true inci-
          dent.

In 169   Treffinger, Carolyn. Li Lun, lad of courage. Nashville:
          Abingdon, 1945.
          A Chinese boy who refuses to go on a first fishing voyage
          learns self-reliance as he grows rice on a lonely mountain.

In 170   Weik, Mary. The jazz man. New York: Atheneum, 1968.
          About a little boy whose parents work and who doesn't
          go to school because his mother feels it is not necessary.
          He cares for himself until his parents come home at night
          from work. One of the ways he amuses himself is by listen-
          ing to the jazz man who lives in the adjoining apartment.
          His parents abandon him; so he lives and dies without help
          from anyone.

In 171   Who runs your life. San Francisco: National Instructional
              TV Center, n.d.   (2-inch video tape--20 minutes, color)
          Relates self-control to freedom in directing one's own
          life. Discusses why rules are necessary for both children
          and adults. Uses photographs to trace the physical develop-
          ment of a young child. Shows how increased physical con-
          trol brings increased freedom and responsibility.

In 172   Wier, Ester. The Loner. New York: McKay, 1963.
          A young boy with no family and no future finds self
          worth.

In 173   Yezback, Steven A. Pumpkin seeds. Indianapolis: Bobbs-
              Merrill, 1969.
          This book, written in the first person, is about a black
          boy who lives with his mother. Since his mother works,
          her son has to fend for himself during the day. Since he
          has done this for so long, he is delighted to be alone and
          independent.

In 174   Yorty, Jeane. Far wilderness. Grand Rapids: Eerdmans,
              1966.
          The Hughes family leaves Albany, New York in the spring
          of 1835 and travels to their newly purchased farm on the
          Flint River in Michigan Territory. Sixteen-year-old Nathan
          takes responsibility for housing, feeding, and protecting his
          mother, sister, and another woman.

                    SELF-RELIANCE: PEERS

In 175   Barrett, Anne. Midway. New York: Coward-McCann,
              1967.
          Mark is dull and ordinary in comparison with members
          of his brilliant family. He is the middle of the five Mun-
          day children, which makes matters worse. Still, at school
          he seems to be the one called on to defend the peculiarities
          of the family. Then, one day while he's sitting on a tree
          limb, Midway comes to visit. Midway, with his green eyes,
          steers Mark away from dullness into success and confidence,
          and he becomes as brilliant as the rest of the family.

In 176   Bishop, Curtis. Little league victory. Philadelphia: Lip-
              pincott, 1967.

Ed Bogart had a hard time making a Little League team
because all the coaches knew about his temper tantrums.
Once he began to play for the Atlas Giants, Ed found things
even more difficult, for his team did not back him up.
Ed's victory over himself leads to a Little League Victory.

In 177 Cretan, Gladys Yessayan. All except Sammy. Boston:
        Little, Brown, 1966.
        All except Sammy Agabashian are musicians in his family
        and he longs to be included in newspaper pictures of the
        "Musical Agabashians." Though he plays championship base-
        ball, he is hopeless as a musician--he has absolutely no
        rhythm and is tone-deaf besides. But at last, in school, he
        discovers another talent and is finally recognized as one of
        the "Artistic Agabashian Family."

In 178 Emery, Anne. Mountain Laurel. New York: Scholastic,
        1948.
        Laurel learns to do things for herself rather than expect-
        ing her friends to help her.

In 179 Holm, Anne. North to freedom. New York: Harcourt,
        1965.
        When David finally escapes from his East European
        prison, he knows only one thing--no one is to be trusted.
        Absorbing odyssey through Europe and how he finally learns
        that he can be independent and still have friends.

In 180 Konigsburg, E. L. George. New York: Atheneum, 1970.
        George was Benjamin Carr's concentric twin--he lived in-
        side of Benjamin. When Benjamin needed an answer to a
        question, he called on George. This relationship lasted un-
        til Benjamin was in the sixth grade; then Benjamin realized
        he needed other people to talk to besides George.

In 181 Rinkoff, Barbara. The watchers. Westminster, Md. :
        Knopf, 1972.
        What can you expect from a boy whose parents fight all
        the time? the neighbors ask. Chris Blake knows bitterly
        what they mean and he himself tells the story of his troubles;
        at home, at school, and no friends except the new kid, San-
        ford, a real loser. Weak and uncoordinated, Sanford is
        overprotected by his parents and bullied by other boys; and
        his loyalty to Chris, who befriends him, is unshakable.
        Little by little, Sanford learns independence and gains cour-
        age.

In 182 Rose, Karen. Single trail. Chicago: Follett, 1969.
        Two boys go to the same school in a Los Angeles neigh-
        borhood. Ricky has learned how to make friends quickly,
        in spite of his family's moving nine times in twelve years.
        Earl doesn't care whether people like him or not--especially
        white people. An effective tale with high identification value.

In 183   Wolley, Catherine. <u>Cathy's little sister</u>. New York: Mor-
            row, 1964.
            At nine Chris has made no friends independently, but
         constantly trails her older sister, Cathy, and her friends.
         She even finds an excuse to stay home from school when
         Cathy is sick, and thus misses out on being in a class play.
         When Cathy has a slumber party and excludes Chris from
         the activities, she is crushed.   On a subsequent overnight
         trip to Detroit with her father, Chris visits a home where
         she has a wonderful time with girls her own age.   She also
         meets a little girl who trails her sister, just as she does,
         and begins to see herself as she is.   Chris returns with
         plans for a slumber party of her own, to which she will in-
         vite school classmates, and she is launched on a program
         of making friends her own age.

Chapter 2

DEVELOPING PERSONAL VALUES

Primary

GENERAL

Va 1   Values. (series) Jamaica, N.Y.: Eye Gate, n.d. (sound
         filmstrip)
         The student of today questions adult standards and values.
         This set is designed to assist the young learner in develop-
         ing a standard of values. Each filmstrip will explore areas
         of social conflict. Both appropriate and inappropriate re-
         sponses will be given without a judgment being made. The
         students can be asked to role play and discuss each problem
         and response, hence developing their own set of values. In-
         cluded in the series: Telling the Truth; What is Stealing?;
         Kindness; Politeness; Responsibility; Citizenship.

FAMILY RELATIONSHIPS

Va 2   Alcock, Gudrun. Duffy. West Caldwell, N.J.: Lothrop,
         1972.
         A warm and poignant story of a young girl whose home
         life was struck by tragedy. Duffy was sent from one place
         to another to live. Her values change and she becomes a
         behavior problem for a while. She becomes disillusioned
         with her real mother, but finally comes "safe home to
         port. "

Va 3   Anglund, Joan W. Love is a special way of feeling. New
         York: Harcourt, 1960.
         A book that tells us how we may discover love--what may
         "start in little ways. "

Va 4   Ardizzone, Edward. Little Tim and the brave sea captain.
         New York: Walck, 1961. (book and sound filmstrip)
         Little Tim runs away from home and becomes a stow-
         away at sea!

Va 5   Beim, Jerrold. Kid brother. New York: Morrow, 1952.
         Buzz resents his younger brother Frankie and hates to
         have him tagging along all the time. But Buzz lets Frankie

33

join in the fun when he does him a favor.

Va 6   _____. Too many sisters. New York: Morrow, 1956.
        Mike and his friends decide that girls are all right
when his sisters come to help during an uneven snowball
fight.

Va 7   Bell, Gina. Wanted: a brother. Nashville: Abingdon,
        1959.
        Timothy learns that his younger sister Anne is a good
playmate and a substitute for the brother he wishes to have.

Va 8   Borack, Barbara. Grandpa. New York: Harper, 1967.
        A charming monologue by a small girl, the tender and
humorous illustrations reflecting the mood of the text.
Marilyn describes her grandfather and their relationship in
a lovely way.

Va 9   _____. Someone small. New York: Harper, 1969.
        A tender but matter-of-fact look at some growing years
in the life of a small girl. Life is already full (of possessions, satisfactions, and love) when a baby sister comes
along to disrupt the pattern. The girl asks for a pet bird,
and enjoys Fluffy but finds, as time goes by, that a sister
is more responsive; in fact, in time, she is fun. And in
the fullness of his time Fluffy dies. The little sisters bury
him lovingly, then go on to play. Life changes. The story
is realistic and low-keyed, touched faintly with humor.

Va 10   Bromball, Winfred. Middle Matilda. Westminster, Md. :
        Knopf, 1962.
        Matilda loves being the middle child in a large family es-
pecially when every member of the family comes to her aid
during a minor crisis.

Va 11   Brown, Margaret Wise. The runaway bunny. New York:
        Harper, 1942.
        A bunny tries to run away from his mother, but she can
always find him.

Va 12   Brown, Myra B. Ice cream for breakfast. New York:
        Watts, 1963.
        A little girl and her brother prepare "breakfast in bed"
for their mother on Mother's Day.

Va 13   Brunhoff, Laurent de. Serafina the giraffe. Cleveland:
        World, 1961.
        Serafina visits her grandmother and all her animal friends
help her to bake a cake for grandmother's birthday.

Va 14   Buckley, Helen E. Grandfather and I. West Caldwell,
        N. J. : Lothrop, 1959.
        Grandfather is never in a hurry, and a small boy enjoys

walking, stopping and looking when they go out together.

Va 15 _____. Grandmother and I. West Caldwell, N. J. :
Lothrop, 1961.
A little girl explains that there are times when grand-
mother's lap is better than that of anyone else.

Va 16 _____. My sister and I. West Caldwell, N. J. : Lothrop,
1963.
Two sisters and their war relationship with each other--
one that is closer than that of ordinary playmates.

Va 17 Chandler, Edna Walker. Crystal pie. New York: Duell,
1965.
Ellen, the eight-year-old daughter of divorced parents,
is living happily with her mother and stepfather, but longs
to be adopted by her stepfather (so that her name will be
the same and she won't be branded as a member of a mixed-
up family). Before this is accomplished, however, Ellen
learns to understand her own father and recognize some of
his traits in herself.

Va 18 Child and his world. (series) Chicago: Society for Visual
Education, n. d. (record and tape)
Simple singing story-lessons devised to help little chil-
dren understand themselves, their family relationships and
their surroundings. Included in the series: My family and
I; Taking care of myself; My world; Helping is a good thing;
Magic of words; Laughing and playing.

Va 19 Clark, Ann Nolan. In my mother's house. New York:
Viking, 1951.
The story of the day-to-day life of Tewa Indians of
Tesuque pablo near Santa Fe.

Va 20 Duncan, Lois. Giving away Suzanne. New York: Dodd,
1963.
After she "trades" her little sister for a goldfish, Mary
Kay becomes lonely and comes to realize that her companionship far outweighs the fact that she can also be a
nuisance.

Va 21 Families have fun. (Primary Social Studies--group 1)
Chicago: Society for Visual Education, n. d. (filmstrip)
Shows how everyone contributes to family plans.

Va 22 The family. (series) Cambridge: Ealing, 1969. (sound
filmstrip, color, 39 frs.)
A simple but sensitive introduction to the family as a
social unit. Comparing families with different economic,
ethnic and cultural backgrounds, shows that, though the factors may vary, the basic function of the family remains the
same. The series squarely faces the problems of adoption,

divorce, separation and death, yet avoids any implication
that "broken homes" are necessarily inferior. Included in
the series: Family members and their roles; Each family
is different; Meeting physical needs; From childhood to old
age; Families from other cultures.

Va 23   The family. (series) St. Paul: Minnesota Mining and
              Manufacturing Company, 1967. (overhead transparencies
              8 x 10, color)
         Describes the role and responsibilities of individuals with-
         in the family.

Va 24   Family feelings. (series) New York: Learning Corpora-
              tion of America, 1970. (filmstrips, records)
              Sibling rivalry, a youngster's day with his father, affec-
         tion between children and grandparents--these themes and
         others show children that emotions within all families are
         similar, and expand their understanding of their own place
         within the family framework. Included are: Harvey's
         Hideout; Ronnie; The Grown-Up Day; Your Family Tree;
         and Grandparents Are to Love.

Va 25   Family fun. (Living with your family series) Chicago:
              Society for Visual Education, Inc., 1969. (filmstrip,
              color, 49 frames)
              Portrays recreational facilities and opportunities where
         families can have fun. Shows how leisure time at home
         can contribute to family unity.

Va 26   Flack, Marjorie. Ask Mr. Bear. Riverside, N. J.: Mac-
              millan, 1932.
         Danny does not know what to give his mother for her
         birthday so he asks many animals for their help.

Va 27   _____. Wait for William. New York: Houghton, 1935.
              William's older brother and sister are impatient when
         William lags behind on the way to the circus but they come
         to think better of him and his ways.

Va 28   Francoise. The big rain. New York: Scribner, 1961.
              Jeanne Marie and her family are caught in a flood on
         their farm in France. How they are rescued and help every-
         one clean up after the flood is depicted in fresh colorful
         drawings.

Va 29   Garelick, May. Double trouble. New York: Crowell,
              1958.
         Steve has a bad day when he is kept at home because of
         a cold until he straightens things out with his parents.

Va 30   Guy, Anne. A baby for Betsy. Nashville: Abingdon, 1957.
              Betsy and her parents go to the agency and find not one
         baby but twins to bring home to love and cherish.

Va 31   Hawkins, Quail. <u>The best birthday</u>. New York: Doubleday,
         1954.
         Dick ran away when he learned that there was going to
         be a new baby in his house but he returned when he found
         out that his parents could love two children as much as one.

Va 32   Haywood, Carolyn. <u>Here's a penny</u>. New York: Harcourt,
         1944.
         Secure in the knowledge that his new parents love him,
         an adopted boy welcomes another orphan into the family.

Va 33   _____. <u>Penny and Peter</u>. New York: Harcourt, 1946.
         Peter is adopted by Penny's new parents and the two
         boys have many good times together and share in earning a
         Christmas present for their "adopted" parents.

Va 34   Heilbroner, Joan. <u>The happy birthday present</u>. New York:
         Harper, 1961.
         Pete and Davey visit nearly every store in town before
         they find the "just right" birthday gift for their mother.

Va 35   Hill, Elizabeth Starr. <u>Evan's corner</u>. New York: Holt,
         1967.
         Evan, who lives with his mother, father and five brothers
         and sisters in a two-room Harlem flat, longs for privacy
         and a place of his own. Evan's understanding mother has
         a fine idea and suggests that each member of the family
         choose for his very own, one of the eight corners of the
         flat. Evan works hard to fix up his corner with a picture,
         a flower, orange crate furniture and even a pet turtle, but
         he discovers that something is missing. He finds the joy
         of sharing and helping others when he helps his little broth-
         er Adam fix up his corner, too.

Va 36   Hoban, Russell. <u>Little Brute family</u>. Riverside, N. J. :
         Macmillan, 1966.
         Mother, father and the three Brute children are ugly and
         mean, but one day, Baby Brute finds a "little wandering lost
         good feeling." After that, everyone becomes nice.

Va 37   <u>Learning to live with others</u>. (series) Chicago: Society
         for Visual Education, n. d. (filmstrip)
         Delightful stories, featuring full-color photography and
         accompanying narration, emphasize the importance of basic
         life values, as applied to the individual. Students will read-
         ily identify with the everyday situations presented in the
         filmstrips. This series is especially designed to help chil-
         dren think for themselves--to feel and grow. Parents and
         the family unit are presented in a supporting role, guiding
         children into discovering positive human values for them-
         selves. The children in these filmstrips reflect a variety
         of ethnic and economic backgrounds. Included in the series:
         Learning to be your best self; Learning about listening;

Learning what giving is all about; Learning to be responsible; Learning to trust people; Learning to keep a promise;
Learning about patience; Learning to face up to mistakes.

Va 38   Lenski, Lois. Surprise for mother. Philadelphia: Lippin-
         cott, 1934.
            Niddy gets the milk, Noddy gets the eggs, and Nancy
         gets the flour, sugar and baking powder so as to surprise
         Mother with a birthday cake.

Va 39   Lindman, Maj. Flicka, Ricka, Dicka bake a cake. Racine,
         Wis.: Whitman, 1955.
            Three little sisters bake a beautifully frosted cake as a
         birthday surprise for their mother.

Va 40   _____. Snipp, Snapp, Snurr and the red shoes. Racine,
         Wis.: Whitman, 1936.
            Three young Swedish boys work at different jobs so that
         they will earn enough money to buy a birthday present for
         their mother.

Va 41   Lord, Beman. Our new baby's ABC. New York: Walck,
         1964.
            Two children tell about their new baby brother and every-
         thing that he does.

Va 42   Mammen, Edward W. The Buttons go walking. New York:
         Harper, 1940.
            About a happy family that enjoyed working and playing
         together.

Va 43   Martin, Patricia Miles. The pointed brush. West Cald-
         well, N.J.: Lothrop, 1959.
            Little Chung Yee, small sixth son, is less help in the
         rice fields than the other children and so is chosen to learn
         to read and write. But when Chung Yee shows "the power
         of the written word" to release Elder Uncle, unjustly im-
         prisoned Honored Father decides all his sons shall sit at
         the feet of the teacher and grow wise and powerful.

Va 44   Mother cares for the family. 2nd ed. (Cooperative Living
         Series) El Cerrito, Cal.: Long Filmslide Service, 1954.
         (color filmstrip, 26 frs.)
            Shows a family--mother, father, and four children--at
         work and play. Emphasizes the need for cooperation within
         the family as a basis for democratic living. Stresses,
         healthful living, safety, courtesy, thankfulness, toleration
         and affection.

Va 45   Neville, Emily. It's like this, Cat. New York: Miller-
         Brody, 1970. (cassette)
            Dave gives this account of his life in New York City.
         He is ever engaged in a struggle with his father. He chooses

a cat to be his best friend as an act of defiance toward his
father.   Dave gradually learns to understand his father's
value system as being slightly different from his.   He also
begins to realize that many people have value systems that
will differ from the one he is developing.

Va 46   Orgel, Doris.   Sarah's room.   New York: Harper, 1963.
Little Jenny proves herself big enough to play in her
sister's room where there is not "a single trace of any
kind of messiness, the toys are all in place."

Va 47   Place in the family.   (Two Sides to Every Story Series)
Los Angeles: Churchill Films, 1970.   (color filmstrip,
37 frs.)
Presents a different point of view in which children can
see themselves in relation to others and to situations.

Va 48   Schlein, Miriam.   Laurie's new brother.   New York:
Abelard, 1961.
Through the warmth and understanding of her parents,
Laurie comes to accept the new baby as a permanent addi-
tion to the family.

Va 49   School and family relations.   Philadelphia: Educational Projections, Inc., n.d.   (cassette-trans.)
Lessons about everyday activities to help children understand themselves and others, and how they can have more
fun through cooperation and working together.   Concepts for
developing positive self-concepts and favorable attitudes.
Included are: Our Family at Home; School Is Our Other
Home; Did you Ask Permission?; Cooperating Is Fun; Working Together at Home; Do It the Right Way; and Fun with
the Family.

Va 50   Scott, Sally.   Judy's baby.   New York: Harcourt, 1949.
Judy felt out of it when Mother spent so much time with
the new baby until she realized how much fun it was to work
with Mother rather than indulge in jealous thoughts.

Va 51   Shotwell, Louisa.   Roosevelt Grady.   Cleveland: World,
1963.
Roosevelt Grady and his family are migratory workers.
Roosevelt lives in a loving family of five.   He shares a
private dream with his mother--that one day they will have
a home, a school and friends.

Va 52   Sonneborn, Ruth A.   Friday night is Papa night.   New York:
Viking, 1970.
The story of a Puerto Rican family in which Pedro and
his brothers and sisters wait for "Papa's night" (Friday)
when Papa is home from two jobs.

Va 53   Wasson, Valentine P.   The chosen baby.   Philadelphia:

Lippincott, 1950.

A man and his wife were very happy except that they had no baby.   So they went to a Home and picked Peter from many others to be their own.

Va 54   What do you think about helping your family.   (What Do You Think Series)   Los Angeles: Churchill Films, 1969. (filmstrip)

Focuses on some of the answers to how a boy can contribute to his family, why he should, and what he will gain by it.

Va 55   What will Christy do?   New York: Doubleday, 1968. (16mm film)

A dramatization about family responsibility and ethics.

Va 56   Why fathers work.   (Social Studies Series)   Chicago: Encyclopedia Britannica Educational Corp. , n. d.   (16mm film)

Shows where a father goes, what he does and how his work helps his family, his community and the city.   Illustrates the economic functions of the family as a community unit.

Va 57   Zolotow, Charlotte.   Big brother.   New York: Harper, 1960.

A little girl learns that her big brother really does not mean what he says when he teases her and they learn that playing together without teasing is fun.

Va 58   _____ .   Do you know what I'll do?   New York: Harper, 1958.

A little girl tells her little brother what she will do to please him.

FRIENDSHIP

Va 59   Anglund, Joan Walsh.   A friend is someone who likes you. New York: Harcourt, 1958.

A story of the many different kinds of friends we have and some of the nice things they do for us.

Va 60   Being friends.   Redondo Beach, Cal. :   Jarvis Couillard Assoc. , n. d.   (16mm filmstrip)

Teaches the value and meaning of friendship.   It shows that people may disagree but they can still remain friends.

Va 61   DeLeeuw, Adele.   Donny.   Boston: Little, 1957.

Shy Donny, an only child, didn't know how to get along with other children until he forgot himself in his care for stray animals and, through this project, made a number of friends.

Va 62   <u>Finding a friend</u>. Hollywood: Charles Cahill and Associates,
         Inc., 1970. (16mm film, color, 11 minutes)
         Portrays the predicament of a ten-year-old child moving
         into a new neighborhood and seeking friends.

Va 63   Foster, Joanna. <u>A train ride</u>. New York: Harcourt, 1965.
         Judy is taking her first train ride on her way to visit
         her grandma. On the way some strange incidents happen as
         well as her meeting a new friend.

Va 64   <u>Friendliness for all</u>. (Tune-up in Health Series) Minneapo-
         lis: Radio Station-Minnesota School of the Air-University
         of Minnesota, 1961. (tape, 15 minutes--3 3/4 IPS.)
         Presents a discussion among team members when one of
         the ball players expresses prejudice against one of the Negro
         players. Depicts how the teacher observes the trouble and
         resolves the situation.

Va 65   <u>Friends</u>. Los Angeles: Churchill Films, 1972. (16mm,
         color, 18 minutes)
         A story about the friendship between Nancy, an extro-
         verted, impatient girl, and her vulnerable best friend. Il-
         lustrates what happens to feelings when Nancy goes off to
         play with another girl.

Va 66   Funk, Melissa. <u>Pals</u>. New York: Western, 1966.
         Tells how a little boy discovers that even though his
         friend calls things by different names, they are basically
         the same. For instance, he calls them pajamas and his
         friend calls them nighties; he calls it a nursery and his
         friend calls it a bedroom; and he calls it a biscuit while his
         friend calls it a cracker. But they are all the same thing,
         and the little boy realizes how nice it is to be a little alike
         and a little different, yet be good friends.

Va 67   <u>Getting along with others</u>. Chicago: Coronet, 1965. (16mm
         film--11 minutes)
         Shows children in familiar situations at home, at play,
         and at school. Stresses the importance of fair play, shar-
         ing, helping one another, and taking turns.

Va 68   Greene, Constance C. <u>Girl called Al</u>. New York: Viking,
         1969.
         Al is fat, she doesn't like the clothes her mother buys
         for her, she has to wear her hair in pigtails, she hates
         her name Alexandra, and hates her mother! Then she
         moves into an apartment house where she finds a friend and
         life becomes happier.

Va 69   Holberg, Ruth. <u>What happened to Virgilia</u>. New York:
         Doubleday, 1963.
         Overly shy Virgilia spends a year with her Aunt Emma
         and learns to make friends and to overcome her jealousy.

Va 70   Holland, Isabelle. Amanda's choice. Philadelphia: Lippin-
         cott, 1970.
         A procession of governesses has tried to care for mother-
         less and rich Amanda. She is a very unhappy child, how-
         ever, whom even her father dislikes. But change comes
         when Santiago moves into a nearby cottage. They need each
         other, like each other, and even fight each other occasional-
         ly. A good character study of Cuban-American interaction
         and of growing responsibility for action on the part of two
         children.

Va 71   How friends are made. Hollywood: Shepherd Menken (see
         Aims...), 1968. (16mm film--11 minutes, color)
         Describes the experiences of an elementary grade boy as
         he makes a friend. Reveals some of his own wonder and
         reflection on the event.

Va 72   Learning to live with others. (series) Chicago: Society
         for Visual Education, n. d. (filmstrip)
         Delightful stories, featuring full-color photography and
         accompanying narration, emphasize the importance of basic
         life values, as applied to the individual. Students will read-
         ily identify with the everyday situations presented in the
         filmstrips. This series is especially designed to help chil-
         dren think for themselves--to feel and grow.

Va 73   McNeer, May Y. My friend Mac. Boston: Houghton, 1960.
         When Little Baptiste's pet moose goes off into the woods,
         he finds a much better friend at school.

Va 74   Mathis, Sharon Bell. Sidewalk story. New York: Viking,
         1971.
         The world of Lily Etta and her friend Tanya is thrown
         into chaos when the men come to evict Tanya's mother and
         seven children from their Harlem flat. Lily Etta's mother
         felt she had done all she could to help Tanya's mother. But
         Lily Etta is determined to get help. How she does secure
         help makes a heart-warming story of true friendship between
         two little girls.

Va 75   Miles, Betty. Having a friend. Westminster, Md.: Knopf,
         1959.
         What it means to have a friend, as experienced by two
         little girls who meet at a playground.

Va 76   Minarik, Else H. Little Bear's friend. New York: Harper,
         1960.
         New friends, including a little girl Emily, and her doll,
         Lucy, help make an unforgettable summer.

Va 77   Ness, Evaline. Sam, Bangs and Moonshine. New York:
         Holt, 1966.
         Motherless Samantha (called Sam), living on an island,

has the lonely child's predilection for daydreams: her mother is not dead--but a mermaid, and Sam has at home not
only Bangs, her wise old cat (who could talk), but also a
fierce lion and a baby kangaroo! Her practical fisherman
father is worried. "... for a change, talk 'Real' not 'Moonshine.' 'Moonshine' spells trouble." Not until her wildly
exaggerated 'Moonshine' talk sends her only friend (Thomas)
with her beloved cat to near destruction does Sam realize
the grown-up difference between true imagination and un-
controlled flights of fancy.

Va 78   Ormsby, Virginia H. What's wrong with Julio? Philadel-
        phia: Lippincott, 1965.
        When Julio's classmates learn why he is unhappy, they
help him to overcome his difficulties.

Va 79   Schlein, Miriam. The sun, the wind, the sea, and the
        rain. New York: Abelard, 1960.
        A variant of an old fable of the wind and the sun with
its theme of kindness and gentleness winning over power and
brute strength.

Va 80   Slobodkin, Louis. One is good but two is better. New
        York: Vanguard, 1956.
        It is all right to be alone but when work and fun are
shared with friends or family it is ever so much better.

Va 81   Steptoe, John. Stevie. New York: Harper, 1969.
        Robert tells the story of the intruder, Stevie, who comes
to stay at his house because both parents are working.
Stevie is a pest, tagging along after Robert and messing up
all his toys. But Robert is sad when Stevie leaves because
he knows that Steve liked him and looked up to him. Robert
feels sorry that he didn't treat him more nicely since he
didn't have his parents around most of the time.

Va 82   Udry, Janice May. Let's be enemies. New York: Harper,
        1965.
        John is unhappy because his friend is too bossy and when
he tells him this, the two boys say they will stop being
friends. They resolve the issue and remain friends.

Va 83   _____. Let's be enemies. Weston, Conn.: Weston
        Woods Studios, 1970. (filmstrip)
        Based on book of same title, correlated with cassette
tape. Story of two little boys who decide to be enemies
because one of them is too bossy.

Va 84   Understanding ourselves. (Value Series) Santa Monica,
        Cal.: BFA Educational Media, n.d. (16mm film--color--
9 minutes)
        Uses a story of three boys to present the concept. Every-
one has an idea of the kind of person he is. Explains that

sometimes it seems like it would be more fun to be someone else but each person if he could really choose, would
rather be himself.

Va 85   Understanding ourselves and others.   (Tune-up in Health
          Series) Corvallis, Ore.: Oregon School of the Air
          Radio Station, KOAC-TV, 1961.   (15 minutes, 3 3/4
          IPS)
          Discusses how the children learn to choose friends for
when they are, not what they look like.   Emphasizes the
idea of understanding people.

Va 86   Values--being friends.   Redondo Beach, Cal.:   Jarvis
          Couillard Associates, 1969.   (16mm film, color, 9 min-
          utes)
          Teaches the meaning of friendship.   Shows that people
may disagree but still remain friends.   Emphasizes trust
and helping each other.

Va 87   Values--cooperation.   Redondo Beach, Cal.: Jarvis
          Couillard Associates, 1969.   (16mm film, color, 11 min-
          utes)
          Stresses the value of cooperation by picturing three boys
playing together.

Va 88   Values--playing fair.   Redondo Beach, Cal.: Jarvis Couil-
          lard Associates, 1969.   (16mm film, color, 10 minutes)
          Teaches the value of cooperation by picturing three boys
together.   Stresses the value of cooperation whether at work,
play or school.

Va 89   Waber, Bernard.   Lovable Lyle.   Boston: Houghton, 1969.
          Lyle the crocodile has an enemy who slips notes under
the door of his house.   Mystery: A little girl's feelings
are hurt because Lovable Lyle has attracted her friends to
him and she feels deserted.

Va 90   Wahl, Jan.   Animals' peace day.   New York: Crown, 1970.
          All the animals bring food to a peace day celebration,
but quarrels and fighting soon break out and all resolve to
try again.

Va 91   Wilder, Laura I.   The long winter.   New York: Harper,
          1953.
          Through a long, hard winter which seems to be one con-
tinuous blizzard, the Ingalls family struggles bravely for
mere existence and makes do cheerfully with what it has.

Va 92   Ylla.   Look who's talking.   New York: Harper, 1962.
          All the zoo animals are critical of Oliver the ostrich be-
cause he doesn't talk.   But when the baby leopard makes
friendly overtures it is discovered that the reason Oliver
has not spoken is that he has been waiting for someone to

talk to him instead of about him.

Va 93   You can't buy friendship. Los Angeles: Family Films,
          Inc., n.d. (16mm film, 15 minutes)
          Tells of a boy visiting his cousins in another city who
          learns that winning friends involves Christian attitudes of
          respect.

Va 94   Zolotow, Charlotte. The three funny friends. New York:
          Harper, 1961.
          A little girl who has many exciting adventures with
          three imaginary playmates gladly gives them up when she
          finds a real one.

                              HONESTY

Va 95   Am I trustworthy. Chicago: Coronet, 1951.
          Portrays examples of trustworthiness. Includes return-
          ing borrowed articles, keeping promises, and doing a good
          job with assigned tasks.

Va 96   Brink, Carol Ryrie. The bad times of Irma Baumlein.
          Riverside, N.J.: Macmillan, 1972.
          New in town, Irma lies to impress a friend by claiming
          to own the biggest doll in the world. She steals a manni-
          kin from her great uncle's store to support her boast, but
          finally faces up to the truth when an innocent store clerk
          is reprimanded.

Va 97   Cole, Joanna. The secret box. New York: Morrow, 1971.
          A little city girl named Anne Marie learns to respect
          other people's property after stealing another child's ring
          to put in her special secret box of treasures.

Va 98   Gallant, Kathryn. The flute player of Beppu. New York:
          Coward, 1960.
          Though sorely tempted to keep it, Sato-san gives up a
          flute after he learns the misery its loss has caused its
          owner.

Va 99   Haywood, Carolyn. Eddie's paydirt. New York: Morrow,
          1953.
          When he returns the old Spanish coins he had found,
          Eddie receives a pony as a reward.

Va 100   _____. Two and two are four. New York: Harcourt,
          1940.
          Teddy and Babs have a wonderful summer playing with
          the twins across the road and when they are naughty they
          own up to their faults.

Va 101   Hogan, Inez. Nappy wanted a dog. New York: Dutton,

1942.
Nappy wanted a dog so much that he collected dogs
from neighborhood backyards until he learned not to take
things that did not belong to him.

Va 102   Jerry has a surprise--honesty is the best policy.   (Little
           things that count series)   Jamaica, N.Y.:   Eye Gate,
           n.d.   (filmstrip)
           A guidance series emphasizing the most important basic
           lessons to be learned in character building.   Centering
           around situations and experiences familiar to all children,
           the stories involve the joy of helping others, honesty, per-
           severance, responsibility, respect and good manners.   A
           designated frame can be held on the screen while the class
           discusses ways for resolving the problem facing the chil-
           dren in the story.

Va 103   Lindman, Maj.   Flicka, Ricka, Dicka and a little dog.
           Racine, Wis.:   Whitman, 1946.
           When they return a stray dog to its rightful owner,
           Flicks, Ricka, and Dicka find out that "honesty pays."

Va 104   McGinley, Phyllis.   The most wonderful doll in the world.
           Philadelphia: Lippincott, 1951.
           Duley builds up her lost doll to have been the most won-
           derful doll in the world.   But later she admits that this is
           not quite the truth.

Va 105   Matsuno, Masako.   A pair of red clogs.   Cleveland:
           World, 1960.
           Mako learns that deceit is not a good practice when her
           parents see through her tactic of soiling her red clogs so
           that she can get a new pair.

Va 106   _____.   Taro and the Tofu.   Cleveland: World, 1962.
           When Taro finds that the Tofu peddler has given him an
           extra forty yen in change, he overcomes the temptation to
           keep it and discovers the feeling of warmth and happiness
           that doing right brings.

Va 107   Rockwell, Anne.   The stolen necklace.   Cleveland: World,
           1968.
           While an Indian Princess bathes, a vain monkey steals
           her pearl necklace and hides it.   A clever gardener places
           shining necklaces where all the monkeys can find them and
           in order to prove that hers is prettiest the vain monkey
           shows her stolen necklace.   The gardener snatches the
           pearls from the monkey and returns them to the princess.

Va 108   Spicer, Dorothy Gladys.   13 rascals.   New York: Coward,
           1971.
           All kinds of rascals people this book.   A country bump-
           kin fools three rascals, a husband outwits his wife who too

often speaks out of turn, an abbot proves to the king that his false friends have lied about him, and an honest shepherd refuses to lie and becomes a trusted adviser. All tales prove that honesty and quick thinking will aid men in their times of need.

Va 109   Values--telling the truth. Redondo Beach, Cal.: Jarvis
          Couillard Associates, 1969. (16mm filmstrip, color,
          10 minutes)
          Illustrates the specific value of honesty.

Va 110   Values. (series) Jamaica, N.Y.: Eye Gate, n.d. (film-
          strips)
          The student of today questions adult standards and values.
          This set is designed to assist the young learner in develop-
          ing a standard of values. Each filmstrip will explore areas
          of social conflict. Both appropriate and inappropriate re-
          sponses will be given without a judgment being made. In-
          cluded in the series: Telling the truth; What is stealing?"
          Kindness; Politeness; Responsibility; Citizenship.

Va 111   What do you think about finders keepers? Mahwah, N.J.:
          Educational Reading Services, 1969. (filmstrip, color,
          24 frs.)
          Focuses on what a young girl would do when she finds
          a wristwatch left on the school playground.

Va 112   What do you think about lying. (What Do You Think Series)
          Los Angeles: Churchill Films, 1969. (color filmstrip,
          36 frs.)
          Portrays an opportunity for a young boy to lie about his
          actions as he has seen his parents do.

Va 113   What will Ted do? New York: Doubleday, 1968.
          A dramatization about making exaggerated claims, a
          problem encountered by many children in everyday, school-
          connected situations.

Va 114   What would happen if? Rochester, N.Y.: Modern Learn-
          ing Aids Division of Wards Natural Science, 1969.
          (16mm, color, 9 minutes)
          This film illustrates what would happen if everyone stole
          things. It stimulates the children's oral expression of
          their ideas.

                        INDIVIDUAL DIFFERENCES

Va 115   About myself--my family and other families alike and dif-
          ferent. (series) Glendale, Cal.: Bowmar, 1970.
          (sound filmstrip, color, 33 frs.)
          Introduces the child to similarities and differences that
          exist from family to family.

Va 116   Acceptance of differences.   (Developing Basic Values
          Series) Chicago: Society for Visual Education, n. d.
          (sound filmstrip)
          Biographies of great men and women are used to show
          the insignificance of political, religious, and racial dif-
          ferences in making contributions to society.

Va 117   Bannon, Laura. The other side of the world.   Boston:
          Houghton, 1960.
          As the sun shines in turn on Tommy and on a little
          Japanese boy, they learn of each other and their mutually
          "strange ways. "

Va 118   Beim, Jerrold. Swimming hole. New York: Morrow,
          1951.
          Steve is not accepted by the other boys in the neighbor-
          hood swimming hole until he has learned that the color of
          one's skin is not important.

Va 119   Beim, Lorraine. Two is a team. New York: Harcourt,
          1945.
          A Negro boy and a white boy play together and by exer-
          cising teamwork make good the damage they have done
          with their scooters.

Va 120   Being alike and being different: I hate you.   (Minorities
          and Majorities series) Jamaica, N. Y. : Eye Gate, n. d.
          (tape)
          Deals with the nature of prejudice and bigotry, showing
          how it is taught or tolerated; directly or indirectly deals
          with child to child prejudice, being part of a group, being
          outside of a group and being within a group.

Va 121   Brenner, Barbara. Mr. Tall and Mr. Small. New York:
          Young Scott Books, 1966.
          A giraffe and a mouse argue about which is the better
          size until a forest fire almost traps them and they must
          find a way to safety.

Va 122   Carter, Katherine J. Willie Waddle. Austin, Tex. :
          Steck, 1959.
          Tolerance for those who are different is the moral of
          this story of a little chicken whose over-sized feet enable
          him to rescue the other chicks during a storm.

Va 123   Different. Nashville: Graded Press, Methodist, 1967.
          (sound strip, color, 70 frs.)
          Explains to children that although individuals may be
          different because of color, physical handicaps, facial fea-
          tures and nationality, they have the same basic needs and
          desires.

Va 124   Doss, Helen. All the children of the world. Nashville:

Abingdon, 1958.
How God planned it so that each child born in the world
would be different from all others and how gratefully we
should be that He made each one not only different but
beautiful.

Va 125   . <u>Friends around the world</u>. Nashville: Abingdon, 1959.
About the things that are common to all children in
spite of their differences and why they should all be friends.

Va 126 Duvoisin, Roger. <u>Our Veronica goes to Petunia's farm</u>.
Westminster, Md.: Knopf, 1962.
All the animals were dismayed when a hippopotamus
came to live at the farm but they gradually made friends
with Veronica and found her not so incongruous, after all.

Va 127 <u>Guidance--Does color really make a difference?</u> Hollywood:
Charles Cahill and Associates, Inc., 1969. (16mm
film, color, 11 minutes)
Conflicts are shown in color situations and leaves the
conclusions open for the class to discuss.

Va 128 Lawson, Robert. <u>They were strong and good.</u> New York:
Viking, 1940.
In a book which is more than half big black and white
pictures, the author proudly tells the stories of his four
grandparents of his father and mother--proudly, not because they were great or famous, but because they were
strong and good, and typical of most American forebears.
Done occasionally with humor and always with emotion.
American ideals are inherent in the story and the superb
drawings.

Va 129 Lexau, Joan M. <u>I should have stayed in bed!</u> New York:
Harper, 1965.
It bothered Sam more that his best friend Albert
seemed to have deserted him than that everything else
went wrong that day. But when both boys stay after school
together, Sam knows that they are indeed friends. Sam is
a Negro and Albert is white and they attend an integrated
school.

Va 130 Liang, Yen. <u>Tommy and Dee-Dee.</u> New York: Walck,
1953.
That differences of environment do not mean that people
are not basically the same is the lesson to be learned from
this little story of American Tommy and Chinese Dee-Dee.

Va 131 May, Julian. <u>Why people are different colors.</u> New York:
Holiday, 1971.
Examines major races and their variations, suggests
possible values of distinctive body features and the pre-

historic migration of people.   It makes the point that differences are superficial.

Va 132   Naylor, Phyllis.   The new schoolmaster.   Our World of
            People series.   Morristown, N. J. :   Silver, 1967.
            A new schoolmaster comes to live in a village in North-
         ern India.   He is unable to win the friendship of the boys
         he teaches until the day a little girl spoils his jacket with
         some red powder.   By the time the jacket is fixed, the
         villagers are ready to welcome him.

Va 133   Randall, Blossom E.   Fun for Chris.   Racine, Wis. :
            Whitman, 1956.
            Chris's mother explains to him and to Toby that if
         there is a difference in the color of their skin it is be-
         cause God meant it to be so, and that such a difference
         should not be allowed to spoil their friendship.

Va 134   Robinson, Veronica.   David in silence.   Philadelphia: Lip-
            pincott, 1966.
            David was deaf and when he and his family moved into
         a new town, the children in the neighborhood reacted to
         him with suspicion and hostility.   Only one boy made the
         effort to understand.

Va 135   Rowe, Jeanne A.   City workers.   New York: Watts, 1969.
            Firemen, policemen, postmen, nurses, doctors, file
         clerks, waitresses are just a few of the many different
         types of city workers whose service jobs are described in
         this book.

Va 136   Steiner, Charlotte.   A friend is "Amie. "   Westminster,
            Md. :   Knopf, 1956.
            American Milly and French Lili learn to talk and play
         together and become good friends.

Va 137   Understanding ourselves and others.   (Tune-up in Health
            series)   Corvallis, Ore. :   Oregon School of the Air
            Radio Station, KOAC-TV, 1961.   (Tape, 15 minutes,
            3 3/4 IPS.)

Va 138   What about other people?   Jamaica, N. Y. :   Eye Gate,
            1969.   (sound filmstrip, color, 34 frs.)
            Drawings.   Studies the person in relationship to others
         and discusses the different types of social groups.

                              RESPONSIBILITY

Va 139   Barr, Catherine.   Runaway chimp.   New York: Walck,
            1954.
            Four chimpanzees have a wonderful time in the city un-
         til they learn that their keeper is in jail because they ran

away from the zoo.

Va 140   Be your own traffic policeman.   New York: McGraw-Hill
         Text Films, 1962.
         Uses the motivating concept of learning to help children
         develop safe attitudes in traffic. Suggests things to do in
         traffic to avoid getting hurt and the importance of traffic
         rules.

Va 141   Bishop, Claire Huchet. All alone. New York: Viking,
         1953.
         Marcel and his friend Pierre herd their family's cows
         high on the French Alps. Their experiences illustrate the
         fact that "there is a better way of life than each man for
         himself."

Va 142   Bowen, Vernon. Lazy beaver. New York: McKay, 1948.
         A lazy beaver becomes the busiest beaver in all Beaver-
         town after he mends a hole in the dam.

Va 143   Bromhall, Winifred. Bridget's growing day.   Westminster,
         Md.: Knopf, 1957.
         After Bridget takes care of the household chores while
         her mother is away, she no longer minds if she continues
         to be called "Wee Bridget" for she has come to see that
         size is not the criterion for worth.

Va 144   Burchardt, Nellie. Project cat. New York: Watts, 1966.
         Betsy and a group of girls who live in a project be-
         friend a cat they find under the bushes and feed it there,
         since pets are not allowed in their apartments. Their
         secret pet finally leads them on an exciting visit to the
         mayor and the city council, and the cat surprises them,
         too.

Va 145   Burton, Virginia L. Katy and the big snow.   Boston:
         Houghton, 1943.
         A crawler tractor named Katy takes the lead in digging
         out the city during a winter storm and saves the city.

Va 146   Caudill, Rebecca. Did you carry the flag today, Charley?
         New York: Holt, 1966.
         Charley who is four "a-going-on five" goes to the "Lit-
         tle" summer school at Raccoon Hollow where he finds
         many new things to excite his curiosity--wash basins,
         colored clay, a library! Each day one good child is chosen
         to lead the boys and girls to the bus and carry the flag
         This is the story of how Charley finally came to carry the
         flag.

Va 147   Craig, Jean M. The long and dangerous journey. New
         York: Norton, 1965.
         A simple walk becomes an exciting adventure as a

small boy changes everyday people into awesome beings.
A child's view of parents and authority is shown.

Va 148   Dalgliesh, Alice. Bears on Hemlock Mountain. New
          York: Scribner, 1952.
          When Jonathan has to return after dark, alone over the
          mountain, the small animals and birds help keep up his
          courage. Then he finds there really are bears on the
          mountain!

Va 149   _____. The courage of Sarah Noble. New York: Scrib-
          ner, 1954.
          Sarah, though only eight, was her father's companion on
          a grueling and dangerous journey to build a new home in
          the Connecticut wilderness of 1707, and she succeeded well
          in following her mother's advice to "keep up your courage,
          Sarah Noble." When, however, the log house was finished
          and her father was leaving her with the Indians while he
          went back alone to get the rest of the family, Sarah, who
          had been very brave, confessed that she had lost her cour-
          age. To this her father made the discerning and hearten-
          ing reply, "To be afraid and to be brave is the best cour-
          age of all."

Va 150   Du Bois, William Pene. Lazy Tommy Pumpkinhead. New
          York: Harper, 1966.
          Lazy Tommy does little for himself. He lives in an
          all-electric environment until the power fails.

Va 151   Duvoisin, Roger. Petunia. Westminster, Md.: Knopf,
          1950.
          Petunia, a silly goose, finds a book and thinks that be-
          cause she owns it, she is automatically wise. Considering
          herself as authority on everything, Petunia gives free and
          incorrect advice to her barnyard friends, making them un-
          happier than they were before. Not until an explosion
          which she causes opens the covers of the book does Pe-
          tunia see the writing inside. She realizes then: "It is
          not enough to carry wisdom under my wing, I must put
          it in my heart and in my mind; and to do that, I must
          learn to read." With a new understanding of wisdom, Pe-
          tunia starts her education.

Va 152   Economakis, Olga. Oasis of the stars. New York: Cow-
          ard, 1965.
          Abu lives in the desert. He loves its beauty, especial-
          ly the stars shimmering in the sky at night. But he longs
          for enough water so that his family will not have to move;
          he works hard to find water.

Va 153   Graham, Margaret Bloy. Be nice to spiders. New York:
          Harper, 1967.
          When Billy left his pet spider, Helen, at the zoo, the

animals suddenly became happy and contented, all because
Helen was spinning webs and catching flies. But one day
the webs were swept away. Soon the flies were back again
and the animals were miserable once more. But not for
long!

Va 154   Guidance for the seventies--who's responsible. Santa Mon-
          ica, Cal.: BFA Educational Media, 1972. (color, 19
          minutes)
          Explores the individual's concept of himself through
          group discussion. States that individuals often place the
          responsibility outside themselves. Concludes with the
          message, "I am the cause of my own effects."

Va 155   Holland, Isabelle. Amanda's choice. Philadelphia: Lippin-
          cott, 1970.
          A procession of governesses has tried to care for moth-
          erless and rich Amanda. She is a very unhappy child,
          however, whom even her father dislikes. But change comes
          when Santiago moves into a nearby cottage. They need
          each other, like each other, and even fight each other oc-
          casionally. A good character study of Cuban-American in-
          teraction and of growing responsibility for action on the
          part of the two children.

Va 156   Jim learns responsibility. (A guidance series) Jamaica,
          N.Y.: Eye Gate, n.d. (filmstrip)
          The series emphasizes the most important basic lessons
          to be learned in character building. Centering around situ-
          ations and experiences familiar to all children, the stories
          involve the joy of helping others, honesty, perseverance,
          responsibility, respect and good manners. A designated
          frame can be held on the screen while the class discusses
          ways for resolving the problem facing the children in the
          story.

Va 157   Lexau, Joan. Benjie. New York: Dial, 1964.
          How a little boy living with his grandmother in Harlem
          discovers he can speak when he must.

Va 158   Lipkind, William. Nubber Bear. New York: Harcourt,
          1966.
          Nubber means to be a good bear, but he means to get
          some honey, too, from Middle Wood where he is forbidden
          to go. In the end, all are happy. Nubber gets his honey
          and learns a useful lesson.

Va 159   MacDonald, Golden. The little island. New York: Double-
          day, 1946.
          Children often think of themselves as little islands self-
          contained and with no responsibilities toward others. This
          book explains that the little island is a part of the big
          world, too.

Va 160   The merry-go-round.   New York: Learning Corporation
         of America, n. d.   (16mm film)
         The story of a ragamuffin and his experiences with a
         beautiful wooden merry-go-round horse he adores.   Raises
         the question--does the end justify the means?

Va 161   Ormondroyd, Edward.   Theodore.   Berkeley, Cal.: Par-
         nassus, 1966.
         Theodore is Lucy's smudgy old teddy bear; and he knows
         she loves him and understands him, even though her care-
         lessness causes him to have a terrifying experience at the
         neighborhood laundromat.

Va 162   Slobodkin, Louis.   Thank you--you're welcome.   New York:
         Vanguard, 1957.
         Story of Jimmy who was happy and good and always said,
         "Thank you," whenever he could--until the day he was sad
         because he, too, wanted to say, "you're welcome." Having
         learned how one earns the right to say this, Jimmy is good
         again and the story ends happily.

Va 163   Stover, Jo Ann.   If everybody did.   New York: McKay,
         1960.
         Sketches of the hilarious consequences if everybody were
         to do what all of us do sometimes--slam the door, track
         in mud, eat all the jam.

Va 164   They need me.   (series) Los Angeles: Churchill Films,
         n. d.   (filmstrip, 4 frs.)
         Young children are shown the meaning of responsibility
         and the many ways in which they are important to others.
         Included in the series: My mother and father need me;
         My baby sitter needs me; My friends need me; My dog
         needs me.

Va 165   Udry, Janice May.   What Mary Jo wanted.   Racine, Wis.:
         Whitman, 1968.
         Mary Jo is interested in getting a puppy.   After she
         learns what her duties toward the pet will be, her father
         buys a dog.   The dog is fine but he cries night after night,
         so Mary Jo must find a way to quiet him.

Va 166   Values.   Jamaica, N. Y.: Eye Gate, n. d.   (filmstrip)
         The student of today questions adult standards and values.
         This set is designed to assist the young learner in develop-
         ing a standard of values.   Each filmstrip will explore areas
         of social conflict.   Both appropriate and inappropriate re-
         sponses will be given without a judgment being made.   The
         students can be asked to roly play and discuss each prob-
         lem and response, hence developing their own answers and
         formulating their own set of values.   Included in the series:
         Telling the truth; What is stealing?; Kindness; Politeness;
         Responsibility; Citizenship.

Va 167   What will Christy do? New York: Doubleday, 1967.
          (16mm film, color, 6 minutes)
          A dramatization about family responsibility and ethics.

Va 168   Woolley, Catherine. Two hundred pennies. New York:
          Morrow, 1947.
          After throwing a tantrum when he does not receive a
          train for his birthday, David proves he is worthy of one
          by earning enough money to pay for the track.

Va 169   Zion, Gene. The plant sitter. New York: Harper, 1959.
          Tommy takes care of the neighbors' plants while they
          are on vacation, learns the proper way to do this, and al-
          most turns his house into a jungle.

                        RIGHTS OF OTHERS

Va 170   Aesop's fables. New York: Atheneum, 1971.
          Fifteen of the familiar fables have been gathered in
          this book. Vivid full-page illustrations humorously retell
          the fables, too.

Va 171   Aesop. The Aesop for children. Eau Claire, Wis.:
          Hale, 1962.
          Old-fashioned in appearance, but a comprehensive col-
          lection of about 75 fables, each with a stated moral.

Va 172   Aesop's fables. New York: Viking, 1933.
          This is a collection of beast tales that serve to illus-
          trate a moral or precept, based on old African tradition.

Va 173   Aesop's fables. New York: Western Publishing, n.d.
          Forty illustrated fables of Aesop that lead one to con-
          clusions of morality beneficial to everyday living.

Va 174   Bonsall, Crosby. It's mine. New York: Harper, 1963.
          Mabel Ann and Patrick are good friends until the sub-
          ject of sharing comes up. They each think "what's yours
          is mine." Each wants all the toys, but they finally learn
          the social benefits of sharing and each grows up a little.
          Good illustrations help tell the story.

Va 175   Brown, Margaret Wise. Dead birds. New York: Scott,
          1958.
          A child finds a dead bird and the other children join in
          giving it a suitable burial, placing spring flowers on the
          grave and singing a song.

Va 176   Consideration for others. (Developing Basic Values series)
          Chicago: Society for Visual Education, n.d. (filmstrip)
          Students learn to show consideration when others are
          busy and learn how to help other people.

Va 177   De Regniers, Beatrice Schenk. A little house of your own.
          New York: Harcourt, 1954.
          The importance of a secret house of one's own as well
          as suggestions as to where it may be found are explored
          here in gentle fashion.

Va 178   Ets, Marie Hall. Play with me. New York: Viking, 1955.
          A little girl learns that the creatures of the meadow
          will come to her if she is gentle.

Va 179   Exploring moral values series. Pleasantville, N. Y.:
          Schloat, 1966. (15 filmstrips, color, and phonodisc;
          average 15 frs. each)
          Photographs present forty-four critical situations which
          demand decisive action. The situations involve prejudice,
          honesty, authority, and personal values and provoke in-
          quiry into alternatives and the reason for each choice.
          Contents: Blocking the sidewalk; Fire; Keep off the grass;
          Latin American Christmas; Mind your older sister; Moving
          in; The boys; The bully; The dollar bill; The Hold-up; The
          little brother; The meeting; The Sabbath; The stranger;
          Waiting for a package.

Va 180   Grandpa says. (series) Big Springs, Tex.: Creative
          Visuals, n. d. (Tape, 15 minutes)
          This series of children's teaching stories was created
          and structured not only to be interesting to children, but
          for the values the child will receive from the "moral" of
          the story. This modern "Aesops Fables" idea is expanded
          to current relevance with the everyday life of the child.
          As each story unravels, the moral of the story becomes
          clearer to the listener. "Grandpa" talks to the children
          as if he was really in the classroom, seated in front of
          them. There are thirty lessons in the series. Each tape
          lesson is fifteen minutes in length. There are two lessons
          to each tape. Included are: Honesty; Taking turns; Keep-
          ing your word; Holding a grudge; Respect for others;
          Selfishness; Doing your part; Quarreling; Respect for rules
          and teasing.

Va 181   I beg your pardon. Mahwah, N. J.: Troll, 1969. (film-
          strip)
          Full color drawings of animals illustrate the importance
          of good manners. May be used for group or individual
          study.

Va 182   Keats, Ezra Jack. Peter's chair. Weston, Conn.: Wes-
          ton Woods Studios, Inc., 1969. (16mm)
          This film is based on the above book title. It is a re-
          production of Peter's rebellion against his chair and other
          possessions being taken over by his new sister until he
          realizes that he has outgrown them.

Va 183   Kirn, Ann. Beeswax catches a thief. New York: Norton,
          1968.
          All the animals except Jackal work together to dig a
          pool so that they will have water during the hot dry day.
          When mischievous Jackal stirs up the water and makes it
          muddy, clever Tortoise devises a way to catch him.

Va 184   Krylov. Fables. New York: Macmillan, 1965.
          This is a collection of Russian animal tales that pare
          away at the absurdities of man and society. The tales
          are told in such a way that we can easily recognize our-
          selves or our friends or acquaintances as the real char-
          acters.

Va 185   The lemonade stand, what's fair? Chicago: Encyclopae-
              dia Britannica Education Corporation, 1970. (16mm
              film, color, 14 minutes)
          Focus on the meaning of commitment, obligation and
          responsibility to others.

Va 186   Little citizens. Burbank: Cathedral Films, 1966. (6
              filmstrips)
          Simple stories for developing good character traits and
          better citizenship habits. Contents: Raggedy Elf (friend-
          liness); Mighty Hunter (Indian legends and the stars); Boy
          (theme of home based on Lincoln); Bike Behavior (safety);
          How the Birds Got Their Color (theme of honesty); Little
          Star That Got Lost (theme of obedience).

Va 187   Living with others--citizenship. Madison, Wis.: Demco,
              n.d. (record and tape, 33 1/3 rpm.)
          Presents thirteen dramatized episodes, involving safety,
          honor, responsibility, family and community rules. Tries
          to help each youngster meet his emotional and social needs
          through recognizing and developing his personal, family
          and community responsibilities.

Va 188   Manners at school. (Primary Manners series) New York:
              United World Films, Inc., 1966. (16mm film)
          Shows examples of good and bad manners at school.
          Stresses cheerfulness, kindness and consideration, respect
          for property and good health habits.

Va 189   Moral values. (series) New York: Popular Science, n.d.
              (filmstrip)
          Designed to help children realize moral values. In-
          cludes: Good or Bad; Ideals to Live By; If It Isn't Yours
          --Respect for Property; Striving for Excellence; Who Are
          Your Ideals.

Va 190   Moyer, Mercer. Mine! New York: Simon and Schuster,
          1970.
          A selfish little boy learns that he cannot have everything
          he wants.

Va 191   Parish, Peggy. My golden book of manners. New York:
          Golden Press, 1962.
          Animals join the children to show them the polite thing
          to do in a number of occasions.

Va 192   Peet, Bill. Kermit, the hermit. Boston: Houghton, 1965.
          A greedy crab changes his selfish ways when a boy
          saves his life.

Va 193   Right and wrong. Drayton Plains, Mich.: Portafilms,
          1968. (16mm film, color, 10 minutes)
          Uses animation to examine to moral, ethical, and log-
          ical aspects relating to right and wrong, and truth and
          falsity.

Va 194   The school community. Chicago: Encyclopaedia Britan-
          nica, 1953. (filmstrip)
          Real life photographs of Steve's days at school picture
          his problems and how he learns to deal with them. Varied
          classroom activities illustrate concepts of friendship, lead-
          ership, cooperation, sharing and courtesy, emphasizing
          constructive behavior and group participation. Also con-
          siders school's relationship to the home and the surround-
          ing community.

Va 195   Slobodkin, Louis. Excuse me! Certainly! New York:
          Vanguard, 1959.
          Told in rhyme, this is the story of Willie White, who
          was not polite, but learned from his neighbors that courtesy
          can be fun.

Va 196   Sparrow's don't drop candy wrappers. New York: Dodd,
          Mead and Company, 1971.
          Discusses the do's and don'ts for everyone interested
          in stopping the spread of pollution.

Va 197   Teaching children values through unfinished stories. Free-
          port, N.Y.: Education Activities, Inc., n.d. (film-
          strips-records)
          Thought-provoking, open-ended stories in which each
          pupil can see himself as the central character provide
          children the opportunity to broaden their understanding of
          such recognized values as Integrity, Responsibility, Justice,
          Courage, Reverence and Love. Each colorfully-illustrated
          filmstrip contains six eight-frame sequences to go with the
          recorded stories. All stories were carefully selected for
          their strong appeal to the children and their depiction of
          the particular value to be studied. A teacher's guide gives
          sample questions, generalizations and suggestions for most
          effective use of these sound filmstrips.

Va 198   Understanding others. Redondo Beach, Cal.: Jarvis
          Couillard Associates, 1970. (16mm film, color, 8

minutes)
The film deals with the question of how we can learn to understand others; should we expect them to change? It explains that when we try to understand how others feel, we begin to care more about them.

Va 199   Values: cooperation. Redondo Beach, Cal.: Jarvis
         Couillard Associates, 1969. (16mm film, color, 11
         minutes)
         Stresses the value of cooperation by picturing three boys playing together.

Va 200   Values: play fair. Redondo Beach, Cal.: Jarvis Couil-
         lard Associates, 1969. (16mm film, color, 10 minutes)
         Teaches the value of cooperation by picturing three boys together. Stresses the value of cooperation whether at work, play or in school.

Va 201   What do you think? Los Angeles: Churchill Films, 1969.
         (Set of 6 filmstrips with an average of 34 color frames each)
         Presents actual photographs of situations that illustrate childhood conflicts. Uses open-ended captioning techniques to encourage critical thinking about the differing situations and the viewer's values. Includes the following: What do you think about finders keepers?; What do you think about tattling?; What do you think about lying?; What do you think about helping your family?; What do you think about prom- ises?; What do you think about helping your community? Useful for group or individual study in guidance or lan- guage arts.

Va 202   Yurdin, Betty. Tiger in the teapot. New York: Holt,
         1968.
         A tiger lives in the family's oversized teapot. He is invited out, commanded out, ordered out and threatened to get out by various members of the family. Then lit- tlest sister Josie tries a strategy of compliments and in- vitations--which succeeds.

SHARING

Va 203   Clark, Margery. The poppy seed cakes. New York:
         Doubleday, 1924.
         Andrewshek and Erminka were born in the old country and become friends and share many adventures when they find themselves neighbors in New York City.

Va 204   Lindman, Maj. Snipp, Snapp, Snurr and the red shoes.
         Racine, Wis.: Whitman, 1936. (book and filmstrip)
         Three young Swedish boys work at different jobs so they will earn enough money to buy a birthday present for their mother.

Va 205   Lucy learns to share.   (A guidance series)   Jamaica,
          N.Y.: Eye Gate, n.d.   (filmstrip)
          Emphasizes the most important basic lessons to be
          learned in character building.   Centering around situations
          and experiences familiar to all children, the stories in-
          volve the joy of helping others, honesty, perseverance,
          responsibility, respect and good manners.   A designated
          frame can be held on the screen while the class discusses
          ways for resolving the problem facing the children in the
          story.

Va 206   Udry, Janice May.   What Mary Jo shared.   Racine, Wis.:
          Whitman, 1966.
          Everyone in Mary Jo's class has something to share
          but Mary Jo.   Each day her teacher, Miss Willett, asks,
          "And Mary Jo, do you have something to share this morn-
          ing?"   Each morning her answer is "No" until the beauti-
          ful day when she discovers and shares something wonder-
          ful, but not usually found in school.

Intermediate

GENERAL

Va 207   Understanding values.   (series)   Jamaica, N.Y.: Eye
          Gate, n.d.   (filmstrip)
          The student at this age is evaluating and reforming
          many of his values and standards.   This set of six film-
          strips makes no conclusive moral judgments.   The set
          does not teach answers, instead a chain of logical questions
          is raised from which the individual must take a stand and
          therefore comes to an evaluation and understanding of his
          own values.   Included in the series: Stealing; Cheating
          and chiseling; Lies, half-truths and untold truths; Other's
          values/your values; Who cares/staying involved; Right,
          wrong or maybe.

Va 208   Values: the right things to do.   Redondo Beach, Cal.:
          Jarvis Couillard Associates, 1970.   (16mm film, color,
          9 minutes)
          Presents a story about deciding what is the right thing
          to do and raises the question, should we do what we know
          is right even if we get into trouble?

Va 209   Values: understanding others.   Redondo Beach, Cal.:
          Jarvis Couillard Associates, 1970.   (16mm film, color,
          8 minutes)
          Raises and discusses questions on value: how can we
          learn to understand other people better, should we expect
          them to change?   Explains that when we try to understand
          how others feel, we begin to care about them.

Va 210   Values: understanding ourselves. Redondo Beach, Cal. :
           Jarvis Couillard Associates, n. d.   (16mm film, color,
           9 minutes)
              Through a story of three boys, presents these concepts:
           everybody has an idea of the kind of person he is. Some-
           times it seems like it would be more fun to be someone
           else. Each person, if he could really choose, would rath-
           er be himself.

FAMILY RELATIONSHIPS

Va 211   Alcock, Gudrun. Run, Westy, run. West Caldwell, N. J. :
           Lothrop, 1966.
              Story of Robert Weston, eleven-year-old truant and de-
           linquent, who is obsessed with running away from a home
           which to him is a windowless room.   Presents a realistic
           picture of a detention home and a juvenile court where an
           understanding judge shows how much can be gained when a
           family faces its problems together.

Va 212   Angelo, Valenti. Big little island. New York: Viking,
           1949.
              The pattern of family life in New York today, colored
           and shaped by Italian warmth and vivacity, is the back-
           ground for this moving story of a war orphan's struggle
           to find himself amid the confusion and alien beauty of Man-
           hattan. Valenti Angelo writes of the boy's spiritual lone-
           liness with understanding and justice through perspective,
           with exuberant description of family celebrations and tem-
           pestuous island excursions.

Va 213   Armer, Alberta. Screwball. Cleveland: World, 1963.
              Awkward and lonely, and reluctant to deal with the prob-
           lem of being the twin of a brother not handicapped by
           being crippled with polio, Mike at last finds an all-absorb-
           ing interest and thereby becomes a new person, loses his
           fears, and draws closer to his brother.

Va 214   _____. Troublemaker. Cleveland: World, 1966.
              Joe Fuller is sent by the judge and the court to spend
           the summer with foster parents in a small Indiana town.
           His broken home, his father in prison, his mother hos-
           pitalized with a serious breakdown, all inflict on Joe more
           problems than he can cope with.   His summer with the
           Murrays, his reactions to family life there, his eventual
           improved understanding of his own problems are realis-
           tically narrated.

Va 215   Arthur, Ruth M. Little dark thorn. New York: Athene-
           um, 1971.
              When Merrie was brought by her father from her home
           in a Malaysian jungle to a new home in the quiet English

countryside, she was deeply resentful. She resented the
secrecy of it, she hated the new ways and the different
climate, but most of all she was desperately homesick for
her mother. The two old Aunts called her "Little Dark
Thorn" for her prickly ways and sudden anger. Eventually
both she and her father make a new home, he is remarried, and she grows to love the new mother. A fascinating story of complex relationships in the modern world.

Va 216   Behn, Harry. The two uncles of Pablo. New York: Har-
          court, 1959.
          The wisdom, understanding and sympathy of one little
Mexican boy help to show the fallacy in the lives of two
grown men. Uncle Jiluan is lazy, untruthful, and unreli-
able, although basically kind. Uncle Peco, a poet, but
sad and lonely, has sought happiness in seclusion and self-
centeredness. An outstanding story, beautifully told, that
will be read by the more perceptive child and enjoyed in
family reading groups.

Va 217   Beim, Jerrold. With dad alone. New York: Harcourt,
          1954.
          Bruce and his dad feel their loss greatly after the
death of Bruce's mother, but they come to see that strug-
gling with their problems gives them the strength they
need to go on without her.

Va 218   Bialk, Elisa. Taffy's foal. Boston: Houghton, 1949.
          Her father's remarriage means a new home, a new
step-mother, and a new school for Taffy. But she is a
good sport and makes the necessary adjustments in a realistic way.

Va 219   Blue, Rose. Grandma didn't wave back. New York:
          Watts, 1972.
          A ten-year-old girl learns to accept the fact that her
grandmother is growing old and must be sent to a nursing
home. The problems of senility and its effect on the family, especially children, are treated with warmth and understanding. The soft gray-and-white illustrations are excellent and add much to the appealing book.

Va 220   Blume, Judy. It's not the end of the world. Scarsdale,
          N.Y.: Bradbury, 1972.
          Unwilling to adjust to her parents' impending divorce,
twelve-year-old Karen Newman attempts a last-ditch effort
at arranging a reconciliation. This story tells how her
scheme goes awry when an unplanned confrontation between
her parents sharply illuminates for Karen the reality of
the situation. Eventually Karen comes to accept her parents' divorce and recognizes that it is not the end of the
world for any of them. A believable first-person story
with good characterization, particularly of twelve-year-

old Karen, and realistic treatment of the situation.

Va 221 Bragdon, Elspeth. <u>One to make ready.</u> New York: Viking, 1959.
Minta has a great deal she must learn to accept including a new baby brother and the prospect of a new school.

Va 222 _____. <u>That Jud!</u> New York: Viking, 1957.
Nat Weston, who has been expelled from every school he ever attended, spends a summer with his father and they make the first tentative moves toward each other as Nat becomes aware of others besides himself.

Va 223 Burch, Robert. <u>Simon and the game of chance.</u> New York: Viking, 1970.
Simon feels that his father disapproves of everything that he wants to do. And his father is, in truth, a very strait-laced, stern person. The family is in a major crisis, however, for the mother goes into deep melancholy when the new baby dies and she has to spend a year of treatment in an institution. An unusual tale of family misery in the Depression, in which Simon learns to understand his father and himself.

Va 224 Calhoun, Mary. <u>Katie John.</u> New York: Harper, 1960.
Katie John and her family move into an inherited home in order to sell it, but grow to love it and decide to stay. Her friend Sue claims the house is haunted and together they find the explanation.

Va 225 Carlson, Natalie Savage. <u>A brother for the Orphelines.</u> New York: Harper, 1959.
In this follow-up story of The happy Orpheline Josine finds a deserted baby at the door of the orphanage. The other fourteen Orphelines are delighted at Josine's find.

Va 226 _____. <u>The family under the bridge.</u> New York: Harper, 1958.
When the old French hobo, Armand, finds his winter quarters occupied, he plans to move on. However, the three children change his plans and end his hobo days.

Va 227 Carol, Bill J. <u>High fly to center.</u> Austin, Tex.: Steck, 1972.
Thirteen-year-old Mickey Ortega, forced to join his family on their lakeside summer vacation, decides to run away from home and rejoin his much loved little league team. A story of sports, survival, and growth of character.

Va 228 Chaffin, Lillie D. <u>Freeman.</u> Riverside, N.J.: Macmillan, 1972.
Freeman didn't understand many things clearly--chiefly

the mysterious "accident" resulting in his separation as a
baby from his parents--but he deeply loved "Mom" and
"Pop" Sloan. He knew his life with them was easier in
the Kentucky coal mining area but breaking through the
feeling of pride, anger at circumstances beyond his con-
trol and understanding, and shame make for many difficulties in growing up. A sensitive analysis of twelve-
year-old attitudes and emotions with good use of local
color.

Va 229   Clark, Ann Nolan. Paco's miracle. New York: Farrar,
          1962.
          The miracle of love enriches the life of Paco and the
          simple people who have befriended him now that his elderly
          guardian has fallen ill. Paco has lived always on the
          mountain with the old man who hoped to make him a man
          of love and compassion like St. Francis. The values that
          a child finds in nature, in relationships with animals, and
          in the miracle of Christmas are portrayed in evocative
          and powerful language.

Va 230   Cleary, Beverly. Henry and Ribsy. New York: Morrow,
          1954.
          Henry bargains with his father to keep his dog Ribsy out
          of trouble for two months. His reward will be a salmon
          fishing trip if he is successful.

Va 231   Clymer, Eleanor. My brother Stevie. New York: Holt,
          1967.
          If you live in a big city project with a poor grandmother
          and an eight-year-old brother life seems terribly hard.
          That's how it is for twelve-year-old Annie Jenner until a
          teacher, a dog, and her own courage help change her life.

Va 232   Collier, Jane. The year of the dream. New York: Funk,
          1962.
          Each member of the Brown family makes a real sacri-
          fice so that, together, they can purchase the cabin cruiser
          of their dreams. When their savings must pay hospital
          bills instead, it really does not matter because they realize
          that their work together for a common goal has been, in
          itself, an enriching experience.

Va 233   Cone, Molly. Too many girls. Nashville: Nelson, 1960.
          When Charlie learns that it was his three sisters who
          persuaded his parents that he should have a dog, he de-
          cides that girls are not so bad after all and that he will
          be able to "take" his sisters plus the baby, who also turns
          out to be a girl.

Va 234   _____. The trouble with Toby. Boston: Houghton,
          1961.
          Toby, growing up in the shadow of her older, more

popular sister, tries so hard to impress her schoolmates
that she earns the reputation of being a showoff until she
learns that it is not necessary to be continually trying to
prove oneself.

Va 235   Craig, Margaret M. Now that I'm sixteen. New York:
          Crowell, 1959.
          Beth, who never seems to quite make the grade, at
          first blames her parents and friends but with her teacher's
          help she comes to realize that misunderstandings come
          from not "leveling" and being open with others.

Va 236   Daringer, Helen F. Adopted Jane. New York: Harcourt,
          1947.
          Forced to decide whether to be adopted by a woman who
          lives alone, or by a family where she would have compan-
          ionship of her own age, Jane chooses to become a part of
          the home where she is most needed.

Va 237   _____. Like a lady. New York: Harcourt, 1955.
          Johanna works at many tasks to earn sufficient money
          so that her mother will have a new suit to wear at the
          PTA meeting.

Va 238   _____. Stepsister Sally. New York: Harcourt, 1952.
          Sally Brown acquires a whole new family when her fath-
          er remarries. Eventually--but not without some problems--
          the family proves to be as wonderful as she had hoped.

Va 239   _____. The turnabout twins. New York: Harcourt,
          1960.
          Rachel and Becky, identical twins, are sent away on
          separate vacations and learn to appreciate the different
          qualities that make each one an individual personality.

Va 240   Doss, Helen. A brother the size of me. Boston: Little,
          Brown, 1957.
          Danny makes several unsuccessful attempts to raise
          money so that his family will be able to "afford" a boy of
          his age, and when they decide to adopt Richard, he gives
          his brother-to-be his dog as a token of welcome.

Va 241   Enright, Elizabeth. The four-story mistake. New York:
          Rinehart, 1942.
          The Melendy family moves to a house in the country
          known, because of its queer architecture, as the "Four-
          story Mistake." A secret room, a cupola, a nearby
          brook provide these resourceful children with ample oppor-
          tunity for new exploits and experiences.

Va 242   _____. The Saturdays series. New York: Harcourt,
          1941.
          Contents: The Saturdays; Go-away lake; Return to go-

away. Life of the Melendy family of four children in a
large city. The children seek to overcome boredom by
pooling their allowances and providing each other with
enough money to have an exciting Saturday of varied activities. Their exploratory nature leads the children to discover a haunted house in a ghost community. The family
eventually buys and restores an old ghost cottage.

Va 243   ____. Then there were five. New York: Holt, 1944.
        The Melendy children spend a happy summer in the
country with their newly adopted brother.

Va 244   Estes, Eleanor. The Moffats. New York: Harcourt, 1941.
        Nine-year-old Janey, her family of brothers and sisters,
and Mama are not poverty-stricken, just poor; their life,
however, is never commonplace.

Va 245   Fox, Paula. Blowfish live in the sea. Scarsdale, N.Y.:
        Bradbury, 1970.
        Ben is nineteen and Carrie, his half-sister, is thirteen.
To Carrie, Ben is "hard to figure out, wrapped in his
droopy coat and leather hair thong." Together they take
a bus trip to Boston to see Ben's father. The day and a
half spent with the down-at-heels old man provides a clue--
and solution to Ben's behavior and explains why Ben always wrote on Carrie's window "Blowfish live in the sea."

Va 246   Friedman, Frieda. The janitor's girl. New York: Mor-
        row, 1956.
        Each member of the Langer family reacts in a different
way to their father's new job as superintendent of an apartment building on Riverside Drive.

Va 247   Galbraith, Clare K. Victor. Boston: Little, Brown,
        1971.
        Victor lives in two worlds, the English speaking world
at school and the Spanish speaking world of his home, and
he is having trouble in both until Parents' Night at school,
when his worlds come together.

Va 248   Gardner, Richard A. Boys and girls book about divorce.
        New York: Science House, 1970.
        Discusses in a straightforward manner the fears, anx-
ieties and sorrows which children of divorced parents may
experience. Presents practical advice to help children
solve the problems which may arise. Tells them how to
handle their guilt feelings and angry thoughts, how to find
out if their parents love them, how to get along with a divorced mother and a divorced father and how to get along
with step-parents.

Va 249   Gates, Doris. Blue willow. New York: Viking, 1940.
        (book and record)

Janey's most cherished hope is to find a home and a mantelpiece for her Blue willow plate.

Va 250   _____. Sensible Kate. New York: Viking, 1943.
Kate, who longs to be pretty rather than "sensible," eventually finds out that being sensible is more important after all.

Va 251   Gray, Elizabeth Janet. The cheerful heart. New York: Viking, 1959.
"Little Tomi" helps her mother look on the brighter side of life when the family returns to Tokyo after the war years to find a small inconvenient house built where their former one had stood.

Va 252   Harnden, Ruth P. The high pasture. Boston: Houghton, 1964.
When Tim's mother becomes ill, his father sends him to stay with his Aunt Kate and there he becomes self-reliant enough to be able to accept the fact of his mother's death and to face life without her.

Va 253   Hoban, Russell. A birthday for Frances. New York: Harper, 1968.
Jealous Frances turns her back on the preparation for little sister Gloria's birthday party, managing to make herself feel left out. Mother Badger wisely waits for Frances to think of buying a present with her allowance, and Father Badger gently offers to take care of the gift candy after half of it disappears. At the party, however, Frances' generosity comes to the fore, and she and Gloria exchange words of goodwill.

Va 254   Hunt, Mabel L. Little girl with seven names. Philadelphia: Lippincott, 1936.
A little Quaker girl was proud of being named for her two grandmothers and four aunts until her long name caused teasing at school. But she finds a way to give away two of them without hurting the feelings of her namesakes.

Va 255   Johnson, Annabel. The grizzly. New York: Harper, 1964.
Eleven-year-old David, living with his divorced mother, is doubtful about going on a camping trip with his father. When a grizzly injures the father and disables the truck, David surprises both himself and his father by his resourcefulness. A perceptive story of father-son relationships.

Va 256   Kjelgaard, Jim. The black fawn. New York: Dodd, 1958.
An orphaned boy gradually learns what it means to be loved and wanted after he goes to live on his grandfather's farm.

Va 257   Konttinen, Aili. Kirsti comes home. New York: Coward,

1961.
Kirsti is torn between the advantages of life with wealthy
foster parents and the more simple life at home in the
shelter of her parents' love.

Va 258   Krumgold, Joseph. Onion John. New York: Crowell,
          1959. (book and record)
          Andy's friendship with the vagrant old man "Onion John"
          provides a foil for the conflict with Andy's father in this
          story, set in present-day New Jersey. Excellent for its
          picture of the maturing of a boy and setting of his life
          goal, but demanding reading.

Va 259   Lampman, Evelyn Sibley. Navaho sister. New York:
          Doubleday, 1956.
          Sad Girl, so named because her grandmother was the
          only family she had and the Navahos considered this a sad
          situation, was ashamed of her name and resented the pity
          that she thought she saw in everyone's eyes. When she
          went from her Arizona home to the Chemawa Indian School
          in Oregon, she tried to keep anyone at the school from
          knowing that she had no family. At first her secret
          weighed heavily upon her, and then she came to understand
          that, in a sense, the entire school was her family, and so
          she had found happiness even before the existence of her
          real family was disclosed. Many girls will find in Sad
          Girl's problem and her way of meeting it similarities to
          their own problems.

Va 260   Lattimore, Eleanor F. Little Pear. New York: Har-
          court, 1931.
          Little Pear was disobedient and was continually wander-
          ing off by himself but after he fell into the river, he de-
          cided to be good and never run away again.

Va 261   _____. Molly in the middle. New York: Morrow, 1956.
          As the middle child in a family of nine, Molly takes
          seriously her responsibility of taking charge of her four-
          year-old brother.

Va 262   Lawson, Robert. The tough winter. New York: Viking,
          1954.
          Just as Uncle Analdas predicts, it is a tough winter.
          Severe weather comes early. The folks leave a character
          who not only fails to feed the animals but owns a mean
          dog as well.

Va 263   L'Engle, Madeleine. Meet the Austins. New York: Van-
          guard, 1960.
          A "story of the family of a country doctor, (the Austins),"
          told by the twelve-year-old daughter, during a year in
          which a spoiled young orphan, Maggy, comes to live with
          them. This is an account of the family's adjustment to

Maggy and hers to them.

Va 264   Lenski, Lois. Strawberry girl. Philadelphia: Lippincott,
          1945.
          Birdie Boyer and her hardworking family raise straw-
          berries in Florida, but arouse the enmity of the lazy and
          proud neighbors, the Slaters.

Va 265   Lewiton, Mina. Rachel and Herman. New York: Watts,
          1957.
          The Lessing family have moved Uptown and this story
          follows Rachel and her younger brother, Herman, through
          their trials of getting used to a new school, a new public
          library, a new teacher, and new friends. When Uncle
          Boris comes from Chernovinski, life becomes more excit-
          ing and unpredictable, and eventually Rachel decides she
          likes Uptown better than Downtown.

Va 266   Lexau, Joan M. Benjie. New York: Dial, 1964.
          Benjie hated to talk. In fact about all he enjoyed doing
          was sticking close to Granny. But he changes the day he
          sets out to find Granny's lost earring.

Va 267   _____. The homework caper. New York: Harper,
          1966.
          A mystery in an integrated school. Who took Bill's
          homework paper? Bill's friend, Ken, a Negro, helps him
          solve the mystery and we meet both their families, and
          an understanding teacher, in the process.

Va 268   Little, Jean. One to grow on. Boston: Little, 1969.
          Janie Chisolm is trying to grow up but she attempts to
          get attention by lying and exaggerating. Then she meets
          Lisa Daniels and thinks she has found a friend but Lisa
          is only using Janie to get to know her brother, Rob.
          When Janie's godmother takes her to a beautiful island
          camp for the summer, Janie begins to grow up and to find
          real friends.

Va 269   McGinley, Phyllis. The plain princess. Philadelphia:
          Lippincott, 1945.
          A rich and spoiled little princess is transformed into
          a beautiful young lady.

Va 270   McQueen, Noel. A home for Penny. New York: Watts,
          1959.
          Penny, disconsolate when Lillie May and Joe find adop-
          tive parents, is herself made happy when she finds some-
          one who loves her right in the Children's home.

Va 271   Maddock, Reginald. Danny Rowley. Boston: Little,
          Brown, 1969.
          A story of a very mixed-up boy. When Danny Rowley

discovers his mother is going to re-marry, he feels she
has betrayed him. He smashes street lights, gets involved with a gang of toughs in school, heads for disaster.
But he also suddenly gets help from some Negro boys in
the next street. A really fine tale with excitement and
character development.

Va 272   Means, Florence C. Borrowed brother. Boston: Hough-
          ton, 1958.
          Molly, one of six children, and Jan, an only child,
          trade families for a month and each learns that the size
          of a family is not a criterion for judging the happiness of
          its members.

Va 273   Neufeld, John. Edgar Allan: a novel. New York: Phil-
          lips, 1968.
          Michael Ficket, twelve-years-old, tells the story of the
          events--and motivations behind them--which occurred in
          his family when his parents adopted a little Negro boy,
          Edgar Allan. Edgar Allan's arrival means a testing of
          everything in which Michael believes, including his father's
          actions and motives. Divided loyalties finally make the
          family realize that good intentions are not enough.

Va 274   Norris, Gunilla B. If you listen. New York: Atheneum,
          1971.
          Lia is tired of her father's rags-to-riches story and the
          things which his money can buy. What she really wants
          is a friend, a mother who is interested in the family, and
          a father who really loves his family. Having been forced
          into denying her new found friend, Lia runs away in shame
          and remorse. Father's love causes him to seek her and
          this starts the family on the right track.

Va 275   _____. Lillian. New York: Atheneum, 1968.
          Set in Sweden, this story of an only child's adjustment
          to her parents' divorce and to her mother's suitor has a
          universality and simplicity that make it sharply effective
          despite the rather bland style of writing. Lillian finds it
          hard to understand how two people can stop loving each
          other, and her inevitable worry about losing her mother's
          love adds to the problems of adapting to a new school and
          a working mother. Her reaction to the suitor is natural:
          a mixture of resentment, jealousy, and a reluctant affec-
          tion for a pleasant person.

Va 276   O'Moran, Mabel. State boy. Philadelphia: Lippincott,
          1954.
          Fresh out of reform school, Cloudy learns that not
          everyone is against him and responds to his new "mom's"
          trust in him.

Va 277   Orton, Helen F. Mystery up the chimney. Philadelphia:

1947.
Two city children visit country relatives and by making themselves useful around the house and being "a credit to the family" win for themselves an invitation to return the next summer.

Va 278 Otis, James. Toby Tyler. Cleveland: World, 1946.
Toby, through persuasion of a smooth-talking circus man, runs away from Uncle Daniel and joins the circus. After traveling a great distance and suffering much, he is glad to run away again, this time to his home.

Va 279 Seredy, Kate. The good master. New York: Viking, 1935.
Kate, a headstrong tomboy from Budapest, learns gentle ways when she goes to live with an understanding uncle in the country.

Va 280 Shields, Rita. Cecilia's locket. New York: McKay, 1961.
Just when Cecilia thinks that she and her stepmother are making progress in their relationship with one another, something always seems to happen to upset the apple cart. But her friends, the Luchettis, help to bring them together.

Va 281 _____. Mary Kate. New York: McKay, 1963.
When little Robbie is taken in at the orphanage and becomes Katie's special charge, her happiness is complete for now she has someone who understands her. So it is difficult to release him to his parents when the time comes to do so and Mary Kate is forced to learn the difference between selfish and unselfish love.

Va 282 Simpson, Dorothy. The honest dollar. Philadelphia: Lippincott, 1957.
Janie resents her family's poverty but gradually comes to understand that love is more important than money and decides to do her share to give her baby brother the love that he needs.

Va 283 _____. A matter of pride. Philadelphia: Lippincott, 1959.
Too proud to admit that her father cannot afford to buy her a pair of shoes to wear to school, and at odds with her teacher, Janie plays hooky until she permits her teacher to help her with her problems and learns that there is more than one kind of pride.

Va 284 Smaridge, Norah. Looking at you. Nashville: Abingdon, 1962.
Practical advice on getting along with your family, making friends, becoming more mature. Recommended for sixth grade girls.

Va 285   Sommerfelt, Aimee. The road to Agra. New York: Cri-
              terior, 1961.
          A thirteen-year-old boy walks almost 300 miles to take
          his little blind sister to an eye hospital. Some of the
          work of UNICEF is brought into this story of modern India.

Va 286   Sorenson, Virginia. Miracles on maple hill. New York:
              Harcourt, 1956.
          Ten-year-old Marly and her family move from the city
          to grandmother's old Pennsylvania farmhouse, hoping that
          the outdoor life will restore father's health.

Va 287   Spykman, E. C.   A lemon and a star.   New York: Har-
              court, 1955.
          The four Cares children organize their own fun while
          their widowed father tries (in a preoccupied manner) to
          keep them severely disciplined. The scene is a Southern
          country home in the early 1900's. Theodore, the oldest,
          proves to be a menace to fun and family harmony when he
          is in a bad humor, but he grows into manhood following a
          crisis in which he first rejects and then accepts his fath-
          er's unexpected second marriage. An interesting story of
          brother-sister relationships.

Va 288   Spyri, Johanna.   Heidi.   Riverside, N. J.: Macmillan,
              1952.
          A Swiss girl is heartbroken when she is forced to leave
          her grandfather's home in the mountains to take care of a
          sick child in town.

Va 289   Stanger, Margaret A.   A brand new baby.   Boston: Bea-
              con, 1955.
          Margery watches her Aunt Helen's new baby grow during
          its first year and learns to love it. Then, when her moth-
          er tells her she will soon have a baby brother or sister of
          her own, she receives the news happily.

Va 290   Steele, William O.   Flaming arrows.   New York: Har-
              court, 1957.
          Chad was critical of his father for giving shelter to the
          family of the man thought to be the leader of the Injuns
          attacking their village. But he came to see how wrong he
          had been and how good it was to have folks friendly to-
          gether.

Va 291   _____.   Winter danger.   New York: Harcourt, 1954.
          Jared, a wanderer and hunter, leaves his eleven-year-
          old son to grow up with a family in the Tennessee frontier
          about 1780.

Va 292   Stuart, Jesse.   The beatinest boy.   New York: McGraw,
              1953.
          Davy, an orphan, is so happy living with Grandma

Beverly on her Kentucky farm that he gives her a most
unusual Christmas present.

Va 293   Terris, Susan.   The drowning boy.   New York: Double-
          day, 1972.
          This novel deals with a critical two-month period in the
life of a twelve-year-old boy; a period in which he finds
the demands of his family, especially his sister and father,
unbearable; a period in which he is frustrated by not being
able to cure an autistic child he has befriended.   Charac-
terizations are convincing and the well-written story is en-
grossing and moving.

Va 294   Urmston, Mary.   Mystery of the five bright keys.   New
          York: Doubleday, 1946.
          How the Allen family found the missing keys belonging
to their new house, and fittingly named them, Helpfulness,
Understanding, Neighborliness, Courage and Curiosity.

Va 295   Vance, Marguerite.   Windows for Rosemary.   New York:
          Dutton, 1956.
          Though Rosemary has been blind since birth, she faces
her handicaps objectively and without self-pity.   The story,
told in the first person, centers on the girl's receipt of
a braille typewriter on her ninth birthday.   It depicts warm
family relationships.

Va 296   Van Stockum, Hilda.   The cottage at Bantry Bay.   New
          York: Viking, 1938.
          The O'Sullivans may be poor but when they unexpectedly
come into $50 they generously use it for the cure of Fran-
cie's club foot.

Va 297   _____.   The winged watchman.   New York: Farrar,
          1962.
          Tells of the Verhagen family's activities in the under-
ground movement during World War II, when even the children helped to bring aid to the refugees.   A warm story
of family life that demonstrates that the values of life remain the same whatever the situation.

Va 298   Weber, Lenora.   Leave it to Beany!   New York: Crowell,
          1950.
          Beany learns the hard way that "happiness lies in doing
for others, provided you do what they want and need instead of what you think they should want."

Va 299   What will Linda do: sister-sister loyalty.   (The Unfinished
          Series)   New York: Doubleday, 1968.   (16mm film,
          color, 6 mins.)
          A dramatization about sister loyalty.

Va 300   Wier, Ester.   The loner.   New York: McKay, 1963.

An orphan boy is taken in by a lonely woman sheep-
herder on a Montana farm. Story of his adjustment has
many values for one who has known tragedy.

Va 301   Wilder, Laura Ingalls. Little house in the big woods.
          New York: Harper, 1953.
          Family life can be happy and safe, even in the Wis-
          consin woods, if obedience has its proper place as Laura
          shows when a wild bear threatens her and her mother.

Va 302   _____. Little town on the prairie. New York: Harp-
          er, 1953.
          Neither a job in town nor her life at school is easy for
          Laura but she perseveres in both so that she can help to
          send her sister Mary to a school for the blind.

Va 303   _____. The long winter. New York: Harper, 1953.
          Through a long, hard winter which seems to be one con-
          tinuous blizzard, the Ingalls family struggles bravely for
          mere existence and makes do cheerfully with what it has.

Va 304   _____. On the banks of Plum Creek. New York:
          Harper, 1953.
          About Laura's small disobediences and repentances,
          Ma's calm courage and Pa's refusal to become discouraged
          during setbacks caused by blizzards and swarming grass-
          hoppers during the year the family lived in a dugout in
          Minnesota.

Va 305   Wojiechowska, Maia. A kingdom in a horse. New York:
          Harper, 1965.
          David has receded into himself and stubbornly resisted
          the overtures of his father and of would-be friends, but
          his love for a horse and the sympathetic interest of its
          owner help him to come to terms with himself and to ac-
          cept love and the commitments it imposes.

Va 306   _____. Shadow of a bull. New York: Atheneum, 1964.
          The story of a young boy whose father, a great bull-
          fighter, was killed. Everyone expected the boy to become
          the bullfighter that his father had been. The boy, however,
          did not want to become a bullfighter. He was doing it just
          to please the adults. It shows his courage in showing the
          people he did not want to be a bullfighter but not because
          he was resentful or hateful. He set out on his own life
          without regrets toward the people or the past.

Va 307   Wooley, Catherine. Cathy's little sister. New York:
          Morrow, 1964.
          Chris has trailed after her older sister instead of mak-
          ing friends of her own but while on a visit with a family
          where the same situation exists, Chris begins to see the
          light and takes the first steps toward establishing friend-

ships with girls of her own age.

Va 308   Worth, Kathryn. They loved to laugh. New York: Double-
          day, 1959.
          When Martitia joins Dr. David's family she learns to
          overcome her laziness and to appreciate the joy of achieve-
          ment through sharing in the life and work of the home.

                              FRIENDSHIP

Va 309   Belpré, Pura. Santiago. New York: Warne, 1969.
          Santiago is uprooted from his home in Puerto Rico and
          taken to New York. Worse still, he had to leave behind
          his beloved pet hen, Selina. And Ernie, whom he wants
          to impress, won't believe what he tells him. A beautiful
          picture--story of a boy torn between two worlds.

Va 310   Bonham, Frank. Durango Street. New York: Dutton,
          1965.
          Rufus is forbidden to join a gang because he is on
          parole, but finds that he must in order to survive in the
          street life.

Va 311   Bradbury, Bianca. Two on an island. Boston: Houghton,
          1965.
          During the three days they are stranded on a deserted
          island, Jeff and Trudy discover an affection for each other
          of which they had not been aware.

Va 312   Byars, Betsy. The summer of the swans. New York:
          Viking, 1970.
          Sara takes her mentally retarded brother to see the
          swans; and when he tries to return there, he is lost.
          While looking for Charly, Sara makes friends with a boy
          whom she has said she hated all summer and he asks her
          to go to a party that night after Charly is found.

Va 313   Cameron, Eleanor. Room made of windows. Boston:
          Little, Brown, 1971.
          Julia is a self-centered daughter in a closely-knit family
          of mother, daughter, and son. Her desk for her writing,
          her room with windows looking over the world, her own
          desires are the center of her world. Her friends, Addie
          and Mrs. Moore and Daddy Chandler, all make up a part
          of her small intense world. Julia's consuming ambition
          is to be a writer and this story is an account of her ma-
          turing and getting a bit of wisdom.

Va 314   Carlson, Natalie Savage. Ann Aurelia and Dorothy. New
          York: Harper, 1968.
          Ann Aurelia thinks Mrs. Hicken is the best mother she
          has had since her own went away. She and Dorothy be-

come friends on the playground, make a wondrous mixture
of lemonade, get involved in a mix-up at the supermarket
and even get Mrs. Hicken to join the PTA.

Va 315   _____. The family under the bridge. New York:
              Harper, 1958.
              When the old French hobo, Armand, finds his winter
              quarters occupied, he plans to move on. However, the
              three children change his plans and end his hobo days.

Va 316   Christopher, Matt. Challenge at second base. Boston:
              Little, 1962.
              In learning how to maintain confidence and drive to suc-
              ceed even though he is not the best player on the baseball
              team, Stan begins to understand some of the ways to gain
              friendships worth having.

Va 317   Clark, Ann Nolan. Blue canyon horse. New York: Vik-
              ing, 1954.
              One night a young mare fled from her Utah canyon pas-
              ture and the Indian boy who loved her and took care of
              her, clattering up the stony trail, across the mesa, to
              run with the wild herd. But when the canyon field was
              green again, she came back with her colt, drawn by a
              loyalty deeper than her longing to be free.

Va 318   Cleary, Beverly. Ellen Tebbits. New York: Morrow,
              1951.
              Ellen Tebbits is a typical fourth grader whose life is
              made miserable by long underwear and happy by being al-
              lowed to clean erasers. Ellen's problems are those of all
              fourth graders.

Va 319   _____. Henry Huggins. New York: Morrow, 1950.
              Henry Huggins picks up a stray dog, names him Ribsy,
              and sets out on numerous adventures with him, including
              breeding hundreds of fish and collecting over a thousand
              worms.

Va 320   _____. Otis Spofford. New York: Morrow, 1953.
              Otis Spofford is uncontrollable and creates excitement
              wherever he goes. When he cuts Ellen Tebbits' hair for
              fun she proves to be his match.

Va 321   Colman, Hila. End of the game. Cleveland: World,
              1971.
              When black Donny visits Timmy's house for three weeks,
              he is expected to carry a good behavior pattern with him.
              Instead, Donny allows Timmy's sisters to blame him for
              all the bad things because "an underprivileged ghetto child
              doesn't know any better." When the boys are lost, Donny's
              mother comes to the Stevens home to wait out the search.
              The boys are found and she discovers the truth, but Donny

and Timmy have been honest with each other and part as
friends.

Va 322   Craig, Jean M. <u>The new boy on the sidewalk</u>. New York:
         W. W. Norton, 1967.
         Joey and his new neighbor do not become fast friends
         until they must come to each other's defense in this re-
         alistic urban area.

Va 323   Distad, Audree. <u>Dakota sons</u>. New York: Harper, 1972.
         Tad is faced with a whole summer and no friends to
         play with in a small South Dakota prairie town. Then he
         meets Ronnie White Cloud who is visiting his father's
         friend, the Professor at the nearby school. Through his
         growing friendship with Ronnie and Old Choco, he comes
         to recognize the cruelty in the conversation of some of the
         townspeople and in their acts of discrimination. Unusual
         in its effectiveness in seeing this real problem from the
         Indian boy's point of view.

Va 324   <u>Duet</u>. Santa Monica, Cal. : BFA Educational Media, 1969.
         (16mm, color, 9 minutes)
         Concentrates on human values. The film begins by dis-
         playing friendship at its highest level. The relationship
         undergoes drastic changes when one member acquires a
         Record player which becomes a substitute for one member
         of the team. This launches the team into a duel to outdo
         each other. The value of goods begin to outweigh friend-
         ship. Loyalty disintegrates until friendship ends. The
         makers suggest approaches for use of the film.

Va 325   Epstein, Beryl. <u>Lucky, lucky white horse</u>. New York:
         Harper, 1965.
         Shy Ellen finds a friend all by herself after the family
         moves to a new home and she knows that from now on she
         will be her real self instead of living in the shadow of
         her bossy cousin Hetty.

Va 326   Friedman, Frieda. <u>Carol from the country</u>. New York:
         Morrow, 1950.
         Carol feels and acts superior to the girls in her new
         neighborhood. But after her mother points out that her
         various talents are useless unless she also has a talent
         for friendship, Carol learns to be considerate of others
         instead of trying to make an impression on them.

Va 327   Godden, Rumer. <u>Diddakoi</u>. New York: Viking, 1972.
         Kizzy Lovell is a "diddakoi" (half-gypsy) and her class-
         mates taunt her with it daily. She in turn hates all "gor-
         gios" (non-gypsies). She loves living with Gran in the
         caravan and cooking over the open fire. But when Gran
         dies, her world falls apart. Learning how to accept the
         kindness of Admiral Cunningham and Miss Brooks proves

as great a trial as the continuing cruelties of the school
girls.   And others besides Kizzy learn a great deal, too.

Va 328   _____. Miss Happiness and Miss Flower. New York:
            Viking, 1961.
            A lonesome motherless girl builds a Japanese house
            for two Japanese dolls. As the work grows, she gains
            help from the family. By the time it is completed she
            has made friends with her English cousins and no longer
            misses India.

Va 329   Greene, Constance C. A girl called Al. New York: Vik-
            ing, 1969.
            Told in the first person in a disarmingly casual, amus-
            ing style, the story deals with a few months in the lives
            of two seventh grade girls. The narrator (never actually
            named) is a forthright, good-humored child whose family
            life is stable and secure. Her best friend, Al (short for
            Alexandra), whose parents are divorced, lives in an apart-
            ment down the hall with her busy, distracted working moth-
            er. Al--a bright, overfat girl, proudly tries to be a "non-
            conformist" to hide the hurt and loneliness. Their uncon-
            ventional friendship with Mr. Richards, an elderly ex-bar-
            tender who works as assistant superintendent of the build-
            ing draws the girls together. Both the pre-teen protagon-
            ists and the minor performers--sketched with admirable
            economy--are accurately and affectionately drawn.

Va 330   _____. Unmaking of rabbit. New York: Viking, 1972.
            Paul, whom the boys insist on calling rabbit, is lonely
            and shy and stutters now and then. He loves Gran, with
            whom he lives; most of all he wants to live with his moth-
            er in the city. But at eleven he is still waiting. He
            makes several friends, learns how to handle Freddy, the
            bully, writes the best composition in his class, and learns
            also to be himself. A fine story of growing up and find-
            ing one's identity.

Va 331   Harris, Marilyn. Peppersalt land. New York: Four
            Winds, 1970.
            Tollie and Slocum are like blue and white morning
            glories on the same vine. Slocum visits her Grandmother
            English every summer, while Tollie, a black orphan from
            babyhood, has no other parent except the Grandmother.
            The summer of their twelfth year, both girls lose their
            enchantment over Budding Grove, Georgia. Mr. Cicero,
            the storekeeper, begins to look at the girls differently.
            Also, there is angry, talented, black Howard Jackson.
            The conflict between these two causes Tollie and Slocum
            to flee into the dangerous, viper-infested swamp called
            Peppersalt Land. All are forced to examine themselves
            and take a stand.

Va 332   Holberg, Ruth. What happened to Virgilia. New York:
          Doubleday, 1963.
          Overly shy Virgilia spends a year with her Aunt Emma
          and learns to make friends and to overcome her jealousy.

Va 333   Holm, Anne. North to freedom. New York: Harcourt,
          1965.
          When David finally escaped from his East European
          prison, he knows only one thing: no one is to be trusted.
          This is an absorbing story of his odyssey across Europe
          and of how he finally learns that there is beauty and friend-
          ship in the world.

Va 334   How friends are made. Hollywood: Shepherd Menken
          (see Aims...), 1968. (16mm film, color, 11 minutes)
          Describes the experiences of an elementary grade boy
          as he makes a friend. Reveals some of his own wonder
          and reflection on the event.

Va 335   Lawson, Robert. The tough winter. New York: Viking,
          1954.
          Just as Uncle Analdas predicts, it is a tough winter.
          Severe weather comes early. The folks leave a caretaker
          who not only fails to feed the animals but owns a mean
          dog as well.

Va 336   Lovelace, Maud H. Betsy-Tacy. New York: Crowell,
          1940.
          Betsy and Tacy's friendship makes bearable such prob-
          lems as going to school the first time, losing a baby sis-
          ter, and getting a new baby.

Va 337   Malone, Mary. This was Bridget. New York: Dodd,
          1960.
          In the period following the first World War, Bridget is
          transplanted from New York to a small town to live with
          relatives after the death of her mother. Her small broth-
          er has few problems in adapting to the new problems of
          life; for Bridget this is more difficult.

Va 338   Norris, Gunilla B. If you listen. New York: Atheneum,
          1971.
          Lia is tired of her father's rags-to-riches story and
          the things which his money can buy. What she really
          wants is a friend, a mother who is interested in the fam-
          ily, and a father who really loves his family. Having been
          forced into denying her new found friend, Lia runs away in
          shame and remorse. Father's love causes him to seek her
          and this starts the family on the right track.

Va 339   Rinkoff, Barbara. Member of the gang. New York:
          Crown, 1968.
          Thirteen-year-old Woodie wants to be a member of the

Scorpions. This gang of five would-be toughs steals and
battles the Tops, a rival group. During a rumble between the gangs, Woodie sees his friend, Sonny, stabbed.
When all the others flee, Woodie remains with his friend.

Va 340   Rome, Karen. Single trail. Chicago: Follett, 1969.
          Two boys go to the same school in a Los Angeles neigh-
          borhood. Ricky has learned how to make friends quickly
          in spite of his family moving nine times in twelve years.
          Earl does not care whether people like him or not, es-
          pecially white people. An effective tale with high identifi-
          cation value.

Va 341   Scott, Sally. Jenny and the wonderful jeep. New York:
          Harcourt, 1963.
          "Do as you would be done by" is the lesson of this
          story of a girl to whom friendship was not extended by
          older children until she offered her own friendship to a
          child younger than herself.

Va 342   Sechrist, Elizabeth H. It's time for brotherhood. Phila-
          delphia: Macrae Smith, 1962.
          After a brief comment on how the concept of "Love Thy
          Neighbor" appears in many religions, there are stories of
          individuals and groups whose lives and work have been
          shining examples of the principle of brotherhood put into
          action. A great many facts have been compressed into
          this book.

Va 343   Simpson, Dorothy. A lesson for Jamie. Philadelphia:
          Lippincott, 1958.
          Jamie's jealousy toward her new neighbor from the city
          dissolves when they face a common danger and come to
          appreciate each other.

Va 344   Smith, Fredrika Shumway. Courageous comrades. Chi-
          cago: Rand McNally, 1960.
          This is an adventure tale of two young boys who move
          in 1836 with their families from Massachusetts to what
          will be Milwaukee. The hard work and determination
          shown by these early settlers is fully delineated. The
          boys make friends with Gray Eagle; the Indian family and
          the settlers help one another. Their relationship is per-
          haps idealized, but many details show trust and confidences
          are built.

Va 345   Stolz, Mary. The noonday friends. New York: Harper,
          1965.
          A realistic story of family relationships and of a girl's
          need for friendship. Because she must care for her lit-
          tle brother while her mother works, Franny Davis can see
          her best friend only at lunch hour. The embarrassment
          of having a free lunch pass and the uncertainties of life

when her father is out of work are problems which Franny
faces with courage and good sense.

Va 346   Values.   (series)   Redondo Beach, Cal. :   Jarvis Couillard
             Associates, 1969.   (filmstrips)
             Contents: Values--being friends; Values--the right
          thing to do; Values--understanding others; Values--under-
          standing ourselves.   Presents a segment of the lives of
          three friends, Ted, Phil and Ricky, as they learn about
          disagreements, trust, getting into trouble, telling the truth,
          recognizing that other people may not value the things we
          value and projecting one's self as a means of adjusting to
          different value systems.

Va 347   Van Stockum, Hilda.   Friendly gables.   New York: Viking,
             1960.
             Kindness and love motivate the Mitchell children as they
          extend friendship and a share in their happiness to others.

Va 348   What will Kathy do: friendship versus ability.   New York:
             Doubleday, 1968.   (16mm film, color, 6 minutes)
             A dramatization about friendship versus ability, a dilem-
          ma encountered by many children everyday.   School con-
          nected situations.

Va 349   Williams, Barbara.   Secret name.   New York: Harcourt,
             1972.
             Betsy, a very shy little girl from the Navaho reserva-
          tion, goes to live with a family in Salt Lake City.   Laurie
          (who shares her room with Betsy) is puzzled by Betsy's
          curious customs as well as by her irrational fears.   And,
          of course, many of Laurie's customs seem queer and irra-
          tional to Betsy.   Together the girls work out their prob-
          lems of mutual misunderstanding in what is a very unusual
          story of cross-cultural friendship, avoiding the easy an-
          swers.

Va 350   Wooley, Catherine.   Ginnie and the new girl.   New York:
             Morrow, 1954.
             Ginnie feels lonely and hurt when the new girl absorbs
          the time of her best friend.

                              HONESTY

Va 351   Armstrong, William H.   Sounder.   New York: Harper,
             1969.
             The sharecropper was not weak or wicked but crops
          were poor and his children were hungry.   This hunger is
          what causes him to steal and what he steals is a ham and
          some sausage.   But this is enough for the sheriff to come
          with two deputies to arrest the man and nearly kill his
          hunting dog.   A profoundly moving tale of the great cour-

age of a boy, his father, and a dog.

Va 352   Beim, Jerrold. A vote for Dick. New York: Harcourt, 1955.
When Dick cheats on an exam so that he can win a bicycle and membership on the Student Council, his conscience forces him to confess and to accept the fact that success is based upon more than good grades.

Va 353   Carlson, Natalie S. The letter on the tree. New York: Harper, 1964.
A French Canadian boy gives an exaggerated picture of his family's poverty in a note he attaches to a Christmas tree to be sold in the States but comes to see the value of self-respect, honesty and hard work.

Va 354   Cleaver, Vera and Bill. Ellen Grae. Philadelphia: Lippincott, 1967.
Eleven-year-old Ellen Grae is an imaginative tomboy who likes to invent tall tales. But they did not top what simple-minded Ira told her about an attempted death by rattlesnake venom and the burial of his parents in a near-by spot. Now knowing Ellen must make a choice--whether to use her own integrity or do what society demands of her. A strange ending that makes you wonder about the adult world and society.

Va 355   Corbett, Scott. The limerick trick. Boston: Little, 1964.
When Kerly calls upon Mrs. Graymalkin to help him compose a prizewinning poem, her "magic" backfires and he learns to rely on his own powers.

Va 356   Exploring moral values: pts. 12-15, Honesty. Pleasantville, N. Y.: Warren Schloat Productions, Inc., 1966. (sound filmstrip, 166 frs., black and white)
Presents a wide variety of situations, raising relatively minor to quite serious violations for acceptable behavior.

Va 357   Friedman, Frieda. Ellen and the gang. New York: Morrow, 1963.
Ellen is lonely and insecure and as a result, becomes involved with a group of juvenile delinquents. But with her family and younger children on the playground, she pulls herself out of this dilemma.

Va 358   Haywood, Carolyn. Eddie's pay dirt. New York: Morrow, 1953.
Eddie Wilson returns from Texas with, among other things, a parrot, a snake, a pail of pay dirt (given to him by his friend Manuel), and a saddle but no pony. These additions to his valuable property collection bring hilarious experiences for Eddie and his friends, climaxed when Eddie finds $500 worth of old Spanish coins in the pay dirt.

He returns them to Manuel and is rewarded for his honesty; his uncles give him the pony he wants.

Va 359   How honest are you? Chicago: Coronet, n. d. (film)
          Dramatizes some of the elements in honesty. Bob returns to the basketball locker room for the whistle needed in practice. Don sees Bob searching Ben's pockets and tells the gang Bob is a thief. At skill practice, Coach Baker makes the boys realize jumping at conclusions is dangerous and that good intentions are not the same as truth.

Va 360   Human values: Integrity. North Hollywood, Cal. : Format Films, Inc. , n. d. (16mm film, color, 11 minutes)
          Features elementary students photographed in reconstructions of classroom incident challenging the honesty of a boy; discusses courage for admitting his act.

Va 361   Lewiton, Mina. That bad Carlos. New York: Harper, 1964.
          Ten-year-old Carlos finds much to fascinate him. His proneness to be impulsive and easily influenced by friends, and his great desire to ride a bicycle, soon have Carlos in repeated trouble. When it is discovered he has been riding a stolen bike, his family and an understanding teacher prevent more serious involvement with the law and help Carlos to understand the importance of responsible behavior.

Va 362   Little, Jean. One to grow on. Boston: Little, 1969.
          Janie Chisolm is trying to grow up but she attempts to get attention by lying and exaggerating. Then she meets Lisa Daniels and thinks she has found a friend but Lisa is only using Janie to get to know her brother, Rob. When Janie's godmother takes her to a beautiful island camp for the summer, Janie begins to grow up and to find real friends.

Va 363   Stealing. Hollywood: Oxford Films, Inc. , 1971. (16mm film, color, 12 minutes)
          Presents principles of honesty through the story of Johnny, a newspaper boy. Focuses on the moral issues which affect one's decision to steal from the moral decision making series. The series include: Being friends; Cooperation; Playing fair; The right things to do; Telling the truth; Understanding others; Understanding ourselves.

Va 364   Stuart, Jesse. A penny's worth of character. New York: McGraw-Hill, 1954.
          Shan learns the real meaning of honesty when he is sent on an errand to the store by his mother.

Va 365   Weaver, Stella. A poppy in the corn. New York: Pan-

theon, 1960.
A European war orphan, Teresa, comes to live with a
family on the Cornish Coast. The children are left alone
and it develops that Teresa has been stealing. The children solve the problem themselves and the interpretation
of characters makes a most interesting story for mature
readers.

Va 366   What will Bernard do? Gratitude versus cheating. New
          York: Doubleday, 1968. (16mm film, color, 6 minutes)
          A dramatization about gratitude versus cheating.

Va 367   William, Jay. Danny Dunn and the homework machine.
          New York: McGraw-Hill, 1958.
          Danny and another boy use a calculating machine to do
          their homework, but the teacher finds out and the boys
          have to suffer the consequences.

Va 368   Wilson, Hazel. Jerry's charge account. Boston: Little,
          Brown, 1960.
          Jerry learns the difference between honesty and deceit
          when he opens a charge account without his father's per-
          mission just so that he can get a gift.

                     INDIVIDUAL DIFFERENCES

Va 369   Alcott, Louisa M. Little men. Riverside, N. J. : Mac-
          millan, 1957.
          Continues the now classic story of Little Women. It
          tells of the remarkable school that Jo and Father Bhaer
          founded at Plumfield; a happy rollicking home for boys and
          girls. Meg's children and Jo's own small boys are in
          the thick of the run and Marmee, Aunt Amy, Uncle Laurie,
          and other old friends help to make them happy.

Va 370   _____. Little women. Riverside, N. J. : Macmillan,
          1962.
          The story of the New England home life of the four
          March sisters. "Jo's quick temper and restless drive
          for the freedom of a boy's life; Meg's hatred of poverty
          and her longing for pretty clothes; Amy's all-engulfing
          self-interest; and gentle Beth's love of home and family
          characterize at the outset the personality of each 'little
          woman. ' "

Va 371   Allen, Elizabeth. The loser. New York: Dutton, 1965.
          A popular beauty queen in high school, Deirdre meets
          dropout Denny, her world widened as he introduces folk
          singers, art, and poetry to her. He makes her aware of
          her environment. He runs away; she realizes how he
          helped her mature, stretch and listen and reach out in
          life.

Va 372   Brown, Virginia. The hidden lookout. New York: Mc-
          Graw-Hill, 1965.
          How do you act when you have a problem? Here are
          five stories about city families of today. Each story tells
          how a person tried to solve his difficulty, a real problem
          and how he came out.

Va 373   Christopher, Matthew F. Baseball flyhawk. Boston: Lit-
          tle, Brown, 1963.
          Chico feels that if he were not a Puerto Rican his team-
          mates would not hold his lack of skill against him. But
          he finds that he can win their friendship and respect if he
          will only stop trying so hard.

Va 374   De Angeli, Marguerite. Bright April. New York: Double-
          day, 1946.
          Phyllis comes to realize that she and April are alike
          except for the color of their skins, so she no longer re-
          sents April's membership in the Brownie Troop.

Va 375   De Jong, Meindert. The wheel on the school. New York:
          Harper, 1954. (book and record)
          Children of Shora, a Netherlands village, are deter-
          mined to bring storks back to their town.

Va 376   Enright, Elizabeth. Gone-away lake. New York: Har-
          court, 1957.
          The Melendy children discover an old settlement in a
          swamp, befriend the recluses who live there, and find a
          new home for themselves.

Va 377   Estes, Eleanor. The hundred dresses. New York: Har-
          court, 1944.
          Maddie and Peggy make Wanda, a recent Polish immi-
          grant, the brunt of heartless teasing.

Va 378   Faulkner, Georgene. Melindy's happy summer. New
          York: Messner, 1949.
          Melindy learns to think before she speaks when she
          learns that the boastfulness with which she has covered
          up her shyness has not contributed to the hoped-for good
          results when she is sent to spend a vacation with a white
          family in Maine.

Va 379   Friedman, Frieda. The janitor's girl. New York: Mor-
          row, 1956.
          Each member of the Langer family reacts in a differ-
          ent way to their father's new job as superintendent of an
          apartment building on Riverside Drive.

Va 380   Fry, Rosalie K. Promise of the rainbow. New York:
          Farrar, 1965.
          A group of children of Anglican, Methodist and Catholic

backgrounds recondition an abandoned chapel and learn
something about inter-religious understanding in the process.

Va 381   Gates, Doris. Little Vic. New York: Viking, 1951.
           Through his experiences in training his horse for the
great race, Tony learns that the fact that he is a Negro
has no bearing on his abilities one way or the other.

Va 382   _____. North fork. New York: Viking, 1945.
           Drew is snobbish and antagonizes the Indians who work
at the sawmill until he learns to recognize their true value.

Va 383   Hall, Natalie. The world in a city block. New York:
           Viking, 1960.
           Nick discovers the whole world is right next door as
he visits the shopkeepers on his city block.

Va 384   Hayes, Florence. Skid. Boston: Houghton, 1948.
           When Skid's family moves up north and he is the only
Negro in his new school, his adjustment to a new way of
living is difficult but he finally makes a place for himself.

Va 385   Hoffine, Lyla. The eagle feather prize. New York: Mc-
           Kay, 1962.
           Billy Youngbear, on a contemporary Mandan Indian
reservation, faces many alternatives. He visits an Indian
friend whose family values highly the way of the past; another friend shows him life on a modern ranch. Billy's
father has gone to college; his beloved grandmother lives
in her tipi during the summer. The book shows Billy
making choices which deny neither way of life.

Va 386   _____. Jennie's Mandan bowl. New York: McKay,
           1960.
           Jennie is ashamed of her Indian ancestry until she
comes to realize that each of her cultures has aspects
of which she can be proud.

Va 387   Jackson, Jesse. Anchor man. New York: Harper, 1947.
           Charley, anchor man of the track team, runs into dif-
ficulty when other Negroes register as students at Arlington High, but in the ensuing difficulties he is loyal both to
his white friends.

Va 388   _____. Call me Charley. New York: Harper, 1945.
           The only Negro boy at Arlington Junior High has quite
a struggle before he is accepted by his schoolmates.

Va 389   Johnston, Johanna. Together in America. New York:
           Dodd, 1965.
           This book is an attempt to show that people of both
European and African descent have contributed to America's

discovery, growth and strength from the beginning--that the contribution of some who have labored under brutal disadvantages have been remarkable; and that the needs and pressures of the times have played a part in what happened and what was accomplished in every era.

Va 390   Just like me. (Social Studies Series) Lafayette, Ind. : Karl B. Lohmann, Jr. , 1965. (16mm film, color, 8 minutes)

Examines the question of why people are different by following a boy and his father as both try to imagine the consequences of having four identical friends.

Va 391   Lerner, Marguerite. Red man, white man, African chief: the story of the color of your skin. London: Medical Books, 1960.

An explanation of pigmentation in human beings.

Va 392   Little, Jean. Kate. New York: Harper, 1971.

Emily's character sketch of her friend seems almost perfect, but she does not mention that Kate is half Jewish because it does not seem a real part of her character. Kate's image of herself changes during the following year as she gains new insight into relationships with her family, her friends and her Jewish heritage.

Va 393   Newell, Hope. A cap for Mary Ellis. New York: Harper, 1963.

Chosen as one of the first Negroes to be admitted to a recently desegregated nursing school, Mary Ellis determines to do so well that the door will be opened to other Negroes as well.

Va 394   Raymond, John. Prejudice and you: A learning experience. Washington, D.C. : National School Public Relations Association, 1972.

A very useful set of media for teachers to use with students for the purpose of increasing racial understanding. Twenty discussion situations are presented on what is prejudice, kinds of prejudice, and what can be done about it. They are particularly appropriate for children 11-15 years old but children as young as eight are able to understand and discuss.

Va 395   Schwartz, Alvin. The night workers. New York: Dutton, 1966.

This book shows how "with night all around men and women go about jobs that are different as walking a policeman's lonely beat, piloting tug boats, baking bread, printing newspapers, taking care of the sick in hospitals and selling fish. "

Va 396   Seredy, Kate. The singing tree. New York: Viking, 1939.

During World War I, Kate and Jancsi open their home
and hearts to all refugees, be they German, Jews, or
Russians.

Va 397   Sterling, Dorothy. Mary Jane. New York: Doubleday,
          1959.
          The realistic story of a Negro girl's experiences in the
          first integrated class in a junior high school.

Va 398   Waltrip, Lela and Rufus. Quiet boy. New York: Long-
          mans, 1961.
          This is a story of a twelve-year-old boy living on a
          present-day Indian reservation in Arizona. Quiet Boy's
          father died in service in the war. In a letter to his son,
          he had told him to learn all he could of the white men's
          ways and language. Thus, Quiet Boy attends a govern-
          ment school. The conflict and the prejudice that exist be-
          tween cultures are clearly and realistically depicted, as
          are conflicts that occur between generations.

Va 399   Who am I. Jamaica, N.Y.: Eye Gate, 1969. (filmstrip)
          Defines psychology and promotes self-evaluation, em-
          phasizing the concept that people are different. Explores
          the basic human needs and categorizes inherited and ac-
          quired traits, such as abilities, interests, and appearances.

Va 400   Wier, Ester. Easy does it. New York: Vanguard, 1965.
          The Reeses, the first Negroes to move into an all-white
          neighborhood, are boycotted, to the displeasure of eleven-
          year-old Woodman. He likes the Reese boy, who is his
          age. Problems arise but all works out in the end.

                              RESPONSIBILITY

Va 401   Agle, Nan H. Three boys and a lighthouse. New York:
          Scribner, 1952.
          When a heavy fog develops while their father is away
          on an emergency call, Albercrombie, Benjamin, and
          Christopher take care of the lighthouse.

Va 402   Ballard, Martin. The Emir's son. Cleveland: World,
          1967.
          The Emir's son, spoilt and looking for adventure, rides
          with his friends through the countryside, upsetting every-
          thing that stands in the way. One day as he watches the
          people working in the fields so that he will have food to
          eat and clothes to wear, he realizes that his life is worth-
          less. He turns from his foolish rides with his friends to
          study at his father's feet. He, too, can say with the old
          one in the field, "Others have planted, I have eaten; I,
          too, will plant so that others might eat."

Va 403   Binns, Archie. Sea pup. New York: Duell, 1954.
        Clint lives with his family in Puget Sound. He falls in love with an orphan seal, Buster, who cannot live alone without mischief. The situation develops to the point that Clint has to decide whether keeping the sea pup out of trouble is more important than a chance to go to school in preparation for a career as an oceanographer. Clint struggles to make a meaningful decision.

Va 404   Blegvad, Lenore. Moon-watch summer. New York: Harcourt, 1972.
        Adam resents being sent, together with his younger sister, to spend the summer on his grandmother's farm without a TV to watch the Apollo 11 moon walk. This story tells how Adam gradually learns that larger values must sometimes take precedence over personal disappointments.

Va 405   Bond, Gladys B. A head on her shoulders. New York: Abelard, 1963.
        Brita proves that she has a head on her shoulders when circumstances force her to take care of her younger brothers and sisters during a trip to the Northwest by boxcar.

Va 406   Bragdon, Elspeth. That Jud! New York: Viking, 1957.
        Jud, town ward, convinces the residents that he is a responsible person with something to offer the town.

Va 407   Breck, Vivian. High trail. New York: Doubleday, 1948.
        A girl and her father go mountain climbing for the weekend. When the father breaks his leg, the girl has to prove her courage and accept the responsibility.

Va 408   Brink, Carol R. Winter cottage. Riverside, N.J.: Macmillan, 1968.
        A story set in Wisconsin in 1930. Thirteen-year-old Minty Sparks feels responsible for her family's well being, for although she loves her poetry-quoting father, both he and she realize that his verses and charm will not feed or house them and Eggs, Minty's younger sister. How the Sparks' family manage during this penniless winter is told.

Va 409   Buff, Mary. The apple and the arrow. Boston: Houghton, 1951.
        William Tell fights for Swiss freedom against the infamous Gessler. He is forced to shoot an apple from the head of his son, Walter, through whom the story is told.

Va 410   Burch, Robert. Queenie Peavy. New York: Viking, 1966.
        Queenie is tormented by the taunts of the children that her father is in prison. Although she is very intelligent, she fights back and comes perilously close to being sent to the reformatory. How she learns to face life and be honest with herself makes a story which many readers will be interested in.

Va 411   Church, Richard. Five boys in a cave. New York: Day,
          1950.
          Five boys explore an underground labyrinth discovered
          by John Walters. The secret planning is abetted only by
          John's uncle. The day of adventures and near-tragedy
          teaches each boy something about himself and about the
          qualities of leadership.

Va 412   Clymer, Eleanor. Me and the eggman. New York: Dut-
          ton, 1972.
          Don runs away in the eggman's truck when everything
          seems to go wrong. His older brother, John, has been
          cross since his return from the army; then Aunt Lizzie
          came to live with the fatherless family, but she piled work
          on Donald and favored his sister. At first everyone, the
          family and the eggman, is angry with him. However,
          Donald's hard work helps the eggman and brings harmony
          at home.

Va 413   Daringer, Helen F. Bigity Anne. New York: Harcourt,
          1954.
          Anne, oldest of the motherless Todd family, holds the
          children together and cares for the home in the absence
          of their father.

Va 414   Day, Veronigrie. Landslide! New York: McGraw-Hill,
          1965.
          Five children are marooned in a cottage by a mountain
          landslide and show great courage.

Va 415   De Angeli, Marguerite. Yonie wondernose. New York:
          Doubleday, 1944.
          Left in charge while his father is away, Yonie restrains
          his curiosity and proves that he can be trusted.

Va 416   Drug abuse--Who needs it. Shawnee Mission, Kan.:
          Marsh Film Enterprises, n. d. (film)
          Dr. Richard Davis points out some of the pitfalls of
          drug abuse through a story of a boy who becomes involved
          with drugs. This film is designed for the middle grade
          child.

Va 417   Edmonds, Walter D. Two logs crossing. New York:
          Dodd, 1943.
          A story of adventure in which John Haskell goes fur
          trapping in order to pay back his father's debts and support
          his family.

Va 418   Felsen, Henry G. Boy gets a car. New York: Random,
          1960.
          After a period of time during which he focuses all at-
          tention on his car, Woody begins to mature and change his
          sense of values and responsibilities.

Va 419   Fisher, Laura. <u>Never try Nathaniel.</u> New York: Holt,
          1972.
             Nathaniel is the youngest of five and the only one left
          at home, but he has nephews and nieces. This is good,
          except that his oldest nephew, six-year-old Joe, is braver
          and a better worker than twelve-year-old Than. Than
          tries hard but the dog and one of the cows chase him and
          the horses take their own lead, when he tries to drive.
          When Pa gets hurt, Joe's scorn of Than increases, until
          Than resolves to show everyone his metal. Well written
          account of a boy's battle with himself.

Va 420   Flory, Jane. <u>Mist on the mountain.</u> Boston: Houghton,
          1966.
             None of the eight fatherless Scoville girls wants to ac-
          cept the charity of Uncle Bolivar. Therefore, they work
          hard to help Ma keep their mountainside farm going.
          Though they do not have lots of money, they do have lots
          of fun.

Va 421   Frazier, Neta L. <u>Little Rhody.</u> New York: McKay,
          1953.
             Only when she has grown up sufficiently to accept re-
          sponsibility does Rhoda's birthday wish that she be called
          by her real name come true.

Va 422   Freuchen, Pipaluk. <u>Eskimo boy.</u> West Caldwell, N.J.:
          Lothrop, 1951.
             Young Ivik, who becomes head of his family when his
          father is killed by a walrus, provides food for his hungry
          family through courage and determination.

Va 423   Gage, Wilson. <u>Mike's toads.</u> Cleveland: World, 1970.
             Mike knew from experience that it was not wise to
          proffer other people's help without consulting them, but
          he had thoughtlessly done it again. A friend of his broth-
          er's had asked if David would care for his pet toads while
          he was away. Of course he would, Mike said; but he had
          forgotten that David was going to camp and he himself
          was saddled with the responsibility. His small catastrophes
          are entertaining, and the story--written in an easy, natu-
          ral style--incorporates information unobtrusively. The
          outcome is satisfying, the relationships and dialogue feli-
          citous.

Va 424   Harnden, Ruth P. <u>Golly and the gulls.</u> Boston: Houghton,
          1962.
             Golly learns the difference between being brave and being
          foolhardy after being reprimanded by his grandfather for
          going out alone to rescue the gulls from icebound waters.

Va 425   Haywood, Carolyn. <u>Ever-ready Eddie.</u> New York: Mor-
          row, 1968.

Eddie Wilson returns to school late and misses the opportunity of becoming a candidate for student council elections. Nevertheless, he takes on the job of campaign man-
ager for Boodles Cary and discovers in the process that
voting for the right man is more important than voting for
a friend.

Va 426   Justus, May. Use your head, Hildy. New York: Holt,
         1956.
         Story of twelve-year-old Hildy who lives in the Tennes-
         see mountains and of her good sense and sound judgment
         in caring for the family during her mother's absence.

Va 427   Kay, Helen. A pony for winter. New York: Farrar,
         1959.
         Molly loves horses, and more than anything else, she
         wants that pony to board for the winter. She comes to
         know the work and worry, the pride and pleasure of caring
         for a beloved animal, as well as the pain of parting with
         it at the end.

Va 428   Kennedy, John Fitzgerald. Profiles in courage. New
         York: Harper, 1964.
         Young readers edition first published in 1961. The
         1964 memorial edition has a new forward. American
         statesmen who had the courage to make difficult and dra-
         matic moral decisions. President Kennedy has provided
         a special letter for this young readers edition.

Va 429   Krumgold, Joseph. ...And now Miguel. New York:
         Crowell, 1953.
         Miguel earns his family's acknowledgment of his grow-
         ing maturity after he learns to balance privilege against
         responsibility and thus earns permission to take the sheep
         to their grazing fields.

Va 430   Lenski, Lois. Strawberry girl. Philadelphia: Lippincott,
         1945.
         This story contrasts the lives of the industrious Boyer
         family, struggling to make a living from their strawberry
         patch, and the shiftless Slater family who live on an ad-
         joining farm in Florida. The neighborliness of the Boyers
         makes the Slaters not only willing to be friendly but also
         glad to adopt some of the thrifty characteristics of their
         neighbors. The story shows how the work habits of a
         family can influence neighbors in a rural environment.

Va 431   McNeer, May. Armed with courage. Nashville: Abing-
         don, 1957.
         Biographies of seven men and women who dedicated
         their lives to the service of their fellowmen: Nightingale,
         Father Damien, Carver, Addams, Grenfell, Gandhi, and
         Schweitzer.

Va 432   McSwigan, Marie. <u>Snow treasure</u>. New York: Dutton,
          1942.
          A true story of how a group of Norwegian children fool
          the German guards by taking their country's gold out right
          under their noses.

Va 433   Marquis, Helen. <u>Longest day of the year</u>. Des Moines:
          Meredith, 1969.
          Thirteen-year-old Cissy is proud to be left in charge
          of her younger sister, eleven-year-old Margie, and broth-
          er, seven-year-old Tim, when her parents go to deliver
          Christmas gifts. When a blizzard strikes the parents are
          forced to remain in town. Cissy then makes a good
          Christmas for Tim, who believes in Santa, and keeps both
          Margie and Tim occupied, warm, fed, and happy until her
          parents return.

Va 434   Molarsky, Osmond. <u>Where the luck was</u>. New York:
          Walck, 1970.
          Arnold McWilliams has to walk on crutches for three
          months. His three friends decide he must have aluminum
          crutches, but they cost $24.50. This is the tale of how
          they established the Arnold McWilliams Aluminum Crutches
          Fund, raised the money; and then what they did with it.

Va 435   Peyton, K. M. <u>Fly-by-night</u>. Cleveland: World, 1969.
          Twelve-year-old Ruth faces a conflict when the family's
          finances are strained because of her brother's motor bike
          accident. Should she help her family by giving up her
          pony, Fly-By-Night?

Va 436   Reynolds, Barbara L. <u>Hamlet and Brownswiggle</u>. New
          York: Scribner, 1954.
          Ricky learns to accept responsibility and to remember
          the things he is supposed to do when he is given permis-
          sion to have a hamster as a pet.

Va 437   Robinson, Barbara. <u>Across from Indian shore</u>. West
          Caldwell, N. J.: Lothrop, 1962.
          Luke fails his family several times through his day-
          dreaming and irresponsibility but he snaps to when his
          mother's desperate need causes him to undertake a diffi-
          cult trip in search of help.

Va 438   Sperry, Armstrong. <u>Call it courage</u>. Riverside, N. J.:
          Macmillan, 1940. (filmstrip/record)
          Mafatu, the son of a Polynesian chief, is rejected by
          his people because he has not conquered fear. He seeks
          escape from this rejection by going to sea. While at sea,
          he is shipwrecked and marooned and learns that his sense
          of rejection is needless; that in reality he is a courageous
          person. He returns to face his people, without fear but
          with courage.

Va 439   Stolz, Mary. A dog on Barkham Street. New York:
          Harper, 1960.
          Edward, as well as his friend Rod, want nothing so
much as a dog of their own. But Edward's main problem
in life is his next-door neighbor, Martin "Fatso" Hastings,
the Bully of Barkham Street. When Edward's traveling
uncle comes to visit, he brings his own dog along and
eventually many problems are solved. The same story
is told from the point of view of Martin Hastings, the bully,
in Bully of Barkham Street.

Va 440   Thompson, Mary Wolfe. Two in the wilderness. New
          York: McKay, 1967.
          Tabby and her brother Zeke are left to spend a summer
alone in the wilderness in the Hampshire Grants (later Vermont) while their father returns to the settlement to bring
back their mother, the little children, and, of course, the
cow. Fear and loneliness, adventures with wild animals,
and finally a sudden visit by two Indians, are among the
experiences of these two brave children on the American
frontier. Based on a true incident.

Va 441   Turkle, Brinton. Thy friend Obadiah. New York: Viking,
          1969.
          Obadiah, a 19th century Quaker boy, is miffed that he
is the only person on Nantucket to be followed by a sea-
gull; but when the gull disappears, Obadiah learns some
new aspect of friendship and responsibility.

Va 442   Values--The right thing to do. Santa Monica, Cal.: BFA
          Educational Media, 1971. (16mm, 8 minutes)
          Presents a story about deciding what is the right thing
to do and raises the question should we do what we know
is right even if we might get into trouble.

Va 443   What will Kevin do--Responsibility versus preference.
          New York: Doubleday, 1968. (16mm film, color, 6
          minutes)
          A dramatization about responsibility versus preference.

Va 444   Yates, Elizabeth. Amos Fortune, free man. New York:
          Dutton, 1950.
          A slave buys his freedom and dedicates his life to
helping other slaves.

Va 445   _____. A place for Peter. New York: Coward, 1952.
          While Peter's mother is away from home he is able to
prove to his father that he is grown up enough to accept
responsibility.

Va 446   Yorty, Jeane. Far wilderness. Grand Rapids, Mich.:
          Eerdmans, 1966.
          The Hughes family leave Albany, New York in the spring

of 1835 and travel to their newly purchased farm on the
Flint River in Michigan territory. Sixteen-year-old Nathan
takes responsibility for housing, feeding and protecting his
mother, sister, and another woman.

RIGHTS OF OTHERS

Va 447   Black, Algernon. The first book of ethics. New York:
           Watts, 1965.
           An introduction to the principles and significance of
ethics in the conduct of life. The author describes the
moral codes and concepts concerning right and wrong action which have evolved through the ages and covers in
detail four basic commandments common to the great philo-
sophical and religious teachings of the past and present.
He discusses personal and current social ethical issues,
suggesting ways for making choices in life.

Va 448   Burchard, Peter. Jed: the story of a Yankee soldier
           and a boy. New York: Coward, 1960.
           Jed, teen-age soldier for the Union, steals into enemy
territory to return a small southern boy to his home.

Va 449   Cleaver, Vera. I would rather be a turnip. Philadelphia:
           Lippincott, 1971.
           In this summer of importance, Annie Jelks was twelve
years old and her reputation was being threatened. Calvin, eight years old and her sister Norma's illegitimate
son, was coming to live with her and her father. The
traumatic effects of this event on Annie, the slow growth
of her love for Calvin, and the recognition of the pain in-
flicted by bigotry make another enthralling story of children's problems today.

Va 450   Clown. New York: Learning Corporation of America,
           1970. (film)
           No words are spoken in film about a Paris urchin who
loses his shaggy-haired dog, Clown. After much search-
ing and questioning, he finds Clown with a new master, a
blind man. The boy, after observing the dog's expressed
love for the new master, decides that the blind man really
needs the dog more than he does. He leaves his dog with
the blind man without saying a word.

Va 451   Culture and morals. (series) Big Springs, Tex.: Cre-
           ative Visuals, n. d. (transparencies)
           Few persons live outside a culture; thus the expectan-
cies of behavior and an understanding of the framework of
the culture itself must be understood by the citizen. Cultural morals are treated in conjunction with the contemporary life-style of the student. Extrapolation to complex
generalizations may be done with an eye to the students

who may profit by it--this will be at the discretion of the teacher. Rules are considered in light of their constructive contributions and not as tools of the adults.

Va 452   De Leeuw, Adele. The Girl Scout story. Scarsdale, N. Y. : Garrard, 1965.
          The book traces the growth of Girl Scouting, stressing the importance of scouting in developing international goodwill.

Va 453   Estes, Eleanor. The hundred dresses. New York: Harcourt, 1944.
          Maddie and Peggy make Wanda, a recent Polish immigrant, the brunt of heartless teasing.

Va 454   Guidance--What's right. New York: Educational Film Library Association, 1970. (filmstrip)
          Presents episodes to illustrate morals and manners. Asks the students to find answers to various social questions.

Va 455   Hoke, Helen. Etiquette: your ticket to good times. New York: Watts, 1970.
          Briefly, in an easy, encouraging manner, the author explains to young children the rules of etiquette for making introductions, dining out, being a house guest, giving and attending parties, writing letters, and speaking on the telephone, and points out some manners that apply only to boys or only to girls. Quizzes are given at the end of each chapter so the reader may test himself. The format of the book is open and inviting and the black-and-white drawings most attractive.

Va 456   Leaf, Munro. Fair play. Philadelphia: Lippincott, 1939.
          Explains why we have rules, laws and government, and tells how each of us can make our country a better and happier place for everyone.

Va 457   Living with others--Citizenship--Part I. South Holland, Ill. : H. Wilson Corporation, n. d. (1-7/8 ips. audiotape cassette)
          Presents thirteen dramatized episodes about youngsters who did not do the right thing to help students learn right from wrong.

Va 458   Loeb, Robert H. Manners for minors. New York: Associated Press, 1964.
          Discusses personal appearance, behavior at home and in public, good sportsmanship and prejudice, attitude toward school and homework, reasons for writing and speaking correctly.

Va 459   McKinzie, Ellen Kindt. Taash and the jesters. New

York: Holt, 1968.
When he is about ten, Taash is rejected by the wood-cutter and the villagers. His misery increases when he finds the witch Bargoh has taken him over. His misery is compounded when another witch attempts to take over his mind. A fine story of magic, hard work, and the battle between good and evil.

Va 460   McPeek, Walter. The Scout law in action. Nashville: Abingdon, 1966.
A handy, pocket-sized book which explains incidents from real life or literature and with some poetry selections, the nature of each one of the twelve Scout laws. While intended for Scout leaders, it can also provide useful guidance materials for teachers--as well as for young readers.

Va 461   MacSpadden, J. Walker. Robin Hood and his merry outlaws. Cleveland: World, 1946.
An English epic featuring the legendary outlaw Robin Hood who gathers a circle of lively outlaws who prey upon the rich to feed the poor. Many adventures, some humorous, lead to a misadventure with a fat fellow who turns out to be Richard the Lion-Hearted, who rights their wrongs and receives their loyalty. Concepts of death, treachery, heroism are features of the story.

Va 462   Open-ended stories. Lakeland, Fla.: Imperial Film, 1970. (film)
Presents children in open-ended, realistic conflict situations involving personal judgments and decisions. Several alternatives are suggested. Values presented are integrity, responsibility, courage, friendship, and respect for property.

Va 463   Understanding values. (series) Jamaica, N.Y.: Eye Gate, n.d. (filmstrips)
The student at this age is evaluating and reforming many of his values and standards. This set of six filmstrips makes no conclusive moral judgments. The set does not teach answers, but a chain of logical questions is raised from which the individual must take a stand and therefore come to an evaluation and understanding of his own values. Included in the series: Stealing; Cheating and chiseling; Lies; Half-truths and untold truths; Other's values/your values; Who cares? Staying involved; Right, wrong or maybe.

Va 464   Values. Santa Monica, Cal.: BFA Educational Media, 1972. (8 sets of 8 color prints)
These are 13 x 18-inch color photographs that show a variety of ethical problems common in a child's everyday life. Texts on the reverse side identify the problem and suggest appropriate behavior. Contents: My home; My

family; My friends; People I don't know; My class; My
school; My neighborhood; My community.

Va 465   Values in action. New York: Holt, 1970. (10 filmstrips)
          Portrays familiar and believable social dilemmas lead-
          ing to student participation through role playing and the
          development of values through social experience. One film-
          strip is a demonstration lesson in role playing. Contents:
          Demonstration lesson; Big eye; My best friend; It's all your
          fault; Terry takes a ride; Trouble with Nikki; Over the
          fence is out; Sticky fingers; He hit me first; Benefit of the
          doubt.

Va 466   Vandalism: crime or prank. Far Rockaway, N.Y.: Hori-
          zon Publishing, 1964. (16mm film, color, 6 minutes)
          Shows the effects of young people stealing a knife and
          borrowing an automobile "for fun."

Va 467   White, E. G. Charlotte's web. New York: Harper, 1952.
          The life of Wilbur, the pig, is saved by a girl who talks
          to animals and a spider who weaves strange messages.

                                    SHARING

Va 468   Estes, Eleanor. The Moffats. New York: Harcourt,
          1941.
          Nine-year-old Janey, her family of brothers and sisters
          and Mama, are not poverty-stricken but just poor; their
          life, however, is never commonplace.

Va 469   Lawson, Robert. The tough winter. New York: Viking,
          1954.
          Just as Uncle Analdas predicts, it is a tough winter.
          Severe weather comes early. The folks leave a caretaker
          who not only fails to feed the animals but owns a mean
          dog as well.

Va 470   Sharing. Chicago: Society for Visual Education, Inc.,
          n.d. (slides)
          Panorama of slides about family, friendship, love,
          brotherhood, and celebration.

Va 471   White, E. B. Charlotte's web. New York: Harper, 1952.
          The life of Wilbur, the pig, is saved by a girl who
          talks to animals and a spider who weaves strange mes-
          sages.

Chapter 3

ACCEPTING AND VALUING ONESELF
AS A DEVELOPING ORGANISM

Primary

ACCEPTING ONE'S IDEAS

Ac 1   Bishop, Claire Huchet. Five chinese brothers. New York: Coward, 1938.
    Each of five identical Chinese brothers has a special talent which he uses to save the lives of all.

Ac 2   Ets, Marie Hall. Just me. New York: Viking, 1965.
    A young boy emulates his many animal friends, but finds out that it is more fun just being himself, especially when he's with his father.

Ac 3   Fox, Paula. Hungry Fred. Englewood Cliffs, N.J.: Bradbury, 1969.
    Fred is so hungry he eats everything in sight and finally heads for the woods. There he meets a rabbit who shows him there's more to life than eating fifty meals a day!

Ac 4   Greene, Constance. Unmaking of rabbit. New York: Viking, 1972.
    Paul, whom the boys insist on calling rabbit is lonely and shy and stutters. He loves his Grandmother with whom he lives, but most of all he wants to live in the city with his mother. At 11, however, he is still waiting. He makes friends and learns to handle the bully, writes the best composition in class, and learns to be himself.

Ac 5   Krauss, Ruth. Is this you? Englewood Cliffs, N.J.: Scholastic Book Services, n.d.
    This is a picture book that asks children questions about themselves and encourages them to draw their own answers.

Ac 6   Learning about me. Chicago: Society for Visual Education, Inc., n.d. (sound filmstrip, color)
    Five filmstrips with open-ended situations provide for the exploration of self-concept and for the development of insights enhancing self-concept. Contents: Different shapes; First step; I'm new here; Borrowed friendship; I'm the boss.

EMOTIONS

Ac 7   Beim, Jerrold. Laugh and cry: your emotions and how
        they work. New York: Morrow, 1955.
        Emotions such as anger, sorrow, love, etc. are defined
        with examples familiar to every boy and girl.

Ac 8   Bouchard, Lois Kalb. Boy who wouldn't talk. New York:
        Doubleday, 1969.
        Carlos learns rapidly and understands the English he
        hears, but he is so homesick for Puerto Rico that he re-
        fuses to speak. Instead he uses sign language and pictures
        to communicate. This changes when he meets Ricky, a
        blind boy. Unlike the other children who question a boy who
        doesn't talk, Ricky becomes Carlos' friend. And Carlos
        does talk to Ricky.

Ac 9   Burningham, John. Mr. Gumpy's outing. Englewood Cliffs,
        N.J.: Scholastic, 1970.
        Mr. Gumpy was going on an outing in his boat. Some of
        the animals wanted to go along and Mr. Gumpy said they
        could if they did not squabble, hop, tease, and other things.
        The animals said they wouldn't, but they did and the boat
        turned over. It would be an excellent opening to discuss
        safety on a boat to very young children.

Ac 10   Dandelion. New York: Viking, 1970. (sound filmstrip,
        46 frs.)
        Dandelion learns to be himself when he almost misses a
        party. They didn't recognize him because he had made him-
        self look so silly.

Ac 11   Feelings about others. Detroit: Handy, 1956. (sound film-
        strip, color, 41 frames)
        How do children learn to care about others? Why is it
        important to show tenderness and affection towards our par-
        ents, our friends, and others? These feelings sometimes
        embarrass children and they must learn to handle them.
        The filmstrip explains why we must understand our feelings
        and why we must respect ourselves before we can show love
        for others. Love enhances all we do in life.

Ac 12   Getting to know me. (series) Chicago: Society for Visual
        Education, Inc., n.d. (sound filmstrip, color)
        The subject is developmental tasks and human relations.
        "People are like rainbows" points up that people differ bas-
        ically in their interests: that the prime differences in peo-
        ple is not racial. "Three strikes, you're in" emphasizes
        the need for assessment and realization of personal poten-
        tial and capacities. "Listen, Jimmy" discusses the need for
        a positive self image and the need for recognition. "A boat
        named George" stresses the need to get along with one's
        peers and adults.

Ac 13   Godden, Rumer. The fairy doll. New York: Viking, 1956.
        Elizabeth appeared to be clumsy, timid and even stupid
        until she was given the fairy doll to be her "good fairy."

Ac 14   How do you feel? (series) Mahwah, N. J. : Educational
            Reading Services, 1969. (filmstrip)
        Presents live photography showing both positive and nega-
        tive actions in different situations. Captions help the viewer
        gain a better understanding of himself and others. Includes:
        How do you feel about your home and family? How do you
        feel about your community? How do you feel about other
        children? How do you feel about being alone?

Ac 15   Kangman, Lee. The year of the raccoon. Boston: Hough-
            ton, 1966.
        Through his pet raccoon Joey overcomes his feelings of
        inferiority and inadequacy.

Ac 16   Keats, Ezra Jack. Whistle for Willie. New York: Viking,
            1964.
        Adventures of a little boy who tries to whistle for his dog
        the way big boys do.

Ac 17   Moods and emotions. Elgin, Ill. : Child's World, 1969.
            (8 study prints, 13 x 18 ins. , color)
        Drawings illustrating love, compassion, loneliness, frus-
        tration, joy (pleasure), thoughtfulness, anger, and sadness
        help children to understand these moods and emotions and
        may be bases for discussion of these between the teacher and
        class. On the back of each study print and in a nine-page
        booklet are resource materials and suggested procedures.

Ac 18   Moore, Lilian. I feel the same way. New York: Athene-
            um, 1967.
        Free verse, in deceptively simple form, in which the
        child-poet appears to speak directly to the listener of the
        experiences common to children everywhere, but particular-
        ly in the city. Illustrations interpret the poems.

Ac 19   Talking without words. New York: Viking, 1970. (black
            and white filmstrip, 35 frs.)
        Examines ways whereby thoughts are expressed without
        speech, such as a pointing or beckoning finger, an extended
        hand, a shrug, and a kiss.

                        INDIVIDUAL WORTH

Ac 20   Accepting ourselves. (series) Glenview, Ill. : Educational
            Projections Corporation, n. d. (sound filmstrip)
        The material in these sets is designed to help students
        develop respect for and understanding of themselves and
        others; to encourage desirable social attitudes and ethical

values for daily living; and to show how tolerance, respect
and cooperation can lead to more enjoyable friendships and
a happier, healthier life. Included are "The ugly duckling,"
"The rabbit that wanted to be different."

Ac 21   Andersen, Hans Christian. Ugly duckling. New York:
            Scribner, 1965.
         The story of this duckling leads straight to the triumphant
conclusion: "It doesn't matter about being born in a duck-
yard, as long as you are hatched from a swan's egg." Many
persons think this is also the story of the author's own life.

Ac 22   The ant and the grasshopper. Chicago: Coronet Instruction-
            al Films, n. d. (16mm film, 11 minutes, color)
         One can't play all the time; we must work and save for
a time of need. The ants work to gather food for winter
while the grasshopper plays and laughs at the ants. Then
he finds it hard to survive when winter comes, but the ants
are comfortable and now it's their turn to laugh and play.

Ac 23   Beim, Jerrold. The smallest boy in the class. New York:
            Morrow, 1949.
         The story of a boy who proved that stature is not always
measured in feet and inches. He was called Tiny because
of his size until the day that it was proved that he had the
biggest heart in the class. The solution of Jim's problem
will probably help teachers and parents to find other reme-
dies for children who feel insecure in their groups. For
children there is a lesson in the acceptance of important
values over unimportant ones.

Ac 24   Brenner, Barbara. Mr. Tall and Mr. Small. New York:
            Young Scott Books, 1966.
         A giraffe and a mouse argue about which is the better
size until a forest fire almost traps them and they must
find a way to safety.

Ac 25   Brown, Virginia. (series) Kenny wants to help... New
            York: McGraw-Hill, 1967. (filmstrip)
         Full-color drawings tell the story about a boy whose
willingness convinced everyone that he was not too little to
help people. Focus on a child in a culturally deprived area.
Correlated with Virginia Brown's books, Skyline series, vol.
3. May be used for group or individual study in reading
readiness.

Ac 26   Buckley, Helen E. Michael is brave. New York: Lothrop,
            1971.
         Timid young Michael is afraid to go down a high slide in
the playground. But when the teacher asks Michael to help
a little girl who has climbed to the top of the slide and is
too frightened to move, Michael comes to the rescue and
forgets his own fear.

Ac 27   Different. Nashville: Graded Press, Methodist, 1967.
         (sound filmstrip, color, 70 frs.)
         Explains to children that although individuals may be dif-
         ferent because of color, physical handicaps, facial features
         and nationality, they have the same basic needs and desires.

Ac 28   Fox, Paula. The stone-faced boy. Englewood Cliffs, N. J. :
         Bradbury, 1968.
         The story is a perceptive character study of a lonely,
         timid middle child in a family of five self-possessed, in-
         dividualistic children.   To save himself from teasing by
         classmates and siblings, Gus Oliver has learned to mask
         his feelings so well that he has lost all ability to show emo-
         tion.   Even the startling and unexpected arrival of an eccen-
         tric, outspoken great aunt appears to leave Gus unmoved.
         But the night his sister convinces him into going out in the
         dark and the cold to rescue a stray dog, he gains a new-
         found confidence in himself.

Ac 29   Freeman, Don. Dandelion. New York: Viking, 1964.
         Dandelion, the lion, is invited to a party, but he primps
         and preens so much that he is turned away because no one
         recognizes him.

Ac 30   Greene, Constance. Unmaking of rabbit. New York: Vik-
         ing, 1972.
         Paul, whom the boys insist on calling rabbit, is lonely
         and shy and stutters now and then.   He loves Gran, with
         whom he lives; most of all he wants to live with his mother
         in the city.   But at eleven he is still waiting.   He makes
         several friends, learns how to handle Freddy, the bully,
         writes the best composition in his class, and learns also to
         be himself.   A fine story of growing up and finding one's
         identity.

Ac 31   Guessing Games. Chicago: Encyclopaedia Britannica Edu-
         cational Corporation, 1969.   (16mm, color, 7 minutes)
         Uses a split-screen technique to show pantomimists or
         children miming various activities involving objects, and to
         show on the other half of the screen the object which is being
         described.

Ac 32   How can I improve myself? Jamaica, N. Y. : Eye Gate
         House, Inc. , 1969.   (sound filmstrip, color, 26 frs.)
         Studies the development of socially accepted behavior,
         emphasizing personality improvement.   Explains traits char-
         acteristic of popular people and lists those causing unpopu-
         larity.

Ac 33   The importance of you. (series) Santa Monica, Cal.:
         BFA Educational Media, n. d.   (sound filmstrip, color)
         Self-understanding is the underlying purpose of this series.
         Physical qualities, interests, all of the things that make each

child unique are reviewed. An appreciation for his individu-
ality is developed within the child. Reviewing the family
unit, the child examines the variety of experiences shared,
the way in which emotions are handled and the need for people to have time alone. Relationships with friends, learning
to know one another, feelings of love, anger, sadness, excitement and fright are discussed in a way that helps the
child understand other people, but more important, himself.
Included are: "You are somebody special"; "Who's in your
family?" "Why are your friends?" "Your feelings."

Ac 34   Lionni, Leo. Fish is fish. New York: Random, 1970.
        Shows that it is nice to listen to experiences of others,
but that we must each be ourselves and not try something
or want something just because someone else does or has
the thing. The little fish listens to the frog tell of all the
things he sees out of the water. The fish just can't get his
mind off the things and tries to jump out of the water so he
can see all of the wonders. But he finds that he cannot
breathe. The frog helps him back into the water and he becomes content with himself and his life as it is.

Ac 35   Newman, Robert. The boy who could fly. New York:
        Atheneum, 1967.
        Mark and Joey are two brothers who go to spend a year
with their aunt and uncle in a suburban town, after their
mother and father both die. Naturally they are very close,
but Mark feels he must take particular care of Joey, not
just because he is much younger but because he is very
"special." He cannot only tell what other people are thinking but has other unusual skills. You may be surprised at
the outcome--though transference.

Ac 36   Piper, Watty. Little engine that could. Bronx, N.Y.:
        Platt & Munk, 1961.
        When no other engine is willing to help, the little shiny
blue engine gives her all to get the toys and food over the
mountain to the boys and girls. Her theme is "I think I
can."

Ac 37   Slobodkin, Louis. Magic Michael. New York: Macmillan,
        1944.
        Little brother has a vivid imagination and pretends to be
many different things until a gift of a bicycle makes him
wish to be a "boy."

Ac 38   They need me. (series) Mahwah, N.J.: Educational Read-
        ing Service, n.d. (filmstrip, 4 frs.)
        Presents children in everyday situations which show the
emotional and social interdependencies between them and their
family members and friends. Shows situations dealing with
the responsibility of the child in everyday relationships.

Ac 39   Understanding my needs. (Basic Human Values series)
             Wichita, Kan.: Learning Arts, n.d. (filmstrip)
         The importance of self-understanding in the pursuit of in-
         dividual goals. Suggests various means valuable to students
         in the determination of who and what they are. Encourages
         group participation in establishing ethical values and judg-
         ments. Examination of what the child is and what he wants
         to become.

Ac 40   Who am I. (series) Jamaica, N.Y.: Eye Gate House, Inc.,
             1969. (sound filmstrip, color, 30 frs.)
         This first in a series of sound filmstrips by Edward
         Carina and Maria Callas is concerned with the special world
         of small children in their own environment. One objective
         of this set is to help the child develop a concept of self and
         feel good about himself. Excellent color films for children.
         Included in the series: The joy of being you; Nothing is
         something to do; People packages; All kinds of feelings; Do
         you believe in wishes.

Ac 41   Who cares. (Skyline series) New York: McGraw-Hill,
             n.d. (filmstrip, 39 frs.)
         Full-color drawings tell a story about how a young boy's
         enthusiastic love of music helps him change a defeated atti-
         tude to becoming a part of the classroom activities.

Ac 42   Will. The little tiny rooster. New York: Harper, 1960.
         A story about a small rooster who is scorned by his fel-
         low creatures in the barnyard because of his size until they
         realize the value of his voice. He then becomes one of the
         exclusive groups of roosters who crow in the morning to
         announce the coming of dawn.

                        PHYSICAL CHARACTERISTICS

Ac 43   After everything I doodle, doodle, doodle do. Detroit:
             Jam Handy School Service, Inc., 1969. (filmstrip, color,
             23 frs.)
         Cartoon-like art illustrates the song about the importance
         of washing after each activity is completed. Includes words
         and music for viewer participation. Useful for teaching
         cleanliness to preschoolers and kindergarten through grade
         2. Series provides musical expression as well as teaching
         good health practices and developing reading readiness.

Ac 44   Balestrino, Philip. The skeleton inside you. New York:
             Crowell, 1971.
         The human skeleton is explained and depicted in charm-
         ing text and illustrations. Simply the author discusses how
         the body is joined together and how the body structure changes
         as you grow. Also, what happens if you break a bone is ex-
         plained to children.

Ac 45   Beim, Jerrold. The smallest boy in the class. New York:
          Morrow, 1949.
          Story of a boy who proved that stature is not always
          measured in feet and inches. He was called Tiny because
          of his size, until the day it was proven that he had the big-
          gest heart in the class. There is a lesson in the acceptance
          of important values over unimportant ones and remedies for
          children who feel insecure because of size.

Ac 46   Bridwell, Norman. A tiny family. Englewood Cliffs, N. J. :
          Scholastic, 1972.
          A family of imaginative tiny people has many amusing
          problems in a real world of normal sized people.

Ac 47   Brush up on your teeth. New York: Bristol Myers, n. d.
          (filmstrip, color, 46 frames)
          Shows how to take care of the teeth. Includes proper
          food and emphasizes regular visits to the dentist.

Ac 48   Charlip, Remy. Mother, Mother, I feel sick, send for the
          doctor quick, quick, quick. New York: Parents Maga-
          zine Press, 1966.
          A hilarious story of a little boy with a most unusual
          stomach ache. An excellent opportunity to talk about the
          doctor and how he helps keep your body healthy.

Ac 49   The dentist. Inglewood, Cal. : Popular Science Publishing
          Company, 1968. (8mm silent cartridge, 4 minutes, color)
          This pictures the child's first visit to the dentist, and
          demonstrates the correct way to brush teeth. It is from the
          Community Workers Series.

Ac 50   Friedman, Frieda. Dot for short. New York: Morrow,
          1947.
          A girl learns to adjust to her small size.

Ac 51   Getting to know me. Wichita, Kan. : Learning Arts, n. d.
          (records, 33-1/3)
          Emphasis on self-awareness as one of the most important
          things that children in early grades have to learn. Includes:
          People are like rainbows (Theme--The importance of being
          yourself); A boat named George (Theme--Working with others);
          Listen Jimmy (Theme--Succeeding the right way); Strike
          three you're in (Theme--Recognizing abilities).

Ac 52   Getting to know myself. Jamaica, N. Y. : Eye Gate House
          Inc. , n. d.   (tape)
          An introduction to learning for the younger child. Covers
          many areas including, awareness of body image and the
          body's position in space; identification of body places; ob-
          jects in relation to body planes, body part identification;
          movements of the body, laterality of body, feelings and
          moods.

Ac 53   I see you and me. (series) Holyoke, Me.: Scott Education Division, 1971. (sound filmstrip)
A delightful presentation designed to heighten the young
child's awareness of self, encouraging him to see himself
as a separate and distinct entity, and helping him to per-
ceive his relationship to the people around him. The four
sound filmstrips show primary grade children in natural,
everyday situations. The young viewer absorbs, in an entertaining manner, a solid understanding of his own body parts
and how they relate to each other. The resulting physical
awareness of self then provides the basis for a sound psycho-
logical awareness of self. The Teacher's Guide provides a
wide assortment of motivational questions and activities,
plus evaluation ideas. Includes: Faces; Hands and arms;
The body; Expression.

Ac 54   Krasilovsky, Phyllis. Very little boy. New York: Doubleday, 1962.
He was smaller than all the other little boys on the street
but he grows and grows until he is no longer a "very little
boy."

Ac 55   _____. Very little girl. New York: Doubleday, 1953.
A tiny little girl grows and grows until she is big enough
to be the big sister for a new baby brother.

Ac 56   _____. The very tall little girl. New York: Doubleday,
1969.
"For a very young girl who is taller than her contempor-
aries, a bit of reassurance. The little girl here is six
inches taller than most girls her age, which creates all sorts
of problems: school desks are uncomfortable, dresses are
hard to fit (why not just get the next size line?) and adults
expect more of her. On the other hand, she gets to clean
the top of the blackboard and can see over the heads of her
classmates and is the first girl in the neighborhood to get a
full-sized bicycle. All ends on the happy note that being
tall means being different and therefore special."

Ac 57   Kraus, Robert. Leo the late bloomer. New York: Wind-
mill/Simon & Schuster, 1971.
"Leo is a small, sad-eyed creature, who looks more tiger-
ish than leonine in orange with gray-blue stripes. Everybody
writes and reads but Leo. He's just a late bloomer, mother
assures father. Father watches and worries. 'A watched
bloomer doesn't bloom,' says Leo's mother. Father stops
watching, but he peeks. No bloom. Spring comes, and one
day, in his own good time; Leo blooms. He reads! He
writes! He eats neatly! And he speaks a whole sentence:
'I made it!' Artfully bland, sunny, and reassuring for other
late bloomers."

Ac 58   Krauss, Ruth. The growing story. New York: Harper,

1947.
A little boy watches the things around him growing all spring and summer and is delighted when the time comes to put on winter clothes again to discover that he has grown, too.

Ac 59   Learning about growth and exercise. Chicago: Encyclopae-
        dia Britannica Education Corporation, 1969. (sound film-
        strip, color, 35 frs.)
        Answers questions about health, neatness, sleep and rest, food, skin, eyes, ears, teeth. Cartoon-like art work. Explains how children grow and how exercise and good health help in growth. Useful for group study. Questions at the end of the filmstrip lead into student discussion.

Ac 60   One-inch fellow. New York: AVI Associates, Inc., 1969.
        (sound filmstrip, color, 55 frs.)
        Japanese folk tale of the exploits of "Tom Thumb," warrior to the Lord of Kyoto, who proves that size is not necessarily the measure of a man when he saves the Lord's daughter from a man eating monster. Background music and art work typical of the country.

Ac 61   Questions about health. Chicago: Encyclopaedia Britannica
        Education Corporation, 1969. (filmstrip, color, 35 frs.)
        Cartoon-like artwork introduces the series through the children's interest in their differences and the teachers encouraging them to ask about their ears, their eyes, their skin, their teeth, their hair, food, growth, and exercise. Useful for group study in health and for introduction to open discussion on the subject.

Ac 62   Raskin, Ellen. Spectacles. New York: Atheneum, 1968.
        Even though nearsighted 'Iris swears that there's a fire-breathing dragon at the door, a giant pygmy nuthatch on the lawn, a chestnut mare in the parlor, her readers will see, by flipping the page each time, that its only Great-aunt Fanny, her friend Chester, and the babysitter respectively." Iris detests specs but gets them anyway. May be useful with those children resisting needed glasses.

Ac 63   Schloat, G. W. Your wonderful teeth. New York: Scrib-
        ner, 1954.
        "Two small boys, Warren and Andy, learn about teeth, their usefulness and how to care for them. Some of the work done by dentists is described as Andy visits his regular dentist and Warren goes to a specialist to have his teeth straightened. The only book for children that provides information on dental anatomy and hygiene and on dental science. Some of the unnecessary illustrations could have been replaced with more text."

Ac 64   Someday I'll grow up. Detroit: Jam Handy School Service,

Inc., 1969.   (filmstrip, color, 24 frs.)
This is a cartoon-style filmstrip encouraging audience
participation on good social and health habits.   It emphasizes
that animals and people change as they grow.

Ac 65   Your exercise and posture.   (series) Chicago: Coronet
         Films, 1968.   (sound filmstrip)
         Shows why the body needs exercise for growth and good
health, how one can get the right amount of exercise, why
good posture is important, and how it can be obtained.   Other titles in the series: Keeping well; Keeping clean; Your
food; Your clothes; Your rest and sleep.

Ac 66   Your eyes.   (Basic life science--your health series) Chi-
         cago: Encyclopaedia Britannica Education Corporation,
         n.d.   (16 mm film, color, 7 minutes)
         A movie on the parts of the eye and how to take proper
care of the eyes.

Ac 67   Your rest and sleep.   (Good health habits series) Chicago:
         Coronet Films, 1968.   (sound filmstrip, color, 47 frs.)
         Shows why the body needs sufficient rest and sleep, how
sleep helps the body, and how many hours of sleep primary
age children require.   Useful for individual and group study
in health.

Ac 68   Your teeth.   (Basic life science--your health series) Chi-
         cago: Encyclopaedia Britannica Education Corporation,
         n.d.   (16mm filmstrip, color, 6 minutes)
         A movie on how to take care of your teeth, brushing
properly, eating habits and regular check-ups are described.

Ac 69   Zim, Herbert.   What's inside of me? New York: Morrow,
         1952.
         A clear account of the functions of the internal organs of
the human body, illustrated with charts which clarify the
text.

PHYSICAL HANDICAPS

Ac 70   Greene, Constance C.   Girl called Al. New York: Viking,
         1969.
         Al is fat; she doesn't like the clothes her mother buys
for her; she has to wear her hair in pigtails; she dislikes
her name, Alexandra; and she hates her mother!   Then she
moves into an apartment house where she finds a friend and
life becomes happier.

Ac 71   Kirkland, Jessica.   The monkeys. New York: Doubleday,
         1972.
         The mother of three monkeys, Deaf, Dumb, and Blind,
thought they were doomed because of their defects, but when

the Gorilla tribe attacks the monkeys, they transform their
defects into valuable tools.

Ac 72   Krasilovsky, Jessica. A boy who spoke Chinese. New
         York: Doubleday, 1972.
         Because Nicholas has a speech disorder, no one wants to
         talk to him, but Nicholas solves his problem by finding a
         very special someone to talk to.

Ac 73   Lord, Beman. Guards for Matt. New York: Walck, 1965.
         Matt has double trouble; he is trying to stay on the bas-
         ketball team and wear his necessary glasses and he aims to
         keep secret his success in singing, which at a women's club
         luncheon earns him the money for guards for his spectacles.
         This book can help the young sports player learn that there
         are some physical obstacles that he may need to overcome
         in order to become a participant.

Ac 74   Raskin, Ellen. Spectacles. New York: Atheneum, 1968.
         Iris sees things other people can't. She sees a fire
         breathing dragon that turns out to be her Great-aunt Fanny,
         and a giant pygmy nuthatch that is only her good friend
         Chester. When she sees a huge green caterpillar and
         frightens the teacher, her mother takes her to a blue ele-
         phant who prescribes glasses. Now Iris sees things as they
         are supposed to look, except for special times when she
         likes to see "that red rhinoceros with a tulip in its ear."

Intermediate

ACCEPTING ONE'S IDEAS

Ac 75   Bonham, Frank. Nitty gritty. New York: Dutton, 1968.
         Charlie Matthews, black and quite good in school, wants
         to earn money and to leave home, because his dad sees no
         future in a black boy getting too much education. It takes
         Charlie's Uncle Baron, who steals away with Charlie's
         money, to wake Charlie up to thinking for himself.

Ac 76   Clark, Ann Nolan. Santiago. New York: Viking, 1955.
         A Guatemalan Indian boy is adopted by a Spanish lady and
         later reclaimed by his Indian relatives. He leaves the In-
         dian settlement, however, feeling rejected by both races.
         Santiago's search for identity epitomizes the tragic gap be-
         tween two cultures as well as the terrible gulf between
         wealth and poverty. The message of cultural pride and per-
         sonal freedom of this fine author should speak to many chil-
         dren today.

Ac 77   Craig, John. Zach. New York: Coward-McCann, 1972.
         After the death of his family, an uncle and aunt, in a
         fire on the Canadian Ojibway reservation, Zach Kenebec

finds an unwelcome identity as the last of the Agawas. His
search to find others of the tribe and his odyssey over Canada and the U.S. West involve him with every situation and
type of person. In relationships that ultimately prove meaningful, Zach finds the ties that bind people together are not
blood, age, sex or race, but common values.

Ac 78   Fiedler, Jean. Yardstick for Jessica. New York: McKay,
            1964.
            Sixth grader Jessica saves money for shoes with a big
heel so she will appear taller. By the time she is able to
buy them she discovers that she has grown an inch in height
and much more in personal values.

Ac 79   Green, Mary McBurney. Is it hard? Is it easy? New York:
            Scott, 1960.
            Through examples of real children playing at games,
sports, and hobbies, young readers can learn to appreciate
that everybody, including themselves, can do some things
very well and other things not so well.

Ac 80   Hughes, Langston. Don't you turn back: poems. New
            York: Knopf, 1969.
            Forty-five poems with special appeal for youth. Sections
divided into My people, Prayers and dreams, Out to see,
and I am a Negro. Poems that reach the heart of aspira-
tions and frustrations of blacks in America. Attractive one
poem per page layout will appeal to reluctant readers. Strik-
ing woodcuts in rust and black.

Ac 81   Right and wrong: What's in between? Drayton Plains,
            Mich.: Portafilms, 1968. (16mm filmstrip, color, 10
            minutes)
            Stimulates through use of animated cartoon, attention to
ethical values and interpersonal relations. Delineates that
if something is false, it is not automatically a lie; the intent
of the source must be considered.

Ac 82   Yashima, Taro. Crow boy. Weston, Conn.: Weston Woods
            Studios, 1961. (filmstrip, 48 frs.)
            A very shy boy, under the influence of a very understand-
ing teacher, surprises everyone with his talent.

EMOTIONS

Ac 83   Agle, Nan Hayden. Susan's magic. New York: Seabury,
            1973.
            Tells the story of a very real and believable fourth grad-
er who lives with her mother and older brother. In the
course of the book, Susan begins to grow up and discovers
the contradictions in herself. The action rises quickly and
moves rapidly to a climax. Divorce and absent fathers, an

issue more and more children must deal with, is sensitively and realistically treated.   Fourth and fifth grade girls and boys enjoy this story.

Ac 84   Burch, Robert. **D. J. 's worst enemy.** New York: Viking, 1965.
After a series of near-calamities, D. J. (who tells the story) finally decides to grow up and "become a member of the family. " His brother Skinny Little Renfro, who excels at imitations, and his sister Clara May are among the other persons in this funny and enlightening story.

Ac 85   _____ . Renfroe's Christmas. New York: Viking, 1968.
When Renfroe's older sister accuses him of selfishness Renfroe suspects it is true--especially when he buys a better pocketknife for himself than the one he buys for his brother. How Renfroe overcomes his selfish streak is told in this warmhearted family story set in the South.

Ac 86   _____ . Simon and the game of chance. New York: Viking, 1970.
Simon feels that his father disapproves of everything that he wants to do. And his father is, in truth, a very strait-laced, stern person. The family is in a major crisis, however, for the mother goes into deep melancholy when the new baby dies and she has to spend a year of treatment in an institution. An unusual tale of family misery in the Depression, in which Simon learns to understand his father and himself.

Ac 87   Feelings, Muriel L. Zamani goes to market. New York: Seabury, 1970.
At last Zamani is old enough to accompany his father and his two older brothers to market. After a successful morning of selling, the three brothers are given coins to spend. Zamani purchases a beautiful necklace for his mother. His kindness is rewarded almost immediately when he receives a new kanzu. It is his first gown with orange braid and he plans to wear it when he enters school. A simple warm tale of East Africa.

Ac 88   Feil, Hila. Windmill summer. New York: Harper & Row, 1972.
Arabella is so nagged by her elderly relatives and by the apathy of her mother and father that she decides to spend the summer in the windmill as an escape. She moves over bag and baggage to her perfect haven. But she finds she is responsible for a solitary skunk, an industrious beaver family, and an evasive raccoon. She learns not only how to handle the danger which threatens her animal friends, but also how to cope with her own personal problems.

Ac 89   Fiedler, Jean. Yardstick for Jessica. New York: McKay,

1964.
Sixth grader Jessica saves money for shoes with a heel
so she will appear taller. By the time she is able to buy
them she discovers that she has grown an inch in height and
much more in personal values.

Ac 90   Fox, Paula. The stone-faced boy. New York: Bradbury,
        1968.
        The story is a perceptive character study of a lonely,
timid, middle child in a family of five self-possessed, in-
dividualistic children. To save himself from teasing by
classmates and siblings, Gus Oliver has learned to mask
his feelings so well that he has lost all ability to show emotion. Even the startling and unexpected arrival of an eccen-
tric, outspoken great-aunt appears to leave Gus unmoved,
but the night his sister convinces him into going out in the
dark and the cold to rescue a stray dog, he gains a new-
found interest and confidence in himself.

Ac 91   Le Shan, Eda. What makes me feel this way? New York:
        Macmillan, 1972.
        The author uses specific situations involving such emo-
tions as love, hate, fear, anger, and jealousy to illustrate
the conflicts and confusion every child experiences and to
help the child understand and accept his feelings. This book
is an excellent treatment of a rarely taught subject for ele-
mentary-age children.

Ac 92   Me, myself and I. (series) Jamaica, N.Y.: Eye Gate
        House, Inc., n.d. (sound filmstrip)
        A child who feels good about himself has a head start on
successful learning and living. Through captivating filmstrips, teachers can start every member of a group thinking and talking about himself. Students relate to the lively
youngsters on screen as they discuss their appearance, their
friends, their feelings and interests, their wishes and
dreams. At the end of each filmstrip, frames for discussion invite viewers to join the conversation. Each child is
encouraged to discover himself as a unique, worthwhile individual.

Ac 93   Sachs, Marilyn. Veronica Ganz. New York: Doubleday,
        1968.
        At thirteen Veronica, the bully of her school in the Bronx,
hasn't got a friend. Afraid of being made fun of because
she's so big, she has long since beaten (boys) or slapped
(girls) her classmates into subservience. (She also enjoys
making sport of teachers and a librarian.) Then a new boy
arrives. Although small, Peter is smart and he sidesteps
Veronica's persistent attempts to pulverize him. At last
the big girl and the undersized boy have a confrontation
which brings some pleasant surprises for the belligerent
Veronica.

Ac 94   There's a new you comin'. Shawnee Mission, Kan.: Marsh
         Films, 1972. (sound filmstrip, 53 frs.)
         Provides for boys a broad picture of what growing up is
         all about. Emphasizes responsibility to emotional maturity
         as well as physical development.

Ac 95   Walter, Mildred Pitts. Lillie of Watts takes a giant step.
         New York: Doubleday, 1971.
         An inside look at the family problems, organization, and
         aspiration of a black family in the Los Angeles suburb of
         Watts. Lillie is about to enter 7th grade. A family of eight
         people in a three-room apartment leaves little room for pri-
         vacy. Only one of her problems is her shame at having to
         carry a lunch bag instead of buying lunch in the cafeteria.
         An excellent story of interest to white and black readers.

Ac 96   Welber, Robert. The train. New York: Pantheon, 1972.
         Young Elizabeth is fearful of crossing the meadow near
         her home. The method she employs to gain confidence will
         cause country children, black children (as Elizabeth is black)
         and virtually all children to identify. Coping with something
         which makes you afraid is a common problem we all have
         and sometimes solve.

                           INDIVIDUAL WORTH

Ac 97   Apsler, Alfred. Northwest pioneer. New York: Farrar,
         1960.
         Two Jewish boys from a Bohemian ghetto migrate to the
         West and contribute to the founding of a great city--Portland,
         Oregon. The fictionalized but authentic account of the life
         of Lous Fleischner and of the search of the Jewish people
         for a place to put down roots makes this biography a mem-
         orable one.

Ac 98   Arthur, Ruth M. Portrait of Margarita. New York: Athe-
         neum, 1968.
         Orphaned at sixteen, Margarita Somerville becomes the
         ward of her cousin, Francis. Thereafter, when not in
         school, she makes her home in the small English village of
         Swithins Mill with her guardian. But Margarita is troubled
         about her acceptance because her grandmother is a black
         Jamaican and Margarita's complexion is dark. Cousin Fran-
         cis accepts Margarita but she constantly expects others to
         reject her.

Ac 99   Barrett, Anne. Midway. New York: Coward-McCann,
         1967.
         Mark is dull and ordinary in comparison with members
         of his brilliant family. He is the middle of the five Mun-
         day children, which makes matters worse. Still, at school
         he seems to be the one called on to defend the peculiarities

of the family. Then, one day while he is sitting on a tree limb, Midway comes to visit. Midway, with his green eyes, steers Mark away from dullness into success and confidence and into becoming as brilliant as the rest of the family.

Ac 100   Bragdon, Elspeth. That Jud. New York: Viking, 1962.
          Jud, the town ward, convinces the residents of this town that he is a responsible person with something to offer the town.

Ac 101   Burch, Robert. Doodle and the go-cart. New York: Viking, 1972.
          The first time Doodle saw the go-cart he knew he wanted to own one more than anything in the world. But how does a boy in rural Georgia earn that kind of money ($200). This is a story of a boy determined to achieve the impossible. Doodle's efforts to earn the money, which include a mule transportation service, scarecrow making, and beaver trapping, are related with warmth and gentle humor in a story in which the characterization and setting are strongly realized.

Ac 102   _____. Renfroe's Christmas. New York: Viking, 1968.
          When Renfroe's older sister accuses him of selfishness Renfroe suspects it is true--especially when he buys a better knife for himself than the one he buys his brother. How Renfroe overcomes his selfish streak is told in this warmhearted family story set in the south.

Ac 103   Christopher, Matt. Catch that pass. Boston: Little, Brown, 1969.
          Jim Nardi fears being tackled and in the last three minutes of a crucial game against the Cadets, he fails to catch a pass but knocks it down, causing the Vulcans to lose the game. Then Jim learns the coach had the same weakness but overcame it, and this fires Jim to conquer his own fears.

Ac 104   Coolidge, Olivia. Come by here. Boston: Houghton, 1970.
          "Minty Lou's warm, secure world is shattered when her parents are accidentally killed. She becomes an unwelcomed burden in homes where both money and hope are in short supply. Set in Baltimore in 1900 this book is based on an actual life story of a Black girl who struggled to regain the security she once had known."

Ac 105   De Angeli, Marguerite. Henner's Lydia. New York: Doubleday, 1936.
          This is the beginning of a series of books about the Amish people of early Pennsylvania. Lydia questions the responsibilities placed on her by her religious group.

Sometimes she is ashamed to be one of the group.   Slowly
she realizes that she has worth as a person and that she
can have pride in the religious organization that her family
is a part of.

Ac 106   Estes, Eleanor. The Moffats. New York: Harcourt, 1941.
                Nine-year-old Janey, her family of brothers and sisters
          and Mama, are not poverty-stricken but just poor; their
          life, however, is never commonplace.

Ac 107   Fiedler, Jean. A yardstick for Jessica. New York: Mc-
                Kay, 1964.
                Sixth grader Jessica saves money for shoes with a heel
          so she will appear taller.   By the time she is able to buy
          them she discovers that she has grown an inch taller and
          gained much more in personal values.

Ac 108   Fisher, Laura. Never try Nathaniel. New York: Holt,
                1968.
                Nathaniel is the youngest of five, and the only one left
          at home, but he has nephews and nieces.   This is good,
          except that his oldest nephew, six-year-old Little Joe, is
          braver and a better worker than twelve-year-old Than.
          Than tries hard but the dog and one of the cows chase him
          and the horses take their own lead when he tries to drive.
          When Pa gets hurt, Joe's scorn of Than increases, until
          Than resolves to show everyone his metal.   Well written
          account of a boy's battle within himself.

Ac 109   Greene, Constance. Unmaking of rabbit. New York: Vik-
                ing, 1972.
                Paul, whom the boys insist on calling Rabbit, is lonely
          and shy and stutters now and then.   He loves Gran, with
          whom he lives; most of all he wants to live with his moth-
          er in the city.   But at eleven he is still waiting.   He
          makes several friends, learns how to handle Freddy the
          bully, writes the best composition in his class, and learns
          also to be himself.   A fine story of growing up and find-
          ing one's identity.

Ac 110   King, Helen. Willy. New York: Doubleday, 1971.
                Willy isn't a boy.   Willy isn't the ten-year-old man of
          the house.   Willy is the rat who invades the house and
          makes life miserable for the boy, his mother, grandmother
          and five brothers and sisters.   But the boy tries to be a
          man and get rid of Willy.   Finally he outwits the rat, saves
          precious food, and makes the rest of the family happy.

Ac 111   Lampman, Evelyn Sibley. Navaho sister. New York:
                Doubleday, 1956.
                Sad girl, so named because her grandmother was the
          only family she had and the Navahos considered this a sad
          situation, was ashamed of her name and resented the pity,

that she thought she saw in everyone's eyes.   When she
went from her Arizona home to the Chenawa Indian School
in Oregon, she tried to keep anyone at the school from
knowing that she had no family.   At first her secret
weighed heavily upon her, and then she came to understand
that, in a sense, the entire school was her family, and so
she had found happiness even before the existence of her
real family was disclosed.   Many girls will find in Sad
Girl's problem and her way of meeting it similarity to
their own problems.

Ac 112   Little, Jean.   Spring begins in March.   Boston: Little,
            Brown, 1966.
            Meg Copeland, youngest of the family doesn't feel she
has any fun.   "Whenever I do something somebody doesn't
like it," she said.   At home her older sister Sal, with
whom she shares a room, complains of her disorderliness
and Grandmother, who has come to live with them, complains of her general behavior.   Her teacher complains of
her inattention.   A crisis is reached when Meg brings home
a failing report card.   Putting earlier friction aside, Sal
and one of her friends step in and help by tutoring Meg
every day after school.   This, along with an old diary,
and her grandmother's new interest combine to help Meg
find herself.

Ac 113   Raymond, Charles.   Jud.   Boston: Houghton, 1968.
            Jud Harrow is a spoiled, weak city boy reluctant to help
his parents in any way with home duties.   When the family
moves to the Smokey Mountains, life is very different.
Jud learns the satisfaction of work and the joys of life in
the real country.   Even his father learns that conveniences
also have their value.

Ac 114   Stephens, Peter John.   Towappu: Puritan renegade.   New
            York: Atheneum, 1966.
            "With the mysterious disappearance of John Morris,
friend of the Wampanoags, his son Timothy is left alone
in their wilderness home.   The Plymouth colonists take
Timothy into custody, but he escapes and finds refuge in
the Wampanoag camp.   Adopting the Indian ways and becoming one of them, Timothy is soon enmeshed in the mis-
understandings and events which precede the outbreak of
King Philip's War.   Torn and confused by the conflicting
values of his two cultures, he risks his life to reconcile
Indian and Puritan differences....   Skillfully and incon-
spicuously woven through the story is a wealth of historical
and anthropological information.   Tempo quickens; tension
mounts; sympathy lies with the Wampanoags. "

Ac 115   Stinetorff, Louise A.   Musa, the shoemaker.   Philadelphia:
            Lippincott, 1959.
            In his village in the Atlas Mountains of North Africa,

the shoemaker's apprentice wants above anything to bring
honor to his village and to become a foot doctor, though
crippled himself.

Ac 116   Values: understanding others. (series) Redondo Beach,
                Cal.: Jarvis Couillard Associates, 1969. (16mm film,
                color, 9 minutes)
                Includes the importance of trying to understand others
         as a basis of caring more for them. Questions what to
         do with someone who behaves in a way which you do not
         approve. Suggests how you would feel under similar con-
         ditions.

Ac 117   Wells, Rosemary. Fog comes on little pig feet. New
                York: Dial, 1972.
                Rachel's parents were determined that she go to a very
         fine boarding school and have all the advantages they had
         missed. But from the very first day, it was a disaster.
         What she wanted was time and privacy--time to practice
         the piano, to take walks, to think. And this the school re-
         fused to allow. The experience became truly complex when
         she was thrown with a school runaway, whom she tried to
         protect in a situation in which there was really no one right
         answer. A powerful story of loyalty and honesty, high-
         lighted by the problems of an adolescent.

Ac 118   White, E. G. Charlotte's web. New York: Harper, 1952.
                The life of Wilbur, the pig, is saved by a girl who talks
         to animals and a spider who weaves strange messages.

Ac 119   Who am I? Jamaica, N.Y.: Eye Gate House, 1969.
                (filmstrip)
                Defines psychology and promotes self-evaluation, empha-
         sizing the concept that people are different. Explores the
         basic human needs and categories, inherited and acquired
         traits such as abilities, interests, and appearances.

PHYSICAL CHARACTERISTICS

Ac 120   Adler, Irving. Taste, touch, and smell. New York: Day,
                1966.
                A discussion of touch, a skin sense, and two chemical
         senses, taste and smell. The author describes how these
         senses work through the electrical network of the nervous
         system and what purpose each of them serves.

Ac 121   The beauty and you. New York: Sterling Films, 1970.
                (16mm film, 12 mins)
                Presents three teen-aged girls on a fantasy journey to
         discover their individual beauty styles and learn about
         health and beauty from characters whom they meet along
         the way.

Ac 122   Bibby, Cyril & Morison, Ian T. Your body and how it
          works. New York: American Heritage, 1969.
          The aim of this book is to explain how the body func-
          tions. It shows "what role cells, bones, muscles, nerves,
          teeth, digestive system, heart, lungs, blood circulation,
          reproductive organs, glands, and the five senses play to
          keep the complex and intricate mechanism of ... [the] body
          working smoothly."

Ac 123   Discovering your senses. (series) Chicago: Coronet,
          1971. (sound filmstrip)
          Introduces the five senses, illustrating the unique quali-
          ties of each and how they work together for our protection,
          education and well-being. Inquiry questions help children
          develop greater use of their senses to discover more about
          the world around them.

Ac 124   Eyes, their structure and care. Chicago: Encyclopaedia
          Britannica Education Corporation, n.d. (black and white,
          11 minutes)
          "Shows how Ed's low grades, headaches, and poor base-
          ball playing prompt him to visit an optometrist. Animated
          drawings show the parts of the eye and the path of light
          rays through these structures in myopia, hyperopia, and
          astigmatism. Pictures Ed being referred to an opthalmol-
          ogist by his optometrist and shows him going to the op-
          tician who grinds his glasses. Concluded by showing that
          wearing glasses has helped Ed and by discussing the proper
          care of the eyes."

Ac 125   Gallant, Roy A. Me and my bones. New York: Double-
          day, 1971.
          This delightful little book presents some really amazing
          photographs and a tremendous amount of information de-
          livered in a pleasant, interesting, even cheerful manner.
          The use of highly personalized pictures to demonstrate the
          living body and skeleton is most attractive. This will be
          extremely worthwhile collateral reading for a course in
          biology or health. The terminology is sufficiently simple
          to be appreciated by elementary school children.

Ac 126   Goldsmith, Ilse. Anatomy for children. New York: Ster-
          ling, 1964.
          Explains the structure and function of cells, limbs, and
          Organs of the human body and the complex system of res-
          piration, circulation, digestion, glands, nerves and repro-
          duction. There is also a summary of facts at each chap-
          ter's end.

Ac 127   Hear better: healthy ears. Chicago: Coronet, 1950.
          (16mm, 11 minutes)
          Opens with the many sounds of everyday life, and dis-
          cusses their importance. Uses animation to show the

structure of the ear, and emphasizes the importance of
proper care of the ears, through an incident in which a
group of school children talk to the school nurse, after one
of their number has been hurt on the playground.

Ac 128   Kessler, Ethel. Our tooth story: a tale of twenty teeth.
          New York: Dodd, Mead, 1972.
          Cartoon-like illustrations add to the children's story of
          their visits to the dentist. There is emphasis on the im-
          portance of regular check-ups, the fundamentals of caring
          for the teeth by brushing and good diet, and the ways in
          which the establishment of good dental habits helps protect
          the teeth.

Ac 129   Lauber, Patricia. Your body and how it works. New
          York: Random, 1962.
          "The 'inside' story of how the human body grows to form
          the tissues and organs to carry on the functions of respira-
          tion, circulation, and other life processes. A clear, sci-
          entific account ... for young readers. Simple diagrams,
          drawings and photographs."

Ac 130   Martin, Bill. Knots on a counting rope. New York:
          Holt, 1966.
          A simply and beautifully written story of growing up.
          The full-color illustrations which are in keeping with the
          mood of the lyrical text are expressive and poignant.

Ac 131   Ness, Evaline. Girl and the goatherd. New York: Dut-
          ton, 1970.
          "There once was a girl and she was ugly. And she did
          fret and droop because she was not beautiful." A story in
          the folk-tale tradition of Jacobs, all about how the girl got
          to be beautiful and then how she found out what it takes to
          be happy.

Ac 132   North Shore Committee on the Older Adult. Growing up,
          growing older. New York: Holt, 1964.
          This simply written story follows the life of Johnny as
          he grows and develops from a baby, to young boy, teen-
          ager, young man, middle age, until finally he is a grand-
          father. This book will help enlarge a young child's con-
          cepts about the life cycle of man.

Ac 133   Physical fitness and good health. Kalamazoo, Mich.: Up-
          john Company, n.d. (16mm film, color, 10 minutes)
          Discusses importance of keeping the body physically fit
          and stresses the value of exercise to keep the heart and
          other muscles and organs functioning properly.

Ac 134   Ravielli, Anthony. Wonders of the human body. New
          York: Viking, 1954.
          First the book describes the framework or skeleton,

next the muscles, then there is an account of the central
nervous system. Finally there is a description of the
heart, lungs, and digestive system. This all shows the
body as the most perfect of all machines.

Ac 135   Riedmaw, Sarah R. How man discovered his body. New
          York: Abelard-Schuman, 1966.
          An account of the scientific discoveries and developments
          in physiology from the time of the early Greeks to the
          present.

Ac 136   Schneider, Herman. How your body works. New York:
          Scott, 1949.
          Excellent introduction to physiology. Many simple ex-
          periments and clear illustrations make points easy to under-
          stand.

Ac 137   Showers, Pall. Your skin and mine. New York: Crowell,
          1968.
          Detailed information about the skin, its pigmentation in
          different people, the nature of hair and the importance of
          fingerprints and footprints. Emphasizes the importance
          of cleanliness.

Ac 138   Silverstein, Alvin. The muscle system; how living crea-
          tures move. Englewood Cliffs, N.J.: Prentice-Hall,
          1972.
          An examination of the human muscular system and how
          it works. The Silversteins also discuss locomotion in oth-
          er animals and in the plant world, making frequent com-
          parisons between the human system and that of lower ani-
          mals.

Ac 139   Systems of the human body. (series) Freeport, N.Y.:
          Education Activities, n.d. (sound filmstrip)
          Now! An improved, marvelously simple and magnifi-
          cently illustrated full-color set of sound filmstrips, is
          presented on a level children understand. Complete, self-
          teaching elementary physiology series ... unique in its
          multimedia presentation of a complex subject. An excit-
          ing, clear, concise step-by-step presentation showing how
          the human body systems are adapted to carry out the life
          functions and how all systems work together.

Ac 140   What's inside of you? (series) Paramus, N.J.: Educa-
          tional Reading Service, 1968. (filmstrip, 42 frames,
          color)
          The child is interested and concerned about what goes
          on inside his body. His questions about his own body are
          answered simply as he learns about the brain, nerves, di-
          gestive system and other parts of the body at work.

Ac 141   Your body and its parts. (Basic life science--your health

series) Chicago: Encyclopaedia Britannica Education
Corp. , n. d.   (16mm color film, 12 mins.)
Tells how the systems of the body work together in per-
forming many body functions.

Ac 142   Your exercise and posture.   Chicago: Coronet, 1968.
(filmstrip)
Shows why the body needs exercise for growth and good
health, how one can get the right amount of exercise, why
good posture is important, and how it can be obtained.
Useful for individual or group study in health.

PHYSICAL HANDICAPS

Ac 143   Bigland, Eileen.   Helen Keller.   New York: Phillips,
1967.
When she was nineteen months old a mysterious illness
left her totally blind and deaf.   Anne Sullivan, an understanding young teacher, who had been almost completely
blind herself, directed the child's energies and talents with
wisdom and patience.   When Helen Keller grew up she de-
voted her life to helping the handicapped throughout the
world.

Ac 144   De Angeli, Marguerite.   The door in the wall.   New York:
Doubleday, 1949.
Set in 13th century England (this book) tells the dramatic story of Robin, crippled son of a great lord, who
overcomes his disabilities by craftsmanship and eventually
wins his knighthood by a courageous act.

Ac 145   DuBois, William Pene.   Porko von Popbutton.   New York:
Harper, 1969.
The problems of a fat boy are handled with amiable
good humor in a hilarious story.   It is about a gluttonous
274-pound thirteen-year-old boy who is sent to an American boarding school famous for its hockey teams.   The
chronicle of Pat O'Sullivan Pinkerton, nicknamed Porko
von Popbutton by his star-goalie roommate, relates how the
boy eventually transfers his love of food to hockey as a
result of his amazing performance in a victorious but
ridiculously unorthodox game with a rival Canadian school.

Ac 146   Essex, Rosamund.   Into the forest.   New York: Coward-
McCann, 1963.
A great disaster ravages the earth and brings five children together on the edge between a great forest and the
wasteland.   One is blind, one deaf, one lame.   Together
they set out to find their way through the forest, not really knowing whether there is a world on the other side.   A
fine story with some likeness to the allegory in Pilgrim's
Progress.

Ac 147   Graff, Stewart.   <u>Helen Keller: toward the light</u>.   Champaign, Ill.:   Garrard, 1965.
Although a childhood illness made her blind and deaf she learned to read, write, and speak, graduated from college, and worked to help others like herself.

Ac 148   Little, Jean.   <u>From Anna</u>.   New York: Harper, 1972.
Anna, a nine-year-old German girl is the butt of her family's ridicule because of her clumsiness and learning difficulties, but when her family moves to Canada in 1933 a doctor discovers that her problems stem from weak eyes. A pair of glasses and understanding friends in a special school help change Anna's world for the better.   The writing style and the characterization are excellent and the double theme of loving freedom and understanding the handicapped are values sustained throughout the story.

Ac 149   Southall, Ivan.   <u>Let the balloon go</u>.   New York: St. Martin's, 1968.
This taut, compelling story vividly portrays the emotional tensions and frustrations of an intelligent, imaginative boy who is handicapped by cerebral palsy.   In rebellion against the restraints imposed by overprotective adults, twelve-year-old John Sumner, left alone for the first time, laboriously climbs to the top of a tall tree in his yard. Although this grueling but immensely self-satisfying feat almost ends disastrously, it earns John the right to participate more freely in normal boyhood activities.

Chapter 4

DEVELOPING PHYSICAL SKILLS

ABILITY TO SUCCEED

Ph 1   Conford, Ellen. <u>Impossible possum.</u> Boston: Little, Brown, 1971.
Delightful tale about Randolph, a possum who couldn't hang by his tail, and the many frustrating ways he tried to be like everyone else.

Ph 2   Hoff, Syd. <u>Who will be my friends?</u> New York: Harper, 1960.
A straightforward story about a little boy who has moved into a new neighborhood and searches for someone with whom he can play. Proving himself capable of catching and throwing a ball, he is allowed to join a group of boys playing baseball in a nearby field. Enjoyment of the game as well as making new friends give satisfaction to young readers.

Ph 3   Kessler, Leonard. <u>Here comes the strikeout.</u> New York: Harper, 1965.
A delightful book for beginning independent readers, the engaging illustrations showing Willie, the friend and mentor of the strikeout king (Bobby, a white boy), to be Negro. Bobby, in despair because his batting is weak, tries Willie's lucky hat. No luck! Then Willie coaches Bobby, who practices and practices and finally gets a hit--no instant success, but a combination of hard work and encouragement from Willie. The home attitude is good, too.

Ph 4   _____. <u>Last one in is a rotten egg.</u> New York: Harper, 1969.
Freddy can't swim well enough to go in the deep water; so he doesn't have as much fun at the city pool as do his friends, Bobby and Willie. When some bullies push Freddy into the deep water, he almost drowns. After that frightening experience, he doesn't want to go swimming. Finally, he gets enough courage to return to the pool; and this time he is determined to learn to swim. The book gives safety rules and some simple instructions for learning to swim.

Ph 5   Lord, Beman. <u>Quarterback's aim</u>. New York: Walck,
            1960.
            Allen wanted to play football, but he only weighed fifty-
            two pounds. No matter how many many malts and bananas
            he ate, his weight did not improve; but he had another as-
            set which finally won him his desire.

Ph 6   Shortall, Leonard. <u>Sam's first fish</u>. New York: Morrow,
            1962.
            While he has never caught a fish and does not have a rod
            or reel, a boy longs to catch the biggest fish of all.

PHYSICAL SKILLS

Ph 7   <u>Balance</u>. Cambridge, Mass.: Ealing Corporation, 1969.
            (motion picture--4 minutes)
            Illustrates activities that emphasize balance on various
            body parts and on a combination of body parts.

Ph 8   <u>Balance skills</u>. Studio City, Cal.: Filmfair, Inc., 1969.
            (16mm, 8 minutes, color)
            Illustrates the individual balance skills used in everyday
            life--skates, stilts, etc. Illustrates techniques on the bal-
            ance board and balance beam.

Ph 9   <u>Basic motor and ball skills</u>. Wichita, Kan.: Learning Arts,
            n.d. (33-1/3 rpm.)
            This recording introduces and develops the necessary
            basic motor and ball skills so important in the development
            of growing children and contains compositions of fundamental
            motor skills, including a walk, run, hop, skip, and gallop
            and combinations. It also covers fine compositions involving
            basic ball skills: bounce-catch, toss-catch, and combina-
            tions.

Ph 10   <u>Basic movement skills</u>. Studio City, Cal.: Filmfair, Inc.,
            1969. (16mm film, 10 minutes, color)
            Discusses motor development as it evolves in simple play-
            ground activity--learning the parts of the body.

Ph 11   <u>Beginning swimming</u>. (Beginning to swim series) Chicago:
            Athletic Institute, 1958. (filmstrips)
            Getting used to the water--31 frs. Learning to swim--
            26 frs., color.

Ph 12   <u>Being me</u>. Berkeley, Cal.: University of California, 1968.
            (16mm film, 13 minutes, black and white)
            Hilder Mullen demonstrates her approach to teaching
            dance. Children are used in the film to show what one's
            body can do.

Ph 13   Bentley, William G. <u>Learning to move and moving to learn.</u>

Englewood Cliffs, N. J. : Citation Press, 1970.
This small book gives clear and simple directions for
many activities. Movement education is stressed as it covers: Going places; Battling gravity; Strength and direction;
and many other natural experiences.

Ph 14   Bouncing, hand dribbling, and catching. Cambridge, Mass. :
Ealing Corporation, 1963. (motion picture, super 8mm,
color, 3 minutes)
Loop film mounted in cartridge, includes teachers guide.
Live photography illustrates skills in bouncing, catching, and
dribbling activities.

Ph 15   Developing body--space perception motor skills. New York:
Educational Record Sales, n. d. (33-1/3, albums 1, 2,
3)
This recording helps the child to sense his positional relations in place and space. It uses games and exercises to
enable the child to experience such concepts as front-back;
over-under; and left-right in relation to himself and to other
people.

Ph 16   Flexibility. Cambridge, Mass. : Ealing Corporation, 1969.
(super 8mm, 4 minutes, color)
Live photography explores a wide range of movement in
the joints of the body with illustrations of children rolling on
the floor in a variety of body positions and of children keeping one part of the body stationary and in contact with the
floor as they rotate around that point. May be used for
group or individual study.

Ph 17   Flow of movement. Cambridge, Mass. : Ealing Corporation,
1969. (motion picture, super 8mm, color, 4 minutes)
Loop film mounted in cartridge. Live photograph explores
the concept of flow by showing different ways of moving
joined together in sequence.

Ph 18   Greene, Carla. I want to be a baseball player. Chicago:
Children's Press, 1963.
Benny's older brother explains baseball to him, shows
him how to practice and takes him to a big game.

Ph 19   Harbin, E. O. Games for boys and girls. Nashville:
Abingdon, 1951.
A large collection of indoor, outdoor and playroom games.
Diagram for making needed equipment with simple tools.

Ph 20   Jacobs, Helen Hull. Better physical fitness for girls. New
York: Dodd, 1964.
World famous tennis champion describes simple exercises
for health and grace. Teenager Marjorie Frieger demonstrates them in photographs.

Ph 21   Jumpnastics.   Freeport, N.Y.:   Education Activities, n.d.
      (33 rpm record)
      With guide by the author of exercises. Includes direc-
tions for foot and arm movements to modern tunes with fast
and slow tempos to develop balance, agility, coordination
and dexterity of the performer.

Ph 22   Krisvoy, Juel.   New games to play.   Chicago: Follett,
      1968.
      Sixty-two indoor and outdoor games, each incorporating
a simple verse chant, with typical rhythmic activities in a
variety of childlike situations.

Ph 23   Movement exploration: what am I? Wayne, N.J.:   Leonard
      Peck Productions, 1967. (color, 20 minutes)
      This film introduces children to the concept of physical
education that is concerned with the whole body involvement
in moving, exploring and seeking solution to a problem.
This approach stresses concepts of time, space, force, and
flow.   Each child is encouraged to be individual in analyzing
his body potential and finding the limitations of his own
physical and mental abilities.

Ph 24   Moving in many directions.   Cambridge, Mass.:   Ealing
      Corporation, 1969. (8mm motion picture, 3 minutes)
      Explores the relationship of movement to direction and
illustrates tasks for students to perform.   Can be helpful
for group or individual study.

Ph 25   Musical ball skills.   Madison, Wis.: Demco, n.d.   (rec-
      ords)
      Bouncing, throwing, catching, rolling, passing and drib-
bling balls in rhythmic patterns to music are excellent ways
of increasing coordination and perceptual skills.   Bright and
lively up-to-date musical selections in this album are guaran-
teed to spark eager participation in these group activities.
The rhythm produced when balls strike the floor, hands clap,
and bodies move in unison to these catchy, full-orchestrated
tunes gives your class a feeling of cooperative accomplish-
ment.   Each skill is taught in three stages: Talk-through,
walk-through instructions; music with voice cues; and music
only.

Ph 26   Opie, Iona.   Children's games in street and playground.
      Fair Lawn, N.J.: Oxford, 1969.
      Games: chasing, catching, seeking, racing, guessing,
acting--for all ages of children.

Ph 27   Platt, Mildred.   Children around the world, games and oth-
      er activities.   Elgin, Ill.:   Child's World, 1969.   (8
      prints)
      Children's games in other countries that are selected to
illustrate similarities and differences among people.   All

are outdoors, with background information and other re-
sources on the back.

Ph 28   Rope skipping--basic steps.   Seattle, Wash.: Martin Moyer
         Productions, 1965. (16mm, color, 16 minutes)
         Promotes rope skipping as an all purpose physical fitness
exercise that promotes endurance, agility, rhythm, timing,
and requires little equipment. Presents examples the classroom teacher might use in developing a unit on rope skipping.

Ph 29   Rope skipping-rhythms, rhymes, and routines.   Freeport,
         N.Y.: Education Activities, n.d. (records, 33-1/3,
         Album 12)
         Something for everyone--from the special child to the pro-
fessional. A sequential presentation of rope skipping skills
--from the rudiments to advanced competition. The record
has varied tempo rope skipping music. There is a 166-page
illustrated book that accompanies this record.

Ph 30   Rumbaugh, David.   Fun and fitness for primary children.
         Glendale, Cal.: Bowmar Records, 1966. (33-rpm)
         Includes music for children's physical education, as arm
flip flops, kangaroo jump, bear hug, tight rope walker, etc.
Guide and illustrations of exercises for each tune.

Ph 31   _____. Rope jumping and ball handling.   Valhalla, Cal.:
         Stanley Bowmar Company, n.d. (33-rpm)
         Includes folksongs and other music suitable for rope
jumping and ball handling. Text of rhymes on slipcase.
May be used for group work.

Ph 32   Sing 'n do albums.   Glendale, Cal.: Bowmar, n.d. (phono-
         disc, 45 rmp)
         Simple melodies, both vocal and instrumental, selected
to inspire children to create rhythm--both individually and
in groups. Suggestions on album for teacher, if desired.
Very helpful for both music and physical education. Contents:
Album 1, 2 (Grade 3); Album 3 (Grade 1-6); Albums 4, 5,
6 (Grades K-6).

Ph 33   Sport and games' skills.   Cambridge, Mass.: Ealing Cor-
         poration, 1969. (8mm film loops, color)
         The series of film loops include: Agility; Arm and ab-
dominal strength; Balance; Bouncing, hand dribbling and
catching; Flexibility; Hitting in different ways; Throwing and
catching; and Yarn balls, hoops, ropes and wands.

Ph 34   Think, listen and say--a series.   Jamaica, N.Y.: Eye
         Gate House, Inc., 1967. (4 33-1/3 rpm records)
         Emphasizes the three-R's of listen--Recognizing, Retain-
ing and Recalling. Designed to improve auditory discrimination, aural comprehension, and visual perception.

Ph 35   Winter, Ginny Linville. The swimming book. Stamford,
         Conn. : Obolensky, 1964.
         Simple explanations of swimming; techniques begin with
         "land drills," then floating; finally, various strokes.

Ph 36   Worstell, Emma. Jump the rope jingles. Riverside, N. J. :
         Macmillan, 1961.
         A collection of sidewalk songs and playground songs to
         be used for jump-rope time. Also includes instruction for
         many jump-rope games.

                              SAFETY

Ph 37   Being safe. Jamaica, N. Y. : Eye Gate, 1971. (6 film-
         strips, average 51 frs. each, with 33 rpm phonodisc)
         This series includes teacher's guide. Also available with
         cassettes. Presents rules for safe behavior for primary
         children. Familiar everyday situations, such as walking,
         crossing streets, bike riding, playing, etc. , are illustrated
         with photographs. Contents: Think safe, act safe; Cars,
         bikes and people; Delicious or deadly; Fun or fearful; Watch
         where you go; Helpful or harmful.

Ph 38   Crawford, Thomas. Safety first. Mahwah, N. J. : Troll
         Associates, 1969.
         Full color drawings illustrate safety practices on the
         street, in school, at play, on a bicycle, and at home. May
         be used for group or individual study in safety education or
         guidance.

Ph 39   Leaf, Munro. Safety can be fun. Boston: Lippincott, 1961.
         Appealing to the child's common sense, the "nit-wit" will
         be rejected because his hurt is due to foolishness. Car-
         toons in black and red exaggerate this foolishness while
         sound basic safety principles are promoted.

Ph 40   Safely walk to school. Hollywood, Cal. : Charles Cahill
         and Associates, 1968. (16mm film, 11 minutes)
         Follows the route of Tim and Chuck to school. Stresses
         the importance of safely crossing the street, accepting rides,
         obeying traffic signals, and walking on sidewalks.

Ph 41   Safety in the home. Chicago: Encyclopaedia Britannica
         Films, 1966. (16mm film, 10 minutes)
         Shows children how to think ahead as the first step to-
         ward home safety. Demonstrates through a series of brief
         incidents the importance of making common sense decisions
         of safety to prevent household mishaps.

Ph 42   Safety in the playground. Chicago: Encyclopaedia Britan-
         nica, 1968. (16mm film)
         Illustrates good habits of playground safety, such as

catching, batting, using the see-saw, using the slides and
merry-go-rounds, using swings.

Ph 43   Shapp, Martha. Let's find out about safety. New York:
         Watts, 1964.
         An easy-to-read story about safety at home, at school,
         and on the street.

Ph 44   Wolff, Angelika. Mom! I broke my arm! New York: Lion,
         1969.
         An entertaining and informative little story intended to
         assuage children's fears of breaking a limb, trips to doc-
         tors' offices, new experiences with X-rays and casts, etc.

Intermediate

ABILITY TO SUCCEED

Ph 45   Bishop, Curtis. Little league heroes. Philadelphia: Lip-
         pincott, 1960.
         Joel, the first Negro boy to win a place on the Little
         League team in West Austin, Texas, is encouraged by his
         father, coached by the officials, and finally earns acceptance
         by the team.

Ph 46   _____. Little league, little brother. Philadelphia: Lip-
         pincott, 1968.
         Jesse and Duane Kenton's father has waited for the day
         when he will see his two sons as a catcher-pitcher battery
         on the same Little League team. But a childhood accident
         has left Jesse with a stiff leg and because of him, big broth-
         er Duane's chances for a spot on the "best" team are ruined
         the first year they try out. The next time he tries out he
         is automatically put on his big brother's team. It seems to
         Jesse that he just never will have the opportunity to be some-
         one, all on his own merits.

Ph 47   Christopher, Matt. Catch that pass! Boston: Little,
         Brown, 1969.
         Jim Nardi fears being tackled and in the last three min-
         utes of a crucial game against the Cadets, he fails to catch
         a pass but knocks it down, causing the Vulcans to lose the
         game. Then Jim learns the coach had the same weakness
         but overcame it, and this fires Jim to conquer his own
         fears.

Ph 48   _____. The kid who only hit homers. Boston: Little,
         Brown, 1972.
         Sylvester looks like a poor prospect for the Redbirds
         Baseball Team until the mysterious Mr. George Baruth gives
         him special talent. This story tells how Sylvester handles
         his new fame and what happens to Sylvester's baseball abil-

ity when Mr. Baruth goes away, as he said he would have
to.

Ph 49   _____ . Long shot for Paul. Boston: Little, Brown,
                1966.
           Glenn and Judy Marlette decide to teach their brother
        Paul how to play basketball so he can play with the Sabers
        and get to know other boys. This takes a great deal of
        patience, because Paul is mentally retarded and does not
        learn easily. Coach Manson lets Paul join the team, but
        the other boys often get impatient with Paul's errors and
        ignore him. Paul's hard practice pays off and in a crucial
        moment helps the team win.

Ph 50   _____ . Sink it, Rusty. Boston: Little, Brown, 1963.
           Rusty Young, although only slightly crippled by polio,
        magnifies his inadequacies when he tries to compete with
        his friends on a basketball court. Anxious to participate in
        the games, he feels he is not wanted and is easily hurt.
        Through the careful and judicious help of Alex Dows, whose
        own basketball career was cut short by the loss of his left
        hand, Rusty is encouraged to make use of the capabilities
        he has and proves himself a strong team member, becom-
        ing the hero of the final game.

Ph 51   DuBois, William Pene. Porko von Popbutton. New York:
             Viking, 1945.
           Poor Pat was nicknamed Porko von Popbutton as soon as
        he arrived at the new boarding school. His mother and
        father decided to send him to the new school when at his
        birthday party the two chairs over which he spread his
        weight gave way beneath him. His size was against him
        from the very first day at school--a school which empha-
        sized sports. Jim Finger, Porko's roommate, begins to
        get his "roomie" into "shape" by keeping him as a "slave"
        and having him eat at the Dieter's table. At the end of the
        year Porko becomes a hero in a outrageously funny hockey
        game.

Ph 52   Etter, Les. Cool man on the court. New York: Hastings
             House, 1969.
           Lonnie Jackson is talented at tennis but sensitive about
        being the only black on the courts. He faces not only the
        opponents but also the enmity of a local black gang when he
        begins to enter tournaments.

Ph 53   Hodges, Margaret. The hatching of Joshua Cobb. New
             York: Farrar, 1967.
           A good camp story for boys. Josh has never before
        been away from his widowed mother, and he's apprehensive
        about camp. Will they find out that he keeps one foot on
        the bottom while pretending to swim? (They will.) The
        tough and unpleasant counselor of Josh's cabin is fired when

he disappears for long periods to telephone his girl, and everything improves when the new man takes over. Nothing remarkable happens, except that the boys of Cabin 13 begin to enjoy camp life, and that Josh, who has been a diffident participant, learns to swim, makes friends, and writes a skit for the camp show. Pleasantly low-keyed and smoothly written.

Ph 54   Jackson, C. Paul. Haunted halfback. Chicago: Follett, 1969.
Dale Smith's family has just moved from Central City to Riverville. Dale goes to the Riverville football field to watch the high school team practice. A kicked ball comes toward Dale and he catches the ball. Seeing the tackler coming for him, Dale throws his hand out and evades. Afterward Dale is urged to go out for the team, against his better judgment, for Dale is afraid to play the game.

Ph 55   Keith, Harold. Sports and games. New York: Crowell, 1969.
This introduction to seventeen best-known and most popular sports sets forth the rules and analyzes great athletic achievement.

Ph 56   Laklan, Carli. Olympic champions: why they win. New York: Funk and Wagnalls, 1968.
An informal history of the Olympics, emphasizing the outstanding performers of all time and the qualities aside from physical aptitude and training which made them winners. Among the athletes discussed are Bob Mathias, Wilma Rudolph, Don Schollander, Peggy Fleming, and Jean-Claude Killy.

Ph 57   Shortall, Leonard. Ben on the ski trail. New York: Morrow, 1965.
An exciting sports story for the youngest, this tells how Ben borrows ski equipment and sets out to learn to ski. Awkward and discouraged at first, he perseveres and succeeds to ski well enough so that he joins the ski patrol in a rescue. The lively text and illustrations entertain and inform as they join to tell a true-to-life tale about a winter sport.

Ph 58   Taves, Isabella. Not bad for a girl. Philadelphia: Lippincott, 1972.
Sharon Lee is smart, pretty, and she can play baseball. That a twelve-year-old girl can perform on the baseball diamond better than the average boy is too much for most of the men in Whittier and definitely more than a majority of the Little League coaches can handle. But Sharon gets a chance to play on the club's team and she performs well.

Ph 59   Vance, Marguerite. A rainbow for Robin. New York: Dutton, 1966.

Robin, blind from birth, learns to use her abilities to
participate to the fullest in the world around her. She
swims, crochets, acts in plays, and attends a regular school.
Her first and strongest love, however, is her music. Her
major triumph occurs when her composition wins first prize
in a contest and is played by the local symphony orchestra.
She performs at a recital and, as the culmination of her
dreams, is asked to play with the orchestra at a future contest.

Ph 60   Viereck, Phillip. The summer I was lost. New York: Day,
1965.

An unusually good first-person story with a convincing
setting, unified construction, and polished consistency in
style. Paul, poorly coordinated and suffering from astig-
matism, has never been good at athletics; and, therefore,
when he goes to a summer camp, is dubious about enjoying
it. When he gets lost on a hike, Paul finds that his own
survival is far less dependent on brawn than it is on resourcefulness, persistence, good judgment, and an application of skills learned while camping and fishing with his
father. The story has excellent pace, suspense, and a realistic and satisfying ending.

COMPETITION

Ph 61   Because it's fun. Bloomington, Indiana: National Instructional TV Center, n. d. (video-tape)

Explores the good feelings produced by skillfully engaging
in a physical activity. Introduces Bill who thinks that winning is the only thing that really counts and can't understand
why others enjoy themselves just playing for the fun of it.

Ph 62   Bishop, Curtis. Little league victory. Philadelphia: Lippincott, 1967.

Ed Boggart's parents want him to go to summer camp
but Ed is sure he can be the best Little Leaguer in Austin,
Texas. In fact, he is too aggressive for his own good--
and expects his teammates to work as hard as he does and
be as good as he is.

Ph 63   Carol, Bill J. Touchdown duo. Austin, Tex.: Steck, 1968.

The team is on the 30-yard line, the kicker is ready to
kick a field goal, when three defensive men rush in and
block the kick. The kicker runs around the left side with
a row of blockers and goes in for the touchdown. South
High wins the game because Terry Madden, halfback, and
Jim Tompkins, quarterback, have learned to play together.

Ph 64   Christopher, Matt. Baseball pals. Boston: Little, Brown,

1956.
Paul Karoski is pitcher for the Planets until Captain Jimmie Todd decides he can do the pitching himself. After that nothing goes right for the team until Jimmie faces his own lack of sportsmanship and rights everything.

Ph 65   . Catcher with a glass arm. Boston: Little, Brown, 1965.
Jody overcomes his fear of being hit by the baseball and saves the fame for the team.

Ph 66   . Look who's playing first base. Boston: Little, Brown, 1971.
When Yuri Dotzen, newly arrived from Russia, joins the Checkmates' baseball team, he flubs some important plays. Angry teammates threaten to quit until some new developments teach them all a lesson in sportsmanship.

Ph 67   . The team that couldn't lose. Boston: Little, Brown, 1967.
On the first day of practice, the Cayugans certainly looked like losers. As they won game after game, they realized it was because of the new plays that had been sent to the coach in the mail. Excitement and mystery are packed into this story of an inexperienced team learning to have faith in itself.

Ph 68   Crary, Margaret. Mexican whirlwind. New York: Washburn, 1969.
Under a student exchange program, Maria Estrada comes to Raccoon Valley to live with Taffy Webster's family. Taffy plays on the high school basketball team, but Maria finds the game funny. Then she discovers it is fun to play and she also learns that her skill in dancing is an advantage in playing the game. Differences between Maria and Taffy grow easier and easier to solve as Maria learns to accept United States customs and Taffy learns to respect Maria's Mexican culture.

Ph 69   Jacobs, Helen Hull. Tennis machine. New York: Scribner, 1972.
Thirteen-year-old Vicky Clifton is driven by her father to develop her natural athletic ability into a "tennis machine." The conflict imposes on her own outgoing, friendly personality.

Ph 70   Kessler, Leonard. Kick, pass, and run. New York: Harper, 1966.
Includes football words. An assorted group of animals are quite puzzled over a large brown "egg." The mystery is solved when some boys recover it and continue their football game. Intrigued with this new sport, the animals too play a game. In spite of makeshift balls and unexpected

difficulties, the game goes to an exciting finish.   Lists
famous football players, gives some cheers, and provides
pictorial explanations of football terms in an easy-to-read
vocabulary.

Ph 71   Lord, Beman.   Rough ice.   New York: Walck, 1963.
Eddie MacDougal is afraid he won't live up to his father's
reputation as a former star hockey forward.   He tries out
for goalie in the Pee Wee League when he realizes his weak
ankle will prevent his winning a berth as forward.   Though
he proves to be a good goalie, he can't bring himself to tell
his father he is not following in his footsteps.   Eddie's
problems are finally resolved during an exciting game in
the arena.   Easy reading with lively pictures about an exciting sport.

Ph 72   _____ .   Shot-put challenge.   New York: Walck, 1969.
Tiny Murphy (nicknamed because he was bigger and clum-
sy) felt that there was no event in the elementary school
track meet which he could enter.   His friend, Shena, who
was so good at sports that she sometimes beat the boys,
had a different problem.   She could not dance but wanted to
attend the after-track hop.   The two put their heads together and came up with solutions which were surprising
but effective.

PHYSICAL SKILLS

Ph 73   And the beat goes on for physical education.   Freeport,
         N.Y.:   Education Activities, 1966.   (record)
Includes directions and modern music and sounds for ex-
ercising the individual parts of the body and the whole body.
Valuable for physical fitness activities.   Music includes such
modern tunes as: And the beat goes on; L. David Sloan;
Ode to Billy Joe; and Going out of my head.

Ph 74   Antonacci, Robert J.   Basketball for young champions.
         New York: McGraw-Hill, 1962.
Summary of the rules and instructions in guarding, dribbling, passing, shooting.   Explains games for girls and
boys.

Ph 75   _____ .   Football for young champions.   New York: Mc-
         Graw-Hill, 1956.
Describes formations, positions, equipment, scoring, and
records.   Notes qualifications for and duties of each position.
It also offers exercises and drills for each position.   Useful for boys and girls.

Ph 76   _____ .   Physical fitness for young champions.   New
         York: McGraw-Hill, 1962.
After describing ways of testing physical fitness and ex-

plaining its importance, this book describes many exercises
to improve coordination, muscle power, etc. There are
special chapters on home-built equipment, drills for those
who can't join in sports, and a special chapter for girls.
The economical text and spirited drawings are well coordinated and should inspire action on the part of young people
and perhaps even a parent or two.

Ph 77   Archibald, Joe. Baseball talk for beginners. New York:
             Messner, 1969.
             The author explains the game of baseball through the use
         of definitions, tips on how to play, and baseball history.

Ph 78   Ball skills. Studio City, Cal.: Filmfair Communications,
             n. d. (16mm film, 10 minutes)
             Teaches how to throw, bounce, kick, and hit a ball.
         Tells how to use these skills in a ball game.

Ph 79   Basketball for boys. (Junior Sports Series) El Cerrito,
             Cal.: Longslide Filmslide Service, 1968. (filmstrip,
             38 frs., black and white)
             Shows elementary school children in normal play situa-
         tions; stresses ball handling skills.

Ph 80   Bee, Clair. Make the team in basketball. New York:
             Grosset and Dunlap, 1961.
             How to play the various positions and how to improve
         skills together with self-rating charts, practice and learn-
         ing aids and sequence action shots.

Ph 81   Beginning soccer--controlling the ball. Chicago: Athletic
             Institute, 1964. (filmstrip and record, 48 frames, color)
             Demonstrates proper body coordination, form and tech-
         niques of each game. Includes rules, equipment, and origin
         of the sport.

Ph 82   Beginning sports series. Chicago: Athletic Institute, n. d.
             Contents: Several titles within each of the following sub-
         divisions--Archery, badminton, baseball, basketball, bowling,
         golf, softball, tennis, tumbling, volleyball, wrestling.

Ph 83   Bonner, M. G. How to play baseball. Westminster, Md.:
             Knopf, 1955.
             A guide for young readers who want to learn to play base-
         ball; clear, diagrammatic drawings explain the text.

Ph 84   Brewster, Benjamin. First book of baseball. New York:
             Watts, 1963.
             A simple graphic explanation of fundamentals--terminol-
         ogy, plays, players, scoring, organization--designed for the
         beginner or spectator.

Ph 85   Burns, Ted. Tumbling, techniques illustrated. New York:

Ronald, 1957.
With text and pictures this book covers the basic individual tumbling techniques. The series of stunts, with instruction on how to perform them, appears in logical progression with earlier stunts determining the form and nature of those that follow.

Ph 86   Butler, Hal. Underdog of sports. New York: Messner, 1969.
Action and surprise are the keynotes of these football, boxing, baseball, golf, hockey, basketball, and horse racing tales, each focusing on sure losers who defeat seemingly unbeatable opponents.

Ph 87   Catching in baseball. Chicago: Encyclopaedia Britannica Films, 1971. (16mm film, 10 minutes)
Shows basic fundamental through slow-motion and close-up photography.

Ph 88   Clause, Frank. The complete handbook of junior bowling. New York: Fleet, 1964.
Clear explanation of how to bowl, including choice of ball, approach, and delivery, etiquette, clothing, on AMF alleys.

Ph 89   Cooke, David C. Better baseball for boys. New York: Dodd, 1959.
Basic plays, rules of the game, and techniques are explained in detail and pictures in action photographs. Includes advice and care of equipment and a glossary.

Ph 90   Downer, Marion. Kites: How to make and fly them. New York: Morrow, 1959.
Explicit direction for making and using kites with simple tools. Designed to stimulate interest in this outdoor hobby.

Ph 91   Fitzsimmons, Robert. How to play baseball. Garden City, N.Y.: Doubleday, 1962.
Basic skills of baseball, throwing, catching, and hitting.

Ph 92   Frankel, Lillian. Muscle building games. New York: Sterling, 1964.
This book will help you improve your body's fitness and have fun at the same time. Describes squatting games, moving and balancing games and other more complex exercises for improving muscular tone and fitness. Also includes tests to see how fit you are.

Ph 93   _____. One hundred and one best action games for boys 6-12. New York: Sterling, 1968.
Get acquainted games, stunts and contests and an assortment of indoor and outdoor pastimes for small groups.

Ph 94   _____ and Godfrey Frankel. Bike-ways (101 things to do
             with a bike). New York: Sterling, 1968.
             A revised edition of this cycling guide which features cur-
             rent information on touring and camping throughout the United
             States and Europe, as well as facts about bike clubs and pro-
             grams. Brief information on safety and learning to ride,
             bicycle selection, parts, accessories, care and repairs,
             earning money with your bicycle, and bike photograph.

Ph 95   Freeman, S. H. Basic baseball strategy. Garden City,
             N. Y. : Doubleday, 1965.
             Intended for young baseball players, this is a book so
             packed with useful information that it can be read profitably
             by older players, by amateur coaches, and by fans of all
             ages. No talking down, no fooling around, just facts about
             offensive and defensive play, and about preparation and
             drills. There are, for example, chapters on the squeeze
             play, on the hit and run, on the steal. Mr. Freeman tells
             you when to do what and why ... and when not to and why.
             The illustrative diagrams are helpful.

Ph 96   Hitting in different ways. Cambridge, Mass. : Ealing Cor-
             poration, 1969. (filmloop, 2 minutes)
             Live photography explores patterns of striking the ball
             with the open hand and with paddles.

Ph 97   Hutton, Joe and Vern B. Hoffman. Basketball. Mankato,
             Minn. : Creative Educational Society, 1962.
             Basketball as a sport which can be enjoyed by children
             as well as by older players is described simply and directly.
             Covers history, development, and a long section on playing
             fundamentals and techniques.

Ph 98   Iger, Martin. How to play baseball. Garden City, N. Y. :
             Doubleday, 1962.
             Here are the basic skills of baseball--throwing, catching,
             hitting. The author discusses how to bunt, run bases, slide,
             make a double play, throw a curve ball, and the rules of
             the game. The photographs are self explanatory so younger
             children find it useful.

Ph 99   Introduction to physical fitness. Los Angeles: Bailey Film
             Associates, 1966. (8mm, color, 11 minutes)
             Encourages interest in developing and maintaining indi-
             vidual fitness. Demonstrates proper methods and skills
             used in performing basic physical fitness exercises.

Ph 100   Jackson, C. Paul. How to play better basketball. New
             York: Crowell, 1968.
             Explains the present rules and regulations of the game.
             Whole chapters are devoted to the vital functions of passing,
             dribbling, shooting, individual guarding, and rebounding.
             The author tells the different ways each can be done and

discusses offensive and defensive tactics and how a team's
action must be tailored to the strengths and weaknesses of
each opposing team.

Ph 101   Jacobs, Helen Hull. Better physical fitness for girls.
          New York: Dodd, 1964.
          World famous tennis champion describes simple exer-
          cises for health and grace. Teenager Margery Krieger
          demonstrates them in photographs.

Ph 102   Jarvis, Lindle. How to be a better athlete. New York:
          Holt, 1965.
          Suggests exercises and stunts to help the young athlete
          develop a strong body, endurance, and agility.

Ph 103   Kramp, Harry and George Sullivan. Swimming for boys
          and girls. Chicago: Follett, 1966.
          Written by a swimming coach and a sports writer, this
          book is aimed at the beginning swimmer. Safety and the
          need of a competent supervisor are emphasized. All
          basic strokes--elementary, diving, competition, and a brief
          coverage of lifesaving--are included.

Ph 104   Lanoue, Fred R. Drownproofing: a new technique for
          water safety. Englewood Cliffs, N.J.: Prentice-Hall,
          1963.
          Explanation of a method for learning to swim which is
          required for earning the Boy Scout Merit Badge and is
          taught at Scout Camp. Written by a man who swam like a
          "hunk of concrete" as a boy but who grew up to become a
          leading swimming coach.

Ph 105   Liss, Howard. Football talk for beginners. New York:
          Messner, 1970.
          Numerous diagrams illustrate this dictionary of tech-
          nical terms and phrases used in football.

Ph 106   Loken, Newton C. Tumbling and trampolining. London,
          England: Oak Tree Press, 1970.
          Action photographs demonstrate both basic and advanced
          skills in individual tumbling, individual balance doubles,
          and stunts. Beginning and more complex movements in
          trampolining. National trampolining rules included.

Ph 107   Mulac, Margaret C. The game book. New York: Harper,
          1966.
          More than 600 games and stunts including ideas for
          parties and game programs for every age and occasion.

Ph 108   Pashko, Stanley. How to make your team. New York:
          Putnam, 1968.
          Information for young athletes hoping to make the high
          school team in football, basketball, baseball, and track.

Fundamentals of each sport are given along with basic
skills needed, what to eat, and exercises to keep in shape
for each sport.

Ph 109   Physical education--basic skills--basketball. (Physical
          Education Basic Skills Series) Hollywood, Cal.: Ca-
          hill, 1964. (16mm silent film, color, 3 minutes)
          Depicts basic skills employed in basketball. Slow mo-
          tion photography is used.

Ph 110   Physical education--basic skills--football. (Physical Edu-
          cation Basic Skills Series) Hollywood, Cal.: Cahill,
          1964. (16mm silent film, color, 3 minutes)
          Depicts basic skills employed in football. Slow motion
          photograph is used.

Ph 111   Robinson, Jackie. Jackie Robinson's little league baseball
          book. Englewood Cliffs, N.J.: Prentice-Hall, 1972.
          Using a conversational approach and including many anec-
          dotal instances, the author emphasizes the importance of
          personal attitude, teamwork, and gives solid advice on im-
          proving baseball skills, covering hitting, base running, as
          well as each of the positions in the infield and outfield,
          pitching and catching.

Ph 112   Ryan, Jack. Learning to swim is fun. New York: Ron-
          ald, 1960.
          Gives a brief sketch of swimming through the ages, and,
          after stressing safety rules, proceeds to explain the vari-
          ous types of strokes and how to learn and perfect them.
          The final sections are on diving and water games. A good
          book for the beginning swimmer of any age; it helps to in-
          still confidence through pre-knowledge.

Ph 113   Schiffer, Don. The first book of basketball. New York:
          Watts, 1959.
          A good basic book on basketball explaining rules and
          strategy and offering many pointers on mastering the skills
          and techniques of the games. A glossary of terms is ap-
          pended and many drawings and diagrams of plays are in-
          cluded. While addressed to the player, the book will also
          serve as a guide to the spectator.

Ph 114   _____. The first book of football. New York: Watts,
          1958.
          This book is written for the observer. It begins with
          an explanation of the field, officials, players and ball, and
          then discusses fundamental football skills, rules, forma-
          tions, penalties, and football strategy. Some general tips
          for football players, information on conferences, bowl
          games, All-American teams, and the professionals, and
          a glossary of terms are included. Illustrated with draw-
          ings and with diagrams of plays.

Ph 115   Siebert, Dick and Vogel, Ott. Baseball. New York: Ster-
          ling, 1968.
          A first-rate outline of the basics of the game, comprised
          of clear, relevant photographs and easily understood com-
          mentary on techniques of fielding, hitting, base running,
          sliding, pitching and catching.

Ph 116   Softball series. Los Angeles: Bailey Film Associates,
          1967. (8mm film, 4 minutes)
          This film contains instructions on batting, catching
          above and below the waist, catching grounders, pitching
          and throwing.

Ph 117   Stunts and tumbling for elementary children. Wichita,
          Kan.: Learning Arts, n.d. (33-1/3 rpm. record)
          Children learn stunts and tumbling quickly and easily.
          This record describes the actions using the "whole-part-
          whole" method so the child may learn how each part of
          the action fits into the full routine. Eight stunts and the
          tumbling activities are presented in the order of their de-
          gree of difficulty.

Ph 118   To move is to be. Freeport, N.Y.: Education Activities,
          n.d. (records)
          Happy, catchy, singable ditties and infectious "gotta
          move" electronic music guides the student gently into doing
          his own version of moving, bending, twisting, stretching,
          hopping, walking, running. The singing is contagious, the
          movements are great fun, good exercise, and non-com-
          petitive. Actions may differ but the experiences will both
          elate the student and pave the way for more learning.

Ph 119   Values of exercise. Corvallis, Ore.: KOAC-TV, n.d.
          (audio tape, 15 minutes)
          Presents the physical education instructor as he ex-
          plains the value of certain exercise to Dick. Tells how,
          at a family outing, Dick's physical coordination saves a
          boy's life.

Ph 120   Volleying in different ways. Cambridge, Mass.: Ealing
          Corporation, n.d. (8mm, color, 3 minutes)
          Includes teacher's guide. Live photography explores
          volleying the ball with different parts of the body trying
          to keep it in the air as long as possible. May be used
          for individual or group study with teacher inservice or for
          physical education for students.

                            SAFETY

Ph 121   Bendick, Jeanne. The emergency book. Chicago: Rand
          McNally, 1967.
          Life is full of emergencies--household emergencies, sit-

ter emergencies, emergencies in sports, emergencies in
all kinds of weather, emergencies on the road, and those
that happen in the community. In this self-help guide, the
young person is alerted to ways of preventing emergencies
that need never happen as well as directed in his conduct
once the situation has occurred. Simple, non-technical explanations make this a most practical and useful reference
for young people.

Ph 122   Bicycle safety. (Safety series) Philadelphia: Curriculum
          Materials Corporation, 1958. (filmstrip, color, 30 frs.)
          Based on techniques used in the Disney 16mm Safety
          films, each print is designed to stimulate discussion. Re-
          verse side of every card contains questions, information
          and suggested activities to guide the teacher. Contents:
          Keep your bicycle in good condition; Protect your bicycle;
          Learn to ride in a safe place; Don't be a show off; Obey
          all traffic rules; See and be seen on dark days; Ride on
          the right--single file; Ride the Safest route; Always ride
          under control.

Ph 123   Bolian, Polly. Safety. New York: Watts, 1970.
          "Safety Keys" to guide a reader's actions where safety
          is important: biking, swimming, at school, at home.
          Being alert and using responsible judgment are constantly
          emphasized. The section on home safety is valuable for
          child and adult.

Ph 124   Home safety. Burbank, Cal.: Walt Disney Productions,
          1967. (filmstrip, color)
          Based on techniques used in the Disney 16mm safety
          film, each print is designed to stimulate discussion. Re-
          view side of each card contains questions, information and
          suggested activities to guide the teacher. Contents: Poi-
          sons are dangerous--avoid them; Fall causes injuries;
          Play in safe places; What to do in an emergency; Use
          tools and toys properly; Care for your pets; Electricity
          can be dangerous; and Don't open doors to strangers.

Ph 125   Safety tales. Chicago: Encyclopaedia Britannica Educa-
          tional Corporation, 1958. (filmstrip)
          Presents basic ideas of safety through encouraged stu-
          dent discussion of some of the foolish things done by peo-
          ple that result in tragedy or serious accident. Contents:
          How not to have an accident in the home; I'm no fool as a
          pedestrian; I'm no fool with fire; I'm no fool with a bicy-
          cle; I'm no fool in water; I'm no fool having fun.

PART II

TASKS FOR SOCIAL DEVELOPMENT

Chapter 5

DEVELOPING SYMBOL SYSTEMS

Primary

READING

Sy 1   Appell, Clara and Morey. Glenn learns to read. Des
Moines: Duell, 1965.
A small boy learns to read in a manner that may prove
reassuring to others undergoing the same struggle.

Sy 2   Black, Irma Simonton. The little old man who could not
read. Racine, Wis.: Whitman, 1968.
A man can't read and goes hungry while his wife is away
because of it. He quickly has her teach him to read when
she returns.

Sy 3   Child Study Association of America. Now you can read to
yourself. Riverside, N.J.: Crowell, 1964.
To children for their first adventures into reading--eleven
stories that are not too hard.

Sy 4   Cordts, Anna D. Functional phonics. Jamaica, N.Y.:
Eye Gate, 1969. (set of 12 color filmstrips with records)
Helps children hear likenesses and differences in words
as well as see them. May be used with basal readers or
as supplementary.

Sy 5   Crews, Donald. We read A to Z. New York: Harper,
1967.
An indispensable book that will provide days of fun for
children. Instead of the conventional approach to the alphabet, the author has combined the letters and the illustrations with definite concepts that a child can see and use.
The format is good, the print excellent, and the use of
colors unusual and very appealing to the child's imagination.

Sy 6   Duvoisin, Roger. Petunia. New York: Knopf, 1950.
Petunia, a silly goose, finds a book and thinks herself
automatically wise. She gives out incorrect advice to her
barnyard friends, making them more unhappy. Not until she
sees the writing inside the book does she learn that she
must not just carry around a book to be wise but put it in

her head, heart and mind by learning to read. Petunia
brings across a message to young children who do not see
the value of learning.

Sy 7   Falls, Charles Buckles. The A B C book. Garden City,
            N.Y.: Doubleday, 1933.
            This is a superb alphabet book which illustrates the let-
            ters of the alphabet with decorative wood block color print-
            ings of animals.

Sy 8   Flipper the seal: background for reading and expression.
            Chicago: Coronet, 1953. (16mm film, 11 minutes)
            A group of children at a zoo watch Flipper the seal per-
            form and one boy decides to learn more about seals. While
            he reads such words as "waves," "swimming," and "dive,"
            seals are shown in their natural habitat swimming and div-
            ing, etc. Good material to stimulate a child's reading.

Sy 9   Funk, Tom. I read signs. New York: Holiday House,
            1962.
            While Johnny is on an errand, he reads signs and finds
            out what words mean.

Sy 10   Garden, Jan. The alphabet tale. Westminster, Md.:
            Random, 1964.
            A surprise ABC book where the picture of the tip of a
            tail and a short rhyme are helps in guessing which animal
            each letter stands for.

Sy 11   Gordon, Isabel. The ABC hunt. New York: Viking, 1961.
            Two children find an A in their alphabet soup. This
            sets them off on a search through town for all the letters
            A through Z on signs, labels, and posters. Capital and
            small letters are both given.

Sy 12   Grossbart, Francine. A big city. New York: Harper,
            1966.
            In an appealing ABC way, picture objects of the city are
            presented to the child. A is for antennas. G is for gar-
            bage can. H is for hydrant. Large flat drawings stand
            out against contrasting colors. Vocabulary building book.

Sy 13   Harwood, Pearl Augusta. Mrs. Moon's story hour. New
            York: Lerner, 1967.
            Mrs. Moon introduces a small boy to a city library and
            to travel in the subway.

Sy 14   I can read signs--a series. Flushing, N.Y.: Urban Media
            Materials, n.d. (filmstrip)
            Teaches children about the different signs around the city
            in transportation, signs of warning, and signs with numbers.

Sy 15   Joslin, Sesyle. The night they stole the alphabet. New

York: Harcourt, 1968.
Fantasy and mystery are combined in this amusing, sus-
penseful, fast-moving adventure. Young Victoria is awakened during the night by the noise of robbers. After finding her alphabet wallpaper bereft of its letters and all the
pages blank in her fairy tale book, she sets off on a wild
but delightful adventure to retrieve the 26 stolen golden letters of the alphabet.

Sy 16   Kredenser, Gail. The ABC of bumptious beasts. New
          York: Harlin Quist, 1966.
          The author of these 26 verses and the illustrator who
drew the wrinkled people and dour animals both have a ball
describing all the animals from Aardvark to Zebra, and you
will, too, if you like big words and crazy situations. An
alphabet book but not for the beginner.

Sy 17   Learning the alphabet and its sounds with Amos and his
          friends. Lakewood, Fla.: Imperial Productions, 1966.
          (kit: 12 color prints and phonotape)
          Each card illustrates a letter of the alphabet with a draw-
ing of a familiar object, a sentence and the capital and lower case form of the letter. The tape allows the child to
listen and then sing with Amos and his friends. The listen-
ing is done with the picture charts. The set includes a
teacher's manual and 24 spirit duplicator masters for activity to be done along with the study of sounds.

Sy 18   Lionni, Leo. Alphabet tree. New York: Pantheon, 1968.
          Have you ever heard of an alphabet tree where a funny
red, black and yellow word bug teaches the letters and
makes words? If you read about the alphabet tree, you
will also know about a fuzzy purple caterpillar who teaches
words.

Sy 19   Matthiesen, Thomas. ABC: an alphabet book. Bronx,
          N.Y.: Platt, 1966.
          Familiar objects--shoes, a clock, a balloon--represent
the 26 letters of the alphabet.

Sy 20   Munari, Bruno. ABC. Cleveland: World, 1960.
          Pictures are handsome and simple enough for small
children to identify. The objects are familiar ones and
there are three or more words, adjectives as well as nouns,
for many of the letters. For example, U is represented by
umbrella that is up.

Sy 21   Read as you listen. Madison, Wis.: Demco, n.d. (rec-
          ord series)
          Margie Bell reads childrens stories to help build vocabu-
lary, improve phonics and diction.

Sy 22   Reading for beginners--word shapes. Chicago: Coronet,

1969. (16mm film, 11 minutes)
Discloses that each word has its own special shape that
comes from the number and position of its letters.   Suggests that sometimes you notice the shape of the whole word
and sometimes the shape and placement of certain letters.

Sy 23   Reading for beginners--word sounds.   Chicago: Coronet,
         1969.   (16mm film, 11 minutes)
         Uses Jerry as an experiment with words that begin with
the same sounds, and words that end with the same sound.
Teaches that the same letters usually make the same sounds,
but sometimes do not and that sometimes the same sound is
made by different letters.

Sy 24   Reading is important.   Burbank, Cal.: Avis Films, 1968.
         (16mm film)
         Demonstrates importance of reading, indicating its im-
portance in many everyday activities.

Sy 25   Reading signs is fun.   Chicago: Coronet, 1967.   (16mm)
         This film is about a young boy who learns to read road
signs as he drives with his father.   Also included is a
teacher's guide.

Sy 26   Reading skills--find the vowels.   Chicago: Journal Films,
         1971.
         Combines animation, music and sound-effects with live
film sequences to introduce the concepts that certain letters
in the alphabet are called vowels.   Shows that each word
has at least one vowel in it and that each vowel has a sound.
Asks children to respond verbally so that they may discover
for themselves the sound of each of the vowels.

Sy 27   Rey, H. A.   Curious George learns the alphabet.   Boston:
         Houghton, 1963.
         How his friend, the man in the yellow hat, teaches a
monkey to read.

Sy 28   Sendak, Maurice.   Nutshell library.   New York: Harper,
         1962.
         All-around books to give children an all-around concept
of a lot of things.   Each book is delightful and the child
will never realize that what he thinks is fun is actually
learning! Consists of: Alligators all around; Chicken soup
with rice; One plus Johnny; and Pierre.

Sy 29   Taking a trip with a book.   Mahwah, N.J.: Troll Associates,
         1968.   (filmstrip, 40 frs., color)
         Serves as a good introduction to the world of books and
to the library itself.

Sy 30   Walker, Barbara K.   I packed my trunk.   Chicago: Follett,
         1969.

Book in which 26 alphabetized items, occasionally quite unlikely ones, are stuffed into a trunk.

Sy 31   Wildsmith, Brian. ABC. New York: Watts, 1963.
Each letter of the alphabet is represented by one subject, mostly animals.

WRITING

Sy 32   Easy as A B C. Burbank, Cal.: Associated Film Services, 1970. (film, 14 minutes)
Uses building block method to demonstrate that all writing involves the placing of letters, words, sentences, and paragraphs in the right order.

Sy 33   Felt, Sue. Rosa-too-little. Garden City, N.Y.: Doubleday, 1950.
Rosa learns to write her name so that she can get a library card and go to the library--her dearest wish.

Sy 34   McCain, Murray. Writing. New York: Farrar, 1964.
Points out relationships of alphabet to talking and writing, different ways and kinds of writing, and lists words that express seeing, hearing, knowing and feeling.

CALCULATING

Sy 35   Adler, Irving. Numerals: new dress for old numbers. New York: Day, 1964.
In this book the young reader will learn that every number has a name and that it also has a sign which is a numeral. The author explains that while counting is generally done with the digits 0 to 9, we could count by eights, or twelves, or other numerals, and that giant "thinking machines" which solve complicated problems use only the digits 0 to 1! Illustrated with drawings.

Sy 36   _____. Sets and numbers for the very young. New York: Day, 1969.
Simple black and white pictures and very simple text introduce young readers to the concepts of sets, counting, adding and subtracting.

Sy 37   _____. Time in your life. New York: Day, 1969.
You can tell time by a fiddler crab, a uranium clock, by the rhythm of the stars, and in countless other ways. Included in the revised edition is a brief section on how to make a star clock.

Sy 38   Berenstain, Stan and Jan. Bears on wheels. Westminster, Md.: Random, 1969.

A story told with numbers about one small bear on one small wheel out for a spin. Before they know it, beginning readers will be reading and counting by themselves.

Sy 39   Bishop, Claire. <u>Twenty-two bears</u>. New York: Viking, 1964.
Counting book which describes the antics of a large family of bears in the wild woods of Wyoming.

Sy 40   Brenner, Barbara. <u>The five pennies</u>. Westminster, Md.: Knopf, 1965.
Nicky puts five new pennies in his pocket and goes out to buy a pet. He does not have enough money; so he buys other things but has a surprise and a pet in the end.

Sy 41   Budoney, Blossom. <u>A cat can't count</u>. West Caldwell, N. J.: Lothrop, 1962.
Using the concept of counting and measuring, gay pictures and verse invite the young child to count and see how many objects he can find.

Sy 42   Carle, Eric. <u>One, two, three to the zoo</u>. Cleveland: World, 1968.
After a lone elephant on a flatcar, for number one, this counting book gives groups of animals in ascending numbers on their way to the zoo in open box cars.

Sy 43   _____. <u>The rooster who set out to see the world</u>. New York: Watts, 1972.
Uses collage and fingerpainting, trying to teach children sets. New style of counting book aimed not at learning numbers but learning sets.

Sy 44   Chwast, Seymour. <u>Still another number book....</u> New York: McGraw-Hill, 1971.
Contemporary design and illustrations fill this counting book, which proceeds from one ship, afloat on a purple sea alive with sea animals and plants, to ten jugglers in unusual poses and costumes.

Sy 45   <u>Day without numbers</u>. Detroit: Wayne State University, 1953. (16mm film, 9 minutes)
A second grader's experience during the day without numbers causes him to want to study arithmetic and to realize the value of numbers in everyday living. All the class but Bob enjoy arithmetic. When a puppet with magic powers offers Bob a day without numbers, he gladly leaves the room with the puppet. A series of frustrating experiences caused by the magical disappearance of numbers, such as the disruption of an exciting baseball game, results in Bob's gladly returning to the classroom and the study of arithmetic.

Sy 46   Earle, Eric. <u>One, two, three to the zoo</u>. Cleveland:

World, 1968.
A counting book illustrated with colorful animals traveling
in a zoo train. There is no text but each doublespread page
contains a numeral and a corresponding number in a train
car.

Sy 47   Eichenberg, Fritz. Dancing in the moon. New York: Har-
         court, 1956.
         This book introduces young children to the numbers from
         one to twenty by means of nonsensical counting rhymes.
         The book has real value in teaching number concepts to
         children in that it presents the abstract number symbol in
         the text with a concrete example of what the symbol stands
         for in the illustrations.

Sy 48   Emberley, Ed. The wing on a flea: a book about shapes.
         Boston: Little, Brown, 1965.
         Gay rhymes and lively green-and-blue drawings show chil-
         dren how to identify triangles, circles and rectangles in
         everyday objects.

Sy 49   Epstein, Sam. First book of measurement. New York:
         Watts, 1960.
         Presents the systems that the world uses for measuring
         as well as the history of measurement.

Sy 50   Fisher, Margery M. One and one. New York: Dial, 1963.
         About the numbers from one to ten.

Sy 51   Frances, Marian. Silly number mystery. Mahwah, N.J.:
         Troll Associates, 1969. (filmstrip, color, 42 frs.)
         Full color drawings illustrating the rhyme of the silly old
         man explain the meaning of the numbers one through eleven.
         May be used for group or individual study in arithmetic.

Sy 52   Francoise. What time is it, Jeanne-Marie? New York:
         Scribner, 1963.
         Children can learn to tell time by watching Jeanne-Marie
         spend a happy day filling the hours from early morning to
         late at night with interesting things to do.

Sy 53   Freeman, Mae. Finding out about shapes. New York:
         McGraw-Hill, 1969.
         By looking at the pictures in this book children can dis-
         cover triangles, rectangles, circles and other simple shapes.
         The author describes these various geometrical forms and
         provides readers with instructions on how to make such
         things as triangles, cones, cubes, etc.

Sy 54   Goldberg, Esther. Using a ruler. St. Paul: Minnesota
         Mining and Manufacturing, 1968. (Wollensak teaching
         tape, single track. Includes teacher's guide)
         Leads the listener step-by-step through the processes in-

volved in measuring and drawing lines of varying lengths;
explains the whole and half-inch markings; explains the uses
of the quarter and eighth-inch markings and provides practice related to these concepts. Useful for group and individual study but especially for individual work. For best
results, use with student worksheet.

Sy 55   Gregor, Arthur. **1, 2, 3, 4, 5.** Philadelphia: Lippincott,
             1956.
             Rhymes and photographs show the first and second grader
         how to count.

Sy 56   Hoban, Tana. Count and see. Riverside, N. J.: Macmil-
             lan, 1972.
             A counting book that moves from 1 to 15, then in tens
         to fifty and then to one hundred. The left-hand pages are
         black with large numerals and the number in white, and
         with large white dots to corroborate the counting. The right-
         hand pages are clear photographs in black and white, all ob-
         jects that are easy to recognize; four children, eight windows,
         twelve eggs in a carton, fifteen cookies on a baking sheet,
         forty peanuts, one hundred peas in their pods--ten per pod.

Sy 57   Ipcar, Dahlov. Brown cow farm. Weston, Conn.: Weston
             Woods Studios, 1965. (filmstrip)
             Provides easy lessons in counting, adding, and multiply-
         ing.

Sy 58   Jacobs, Allan D. Arithmetic in verse and rhyme. Scars-
             dale, N. Y.: Garrard, 1971.
             Counting rhymes, poems of adding and subtraction, num-
         ber riddles and verse simply in dealing with number fun.
         Provides a fanciful new aspect to arithmetic that teachers
         may wish to use with reluctant students for an added di-
         mension.

Sy 59   Jenkins, Ella. Counting games and rhythms for the little
             ones. Vol. I. Englewood Cliffs, N. J.: Folkways
             Records, n. d. (33 rpm phonodisc, also available in cas-
             sette)
             Ella Jenkins leads children from Lake Meadows Nursery
         School in Chicago in folk songs, rhymes, and activities that
         teach number concepts to preschoolers through second grad-
         ers.

Sy 60   Jonas, Arthur. More new ways in math. Englewood Cliffs,
             N. J.: Prentice-Hall, 1964.
             This book is for children who do not like arithmetic. Ex-
         plains number, numeral, place value, sentence, systems of
         numeration, and graphing.

Sy 61   Krahn, Fernando. Life of numbers. New York: Simon and
             Schuster, 1970.

Number one lives alone and gets bored so he leaves to find a number friend. All other numbers are not appropriate because of their characteristics. He is sad until zero shows him how they can become ten. Amusing and clever illustrations complement the text.

Sy 62 Langstaff, John. Over in the meadow. New York: Harcourt, 1957.
This old counting rhyme tells of ten meadow families whose mothers advise them to dig, run, sing, play, hum, build, swim, wink, spin, and hop. The illustrations, half in full color, show the combination of realism and imagination which little children like best. The tune, arranged simply, is on the last page and children will have fun acting the whole thing out.

Sy 63 Leaf, Munro. Arithmetic can be fun. Philadelphia: Lippincott, 1949.
The author explains some of the whys and hows of arithmetic--counting, adding, subtracting; so that it makes sense to the beginner or the slow learner. Written a generation ago, it's lighthearted humor and the basic math skills are never outdated.

Sy 64 Lubell, Winifred. Mathematics for children. (series) Irvington on Hudson, N.Y.: Hudson Photographic Industries, 1970.
Designed to teach very elementary mathematical principles to pre-school and primary grades. She loves blueberries (43 frames) tells the story of a pet hamster whose blueberry eating habits form the basis of a lesson in subtraction and addition. Magic fraction garden (37 frames) teaches beginning concepts in fractions, using halves, quarters, and thirds. Measure me (38 frames) describes two caterpillars, a big one and a small one, who disagree about the height of a daisy and proceed to measure it. Includes teacher's guide.

Sy 65 Malinowski, Otylia. Clock arithmetic: problems. St. Paul: Minnesota Mining and Manufacturing, 1968.
Builds skills in applying arithmetic to practical word problems, develops logical steps in problem solving, and provides practice problems in reinforce concepts.

Sy 66 Math made meaningful. Great Neck, N.Y.: Classroom Materials, Inc., n.d. (record)
Presents concepts of counting, addition, and subtraction, encouraging pupils to participate in games and activities which introduce the basic concepts.

Sy 67 Mathematical relationships. Freeport, N.Y.: Education Activities, n.d. (filmstrip)
Introduces principles of the new math. Provides illus-

trations which enable the children to see the relationships
between sets.

Sy 68   O'Brien, Thomas C. Odds and evens. New York: Crowell,
         1971.
         In this explanation of the properties of odd and even num-
         bers, the author includes questions, puzzles, games, and
         experiments. The book will perhaps be more fun if an older
         person shares it with a child or a group of children. The
         reading is a little difficult for nursery school and kindergar-
         ten youngsters, yet they can comprehend the illustrations
         and participate in the exercises.

Sy 69   Oxenbury, Helen. Numbers of things. New York: Watts,
         1968.
         A tall counting book from England, the shape used to
         great advantage for the contrasting facing pages. Presents
         numbers ranging from one to fifty, including one lighthearted
         lion, four melancholy mice, nine beaming birds, twenty
         bright balloons, thirty passive penguins, forty friendly fish
         and fifty laughing ladybugs.

Sy 70   Palmer, Hap. Math readiness--vocabulary and concepts.
         Freeport, N. Y. : Education Activities, n. d. (33 rpm
         phonodisc)
         Lively music and action songs teach the concepts and
         vocabulary needed for an understanding of basic mathematics.

Sy 71   Peppe, Rodney. Circus numbers: a counting book. New
         York: Delacorte, 1969.
         A counting book in which readers encounter 1 ringmaster,
         2 horses, etc. , up to 100 elephants divided into groups of
         10.

Sy 72   Reiss, John J. Numbers: A book. Scarsdale, N. Y. :
         Bradbury, 1971.
         This is a big brilliantly colored picture book which first
         counts from one to ten and then by tens to one hundred and
         ends with the number 1000 (raindrops). It enumerates such
         things as shoes, starfish, arms, beads, crayons, baseball
         players, and kites.

Sy 73   Sendak, Maurice. One was Johnny: a counting book. New
         York: Harper, 1972.
         A book to help you count from one to ten by telling you
         about the queer creatures who infested Johnny's house and
         how he got rid of them.

Sy 74   Waller, Leslie. A book to begin on: Numbers. New York:
         Holt, 1960.
         This book is useful as a supplement to the arithmetic
         lesson. Both the text and lively drawings are light in their
         approach and even very young pupils can painlessly absorb

facts that will add to their concept of numbers.

Sy 75   Watson, Nancy. What is one? Westminster, Md.: Knopf,
         1965.
         Big brother Peter teaches little sister Linda how to count.
         What is one? The lone pine against the sky. What is two?
         Sled tracks in the snow; and so on in simple text and full
         page pictures.

Sy 76   What's missing lotto. Commack, N.Y.: Edu-Cards Cor-
         poration, 1970. (Game--24 word picture cards; 4 large
         scene cards; 2, 3, or 4 players; 15 minutes)
         The object of the game is to identify what is missing from
         a large incomplete scene and then find the word-picture
         cards that pertain to the missing part. A caller calls the
         word-picture cards; the player who has obtained all six of his
         missing objects in the form of the word-picture cards is
         the winner. Has been useful in increasing perception on
         the part of children in kindergarten and first grade.

Sy 77   Whitney, David C. Lets find out about addition. New York:
         Watts, 1966.
         Illustrated book which will help reinforce the child's first
         experience with the new math; covers basic concepts of num-
         ber sets and addition.

Sy 78   _____. Let's find out about subtraction. New York:
         Watts, 1968.
         Black is the opposite of white. Wet is the opposite of
         dry. A wet black dog is the opposite of a dry white cat.
         And subtraction is the opposite of addition. A simply clear
         explanation about subtraction, which includes its uses, im-
         portance and methods.

Sy 79   Wildsmith, Brian. Brian Wildsmith's 1, 2, 3's. New
         York: Watts, 1965.
         The author has illustrated each numeral from 1 to 10
         with a picture made up of three basic shapes--rectangle,
         triangle, and circle in a kaleidoscope of colors. The shapes
         build up to form recognizable objects until the end of the
         book. There are a number of puzzle pictures.

LANGUAGE ARTS

Sy 80   Basic primary phonics--group one. Chicago: Society for
         Visual Education, 1959. (filmstrip)
         Shows pictures of familiar objects that help introduce
         children to sounds as they say and hear the words. De-
         signed for use in sequence with full class participation,
         simple words illustrate the initial consonant sounds, blends,
         two-and-three letter combinations, final consonant and vowel
         sounds.

Sy 81   Early reading recognition skills.   Freeport, N. Y. :   Educa-
         tion Activities, n. d.   (filmstrip)
         Through this carefully-structured filmstrip program, the
         young child is encouraged to recognize, identify, synthesize
         and manipulate vowel and consonant letters, letter combina-
         tions and words.   Careful attention is given to those letters
         and letter combinations which have been found to be the most
         difficult for the young child.

Sy 82   Eastman, P. D.   The cat in the hat beginner book diction-
         ary.   Westminster, Md. :   Random House, 1964.
         An illustrated storybook which explains word meanings
         through pictures and sentences.

Sy 83   Rand, Ann and Paul.   Sparkle and spin.   New York: Har-
         court, 1957.
         The authors deal with the abstract concept of words--
         what they stand for, how they sound, how they are used as
         a means of communication.   Some of the ideas, both in the
         text and pictures, will require adult interpretation but on
         the whole the presentation is as childlike as it is fresh and
         imaginative.

Sy 84   Reading for beginners--words and word parts.   Chicago:
         Coronet, 1969.   (16mm filmstrip)
         Shows the use of a game called "build a word" to teach
         how words are built.

Sy 85   Reading with riddles.   Freeport, N. Y. :   Education Activities,
         n. d.   (filmstrips, records)
         Creates interest in words and their meanings through
         photographic illustrations.   Key words from narrated rid-
         dles are superimposed on filmstrip; rhythmic repetition
         along with solicited verbal response from the children help
         to make this an enjoyable learning experience.

Intermediate

READING

Sy 86   Acker, Helen.   The school train.   New York: Abelard-
         Schuman, 1953.
         John and Tony are left to fend for themselves in their
         cabin in the Canadian woods, while their father goes off to
         hunt and trap in order to earn their living.   They learn of
         the "school train" which the railroad brings and parks near
         them for two weeks at a time.   They learn to read and
         have several exciting adventures.

Sy 87   Beim, Jerrold.   Thin ice.   New York: Morrow, 1956.
         Lee didn't care much about reading well; but when he
         was able to make out the sign that read "Keep Off--Thin

Ice" and thereby save his younger brother from mishap, he decided he could and would learn to read better.

Sy 88   Boy Scouts of America. Reading. North Brunswick, N.J.:
         Boy Scouts of America, 1965.
         Intended as a guide for Boy Scouts working toward a merit badge in reading, this pamphlet contains material on such topics as the importance of good reading, book selection, the card catalog and use of the library. Included is an annotated bibliography of over 225 selected titles arranged under such headings as: Classics; biography; explaining science; understanding music; poetry; time to laugh.

Sy 89   Carlson, Natalie Savage. School bell in the valley. New
         York: Harcourt, 1963.
         Ten-year-old Belle Mundy's opportunity to learn and to read and write is blocked by her fear of being teased.

Sy 90   Carruth, Ella Kaiser. She wants to read. Nashville:
         Abingdon, 1966.
         Born of parents who had once been slaves, Mary lived on a cotton plantation as a child. She spent long hours in the field, but her fierce determination to learn to read was rewarded when at ten she started to school. Scholarships made it possible for her to go to higher education. Wanting desperately to share her knowledge with others of her race, she opened her own school in Florida.

Sy 91   Child Study Association of America Series. New York:
         Crowell.
         Read to yourself storybook. 1954. A collection of 20 stories--chapters from many books. Samples of books may lead to the enjoyment of reading the whole book. More read to yourself stories: fun and magic. 1956. Twelve stories which are told in fun, excerpted or condensed. Now you can read to yourself. 1964. Relevant stories which are not too hard.

Sy 92   Cleary, Beverly. Mitch and Amy. New York: Morrow,
         1967.
         Mitch and Amy Huff were twins. Amy could not resist taunting Mitch over his reading difficulties; yet she was the one who finally found the book her brother first read independently. When Mitch unwittingly became the target of the school bully, Amy kept Mrs. Huff from interfering and together they handled the problem in their own way.

Sy 93   Ends 'n blends. Peekskill, N.Y.: Educational Games, n.d.
         (simulation game)
         A stimulating game to develop reading and spelling ability. Two to four players reinforcing each other. Game is adaptable to several differing objectives. Contents: Count-

ers, spinners, beginning and ending hit/mis cards.

Sy 94   Ervin, Janet Halliday.   More than halfway there.   Chicago:
        Follett, 1970.
        Can you imagine a time when a boy had to use every
        art he possessed to persuade his father to allow him to go
        to school?   This story tells of a day in 1829 when Albert
        Long met Mr. Gentry's clerk, the "reading man," Abe
        Lincoln.   It proved to be the most eventful day in Albert's
        life and the story of it provides an unusual picture of Lin-
        coln as a young man.

Sy 95   Fenner, Phyllis and McCrea, Mary.   Stories for fun and
        adventure.   New York: Day, 1961.
        A special collection of stories for upper elementary
        pupils who usually do not enjoy reading.

Sy 96   Fife, Dale.   Adam's ABC.   New York: Coward, 1971.
        Three black children, Adam and his friends, Arthur and
        Albert, live in the city.   What they do each day at home,
        in school and after school is followed through each letter
        of the alphabet.   Each letter of the alphabet focuses on an
        everyday image in a city which is also the color black--a
        fire escape, the river at night, many umbrellas in a rain-
        storm.

Sy 97   I read, you read, we read, I see, you see, we see, I
        hear, you hear, we hear, I learn, you learn, we learn.
        Chicago: American Library Association, 1971.
        Audio-visual material.   Poems, stories and films to
        help the socially disadvantaged child to read and under-
        stand about his world.

Sy 98   It's fun to read books.   Chicago: Coronet, 1951.   (16mm,
        1 minutes)
        Describes some of the uses of books and discusses ways
        in which one can enjoy a book.   Tells how to use the li-
        brary as a source for books.   Concludes with suggestions
        for the proper care of a book.

Sy 99   Kraus, Robert.   Leo the late bloomer.   New York: Wind-
        mill Books, 1971.
        In this book animals possess human capabilities such as
        reading and writing.   Leo is a young tiger who couldn't do
        anything.   In his own good time, he learns to do all the
        things that other children can do.   This book is a good ex-
        ample of showing that everyone learns and develops at his
        own rate.

Sy 100 Kyle, Elisabeth.   Great ambitions: a story of the early
        years of Charles Dickens.   New York: Holt, 1966.
        An introduction to the life of Dickens from the time he
        was twelve and an apprentice in a blacking factory to his

twenty-seventh year when he achieved fame as an author.

Sy 101   Learning the alphabet and its sounds with Amos and his
          friends.   Lakewood, Fla.: Imperial Productions, 1966.
          (kit--study print)
          Each card illustrates a letter of the alphabet with a
          drawing of a familiar object, a sentence, and the capital
          and lower case forms of the letter. The tape allows the
          children to listen and then sing the sound with Amos and
          his friends. The listening is done with the picture charts.
          The set includes a teacher's manual and 24 spirit dupli-
          cator masters for activity to be done along with the study
          of the sounds.

Sy 102   Lexau, Joan M. Olaf reads. New York: Dial, 1961.
          Here are three stories of Olaf's misadventures in his
          struggle to read and to understand what he is reading.
          One takes place in school; another tells about his mailing
          a letter, and the third is about his unforgettable first visit
          to the library.

Sy 103   McCain, Murray. Books! New York: Simon & Schuster,
          1962.
          A zany exercise in reading about books; intended to mo-
          tivate and perhaps titillate the reader.

Sy 104   Maney, Ethel S. Introducing reading--thinking skills.
          Elizabethtown, Pa.: Continental Press, Inc., 1968.
          (two sets of 37 color transparencies)
          Designed for both readers and non-readers, these 7 x
          10-inch transparencies develop major thinking skills, in-
          cluding classifying ideas, developing sentence sense, un-
          derstanding multiple meanings, making inferences, relating
          pronouns and antecedents, determining analogous relation-
          ships, and organizing ideas in time and order.

Sy 105   Marriott, Alice. Sequoyah: Leader of the Cherokee.
          Westminster, Md.: Random, 1956.
          This is the story of a scholarly Indian who made a
          syllabary of the Cherokee language so that his people could
          learn to read and write.

Sy 106   Martin, Patricia. Pointed brush. West Caldwell, N.J.:
          Lothrop, 1959.
          Chung Yee is sad because his father will not allow his
          five elder brothers to attend school with him. His teacher
          has told him that there is power in the written word and
          he knows his father wishes his sons to be powerful and
          strong. When Elder Uncle is falsely accused of stealing
          a neighbor's water buffalo and put into a bamboo jail, each
          of the five elder brothers attempt to free him by physical
          strength but each fails. Then Chung Yee writes a letter
          declaring his uncle's innocence and fastens it to the tea-

house wall.   The village scholars read the notice and secure Elder Uncle's freedom.   When the father learns that
Chung Yee's letter has affected Elder Uncle's release, he
declares: "All our sons shall go to the teacher.   They
shall grow wise, knowing the written word. "

Sy 107   Peare, Catherina Owens.   Helen Keller story.   New York:
            Crowell, 1959.
            Stirring life of the girl who, despite blindness and deaf-
            ness, learns to communicate with others.

Sy 108   Reader's Digest Services, Inc.   Reader's Digest reading
            skillbuilders.   Pleasantville, N.Y.:   Reader's Digest,
            1958.
            Selections are adopted from regular issues of The Read-
            er's Digest and have high interest value without being
            childish.

Sy 109   Reading motivation.   (series) New York: Parents Maga-
            zine Press, 1968.   (filmstrips)
            These filmstrips present a variety of imaginative stories
            for children.   Each filmstrip is accompanied by a booklet
            which gives the test of the picture book from which the
            strip was made, coordinated with each frame.

Sy 110   Sloane, Eric.   ABC book of early Americana.   New York:
            Doubleday, 1963.
            A brief encyclopedia of all kinds of early American
            things, such as almanacs, hex signs, and a zig-zag fence.

Sy 111   Slobodkin, Florence.   Sarah somebody.   New York: Van-
            guard, 1970.
            Grandma lived in Poland all of her ninety years, and
            she couldn't read or write.   In 1893 few women were edu-
            cated; so there didn't seem much chance that a nine-year-
            old girl in a Polish village would ever have a chance.
            But Miss Chesnov came from Warsaw and taught a small
            group of girls--so Sarah had her chance to become some-
            body.

Sy 112   Sound way to easy reading.   Wichita, Kan.: Learning Arts,
            n.d.   (33-1/3)
            This recording provides a tutoring aid with one hundred
            and twenty-three basic phonic blends and phonic endings,
            rules for unlocking words and seven self-quizzing phonics
            cards.

Sy 113   Williams, Jay.   Danny Dunn and the homework machine.
            New York: McGraw-Hill, 1958.
            Professor Bullfinch leaves Danny in charge of his mini-
            ature automatic computer while he goes to Washington.
            Danny and two friends work out a scheme using the compu-
            ter to do their homework.   Complications develop when a

jealous boy tells their teacher and sabotages the machine.

Sy 114   Why we read. Hollywood, Cal.: Charles Cahill and
          Associates, Inc., 1969. (sound filmstrip)
          Describes a good reader as one who mentally recon-
          structs a book's content for more meaning and enjoyment.
          Emphasizes importance of concentration for continuous
          meaning shows the importance of leisure reading outside
          of school.

WRITING

Sy 115   Blackstone, Josephine. Songs for sixpence. Chicago:
          Follett, 1955.
          A story about John Newbery, the first person to publish
          books for children. The Newbery Award is given in his
          honor.

Sy 116   Cahn, William and Rhoda. The story of writing: from
          cave art to computer. Irvington-on-Hudson, N.Y.:
          Harvey House, 1963.
          Overview of written communication includes relationship
          of English alphabet to other alphabetic scripts, story of
          numbers, invention of paper and the manufacture of paper
          and ink.

Sy 117   Cretan, Gladys Yessayan. Gift from the bride. Boston:
          Little, Brown, 1964.
          A little Armenian girl longs to go to school and learn
          to write as do the boys of her village.

Sy 118   Fitzhugh, Louise. Harriet the spy. New York: Harper,
          1964.
          Eleven-year-old Harriet who goes to a private school in
          New York jots down her thoughts about people, places, and
          things in a notebook, in preparation for a writing career.
          When her classmates obtain the notebook and read about
          themselves they make life miserable for Harriet--until Har-
          riet learns something she never suspected.

Sy 119   Galdone, Paul. That's right, Edie. New York: Putnam,
          1966.
          Edie is too impatient to learn to write. She can't even
          write her name so that it can be read.

Sy 120   Hart, Toney. The young letterer. New York: Warne,
          1965.
          In addition to demonstrating the techniques of hand let-
          tering, this book discusses the history of the development
          of alphabets.

Sy 121   Hodges, Elizabeth Jamison. Song for Gilgamesh. New

York: Atheneum, 1971.
The ancient Sumerian Adaba learns writing and in so
doing is accused of having stolen temple magic. History
blends well with adventure in recreating the ancient Sumerian culture. Fast paced, good character development of
Adaba. A story with timeless appeal.

Sy 122   I want to write. Los Angeles, Cal.: Regional Education
TV Advisory Council, n. d. (video tape)
Presents a lesson in creative writing. Shows how to
find new words and how to rephrase sentences. Includes
examples of the author's phrasing. Developing Characters
in Your Writing (23 mins.); Developing Plot for your Stories
(24 mins.); Inside Story (17 mins.); Key to Treasure A
(20 mins.); Writing Sports Stories (24 mins.).

Sy 123   Improve your handwriting. Chicago: Coronet, 1949.
(16mm film, 11 minutes)
A boy whose handwriting is poor is given some pointers
by the teacher, who also calls attention to the handwriting
of some of his friends. He makes an effort to improve by
practicing the accepted fundamentals of writing.

Sy 124   Johnston, Johanna. That's right, Edie. New York: Putnam, 1966.
Edie is too impatient to learn to write. She can't even
write her name so that it can be read. After all, Mr.
O'Malley, her good friend the postman, not only delivers
Edie's scribbled notes to her friends but also gives them
the messages as well. During her birthday party, Edie is
so happy when a truck arrives with a long wanted bicycle.
But what a catastrophe! The delivery man says, "Somebody named Edie has to sign for this before I can leave
this beautiful bike. "

Sy 125   Jordan, June. Voice of the children. New York: Holt,
1970.
Out of a Saturday workshop for creative writing in
Brooklyn has come this selection of poems and prose by
26 Black and Puerto Rican children. Corrected only for
spelling errors, these words of the city children portray
slums--the crowded apartments, the dirt and debris in
which they live and the violence that is part of their lives.
And yet there are words of hope, for peace and for love,
and for the courage to make it out of the ghetto.

Sy 126   Krauss, Ruth. I write it. New York: Harper, 1970.
Illustrated poem about writing one's name in likely, unlikely, and impossible places. Gay and endearing small
figures romp through the pages. The poetic text bubbles
along. Not until the end does the reader know it is the
children's names that are being written and the last double-
page spread shows proudly scrawled or printed signatures

from many lands and in several alphabets.

Sy 127   Krieger, David. Letters and words. New York: Young
          Scott Books, 1969.
          Presents a colorful double-page spread for each letter
          of the alphabet illustrating both lower and upper case let-
          ters in a variety of printing styles. Also for each letter,
          there are pictures of objects which are familiar to young
          children. The names of these objects start with the letter,
          end with the letter, or have the letter within the word.
          The words have been superimposed upon the objects for
          reading-readiness at home and school.

Sy 128   Taylor, Margaret. Wht's yr nm? New York: Harcourt,
          1970.
          Simple presentation of the origin of written language
          traces the development of writing from the time of the
          Stone Age man to the time of the picture writing, idea
          writing, sound writing, hieroglyphics and writing by the
          Phoenicians, Greeks and Romans.

Sy 129   Writing through the ages. Chicago: Encyclopaedia Britan-
          nica Films, n. d. (16mm film)
          Provides a chronological history of writing, analyzing
          features of early Chinese, Mesopotamian and Egyptian
          writing. Stresses contributions of Phoenicians, Greeks,
          and Romans to our present alphabet.

Sy 130   Yates, Elizabeth. Someday you'll write. New York: Dut-
          ton, 1962.
          A guide to creative writing for young writers-to-be, dis-
          cussing how to choose a subject, plan the story, sustain
          the reader's attention, and above all devote time and en-
          ergies to developing skill in this profession.

CALCULATING

Sy 131   Adler, Irving. Giant golden book of mathematics: explor-
          ing the world of numbers and space. New York: Gold-
          en, 1960.
          Explores fundamental concepts in the various branches
          of the sciences and the relations or application of mathe-
          matics to the world in which we live.

Sy 132   _____. Integers: positive and negative. New York:
          Day, 1972.
          Explains the meaning and use of integers, describing
          how numbers may be positive or negative by comparing
          them with rewards and penalties. It shows how to add and
          subtract integers using checkers, arrows, and a number
          line. Directions for making a slide rule and a simple
          adding machine are also given.

Sy 133   _____ . Numbers: old and new. New York: Day, 1960.
              What's a rectangle number? How many ways can you
        multiply? Who first thought of using fractions? This is
        only a sample of the questions answered in this book that
        will help interest the reluctant mathematician.

Sy 134   _____ . Sets. New York: Day, 1967.
              Stresses the importance of sets because they are used
        every day. It shows the relationship between sets and
        problem solving. The book includes 80 problems to work
        out.

Sy 135   _____ . The tools of science: from yardstick to cy-
              clotron. New York: Day, 1958.
              Explains the basic principles and purposes of the tools
        used by the eager scientist of the present and the past.
        Emphasizes the basic concepts of the scientific method of
        inquiry.

Sy 136   Arithmetic series--set one. New York: McGraw-Hill,
              1969. (6 filmstrips, 44 frames, color)
              A progressive series beginning with elementary number
        concepts and especially planned for introduction, summary
        or review. Contents: reading and writing whole numbers;
        addition and subtraction (1-10); addition and subtraction (10
        or more); what are numbers; multiplication and division;
        solving problems.

Sy 137   Arithmetic series--set two. New York: McGraw-Hill,
              1969. (6 filmstrips, 44 frames, color)
              Advancing from set one, proceeding to more advanced
        skills and understanding; designed to develop basic under-
        standing of concepts rather than merely manipulative skills.
        Contents: decimal fractions; reading instruments; telling
        time; percentage and using money; meaning of fractions;
        working with fractions; measurement.

Sy 138   Arithmetic series--set three. New York: McGraw-Hill,
              1969. (6 filmstrips, 36 frames, color)
              Continued from sets one and two to further advanced
        skills and understanding. While utilizing the traditional
        approach, modern concepts are developed. Contents: fac-
        tors and primes; exponents; properties of numbers; addi-
        tion and subtraction; multiplication and division; geometric
        figures and their measurements; scale drawings and tables.

Sy 139   Asimov, Isaac. Quick and easy math. Boston: Houghton,
              1964.
              Discover shortcuts to use in doing arithmetic problems.
        Covers addition, subtraction, multiplication, division, and
        fractions.

Sy 140   Bendick, Jeanne. How much and how many: the story of

weights and measures. New York: McGraw-Hill, 1947.
The fascinating true story of how weights and measurements have affected trade, science and everyday living
through the centuries. Full of information with tables of
measurements and several hundred expressive pictures and
diagrams by the author.

Sy 141   . Measuring. New York: Watts, 1971.
What measuring is, how we measure, what we measure,
all explained in a simple text which includes many questions for the reader to answer and suggests many experiments he can do.

Sy 142   . Take a number. New York: McGraw-Hill,
1961.
Explanation of numbers from finger counting to computers with facts, ideas and puzzles that make it more challenging than its appearance indicates.

Sy 143   and Levin, Marcia. Take shapes, lines, and
letters: new horizons in mathematics. New York: Mc-
Graw-Hill, 1962.
This book deals with mathematical ideas and relationships rather than with numbers, explaining the concepts of
lines, curves, angles, planes, and shapes. A fresh, stim-
ulating introduction to geometry with eye catching illustra-
tion.

Sy 144   Charosh, Mannis. Mathematical games for one or two.
New York: Crowell, 1972.
Each of these six groups of games--pyramid games,
checker games, shifting games, take-away games, name
games, magic tricks--begin with an elementary version in
a way that illustrates the basic logical or mathematical
principle, so that the reader may develop the game still
further.

Sy 145   Decimals are easy. Chicago: Coronet, n.d.   (10mm film)
Art Barker works out a series of decimal problems to
prove to his family that they could save enough money
from their gasoline allotment for their vacation to buy a
rubber boat. He wins his point and gets his boat. Slightly more difficult problems in addition, subtraction, multiplication and division are summarized at the conclusion.

Sy 146   Dennis, J. Richard. Fractions are parts of things. New
York: Crowell, 1971.
The author makes clear by clever use of colored mathematical shapes the relationships that are 1/2, 1/3, 2/3,
1/4, and 3/4. The text contains questions, suggests activities, and invites discussion and group learning.

Sy 147   Diggins, Julia. String, straightedge and shadow: the

story of geometry. New York: Viking, 1965.
This book tells the basic story of the origin of geometry
by relating how man probably used the simple tools listed
in the title and from this early effort grew the concepts of
geometry.

Sy 148   Dilson, Jesse. The Abacus: a pocket computer. New
            York: St. Martin's, 1968.
            A practical introduction to the use of the abacus, along
            with an anecdotal history of the device is provided in this
            entertaining book. There are ample clear diagrams, in-
            cluding a chapter showing the young reader how to build
            his own abacus with beads, wire and a cigar box. One of
            the sections explains how one can do binary calculations on
            the abacus using the same number systems employed in
            modern computers.

Sy 149   Equations. Ann Arbor, Mich.: Wff'n Proof Publishing,
            1963. (game)
            A simulation game played at several levels of difficulty.
            Centers around idea of use of cubes in formations of equa-
            tions and solving for unknowns.

Sy 150   Expanded numerals. New York: Popular Science Film-
            Strip-of-the-Month-Club, 1966. (filmstrip)
            Explains and discusses the base-10 system, 10 basic
            symbols or digits, place value pattern and the meaning of
            standard and expanded numerals.

Sy 151   Experiments with length. Chicago: Society for Visual Edu-
            cation, 1966. (filmstrip)
            The use of clear measuring devices in the metric sys-
            tem is explained and taught in clear photographs and cap-
            tions, by which a student can learn how to use the metric
            stick, the vernier caliper and the micrometer.

Sy 152   Fractions in common form. New York: AEVAC, Inc.,
            n.d. (transparencies/study guides)
            Attaché-case designed for total experience with fractions
            --conceptual and computational. Useful with a graded or
            non-graded program.

Sy 153   Hogben, Lancelot. The wonderful world of mathematics.
            Garden City, N.Y.: Doubleday, 1968.
            This book shows how the growth of mathematics as a
            science has arisen from the growth of civilization. It also
            explains such basic mathematical concepts as the workings
            of the decimal system, the measurement of angles, the solu-
            tion of equations, and the measure of change on a graph.

Sy 154   Jonas, Arthur. New ways in math. Englewood Cliffs,
            N.J.: Prentice-Hall, 1962.
            A survey of man's progress in theoretical and practical

mathematics emphasizing and explaining modern mathematics with its binary systems, computers, arithmetic-without-numbers, probability, and other developments. Includes puzzles for readers to try.

Sy 155   Malinowski, Otylia. Problem solving: enough information? St. Paul: Minnesota Mining and Manufacturing Company, 1968. (phonotape)
Leads to the recognition of facts in order to solve a given problem, emphasizing careful reading, complete comprehension, and selection of necessary facts. Useful for group or individual study, especially individual in mathematics.

Sy 156   The metric system. (Mathematical Relationships Series) New York: McGraw-Hill, 1966. (16mm film)
Presents an animated film on the metric system.

Sy 157   Metric system skills. Freeport, N.Y.: Education Activities, n.d. (records)
This sequential, developmental series of skill and drill records promotes mastery of the fundamental units of the metric system. Each recording teaches four complete, single concept, self-directing, self-correcting lessons. No other materials except paper and pencil are needed. Prior to each series of questions the material is taught and examples are given. Answers are given after each lesson for immediate reinforcement. Recordings may be used over and over again for regular practice. May be used by individuals, small groups or entire class.

Sy 158   O'Neill, Mary. Take a number. New York: Doubleday, 1968.
A collection of poems about numbers and mathematical concepts with a brief look at size, space, sets, symbols and time.

Sy 159   Powers, Virginia. Strike three, you're in! Burbank, Cal.: Cathedral Films, 1969. (filmstrip, color, 44 frames; phonodisc 1s, 12-in., 33 rpm)
Shows the importance of recognizing abilities through the story of Tim who cannot play baseball but becomes the team scorekeeper because he is good at mathematics.

Sy 160   Rogers, James T. The Pantheon story of mathematics for young people. New York: Pantheon, 1966.
From finger counting to the modern computer age, the complete story of mathematics, telling of man's major achievements through the lives of great mathematicians. Illustrated with over 200 photographs, diagrams, and reproductions.

Sy 161   Russell, Solveig Paulson. Lines and shapes: a first look

at geometry. New York: Walck, 1965.
Seeks to relate the basic concepts of geometry to our
everyday life by helping the reader gain skill in locating
basic kinds of geometric figures in the immediate environment.

Sy 162   . One, two, three and many: a first look at numbers. New York: Walck, 1970.
Traces the history of numbers from early development
to the use of present day machines and how we use numbers from day to day.

Sy 163   Singing multiplication tables.   Freeport, N.Y.:   Education
Activities, 1971. (records)
Melodic jingles sung to swinging music, with rock, folk,
or jazz flavor, encourage children to master, painlessly,
the multiplication tables through 12 times 12.   Each table
is first sung twice with the correct answers and then sung
again without the answers so the student can insert them.
The final side of the series contains a quiz with mixed-up
multiplication fact problems.   Learning can be fun for both
fast and slow achievers.

Sy 164   Six wonderful records of facts: addition, subtraction,
multiplication, division. Canoga Park, Cal.: John D.
Caddy, 1960. (phonodisc--33 rpm)
Designed to challenge the children to clinch the memori-
zation of the facts.   Provides a quick, easy method for
diagnosing children's difficulties with the facts and for
group or individual practice in addition, subtraction, multiplication, and division facts.   Very good for remedial work
with the facts in the upper grades.   Includes charts and
teacher's manual.

Sy 165   Spearing, Judith. Ghosts who went to school. New York:
Atheneum, 1966.
Mortimer and Wilbur Temple are two young ghosts who
want more than anything else to go to school.   When they
do, the teachers are dismayed and confused, and the children are greatly amused, and Willie suddenly can make
good grades in arithmetic and spelling.

Sy 166   Stonaker, Frances Benson.   Famous mathematicians.
Philadelphia: Lippincott, 1966.
Do you ever wonder about the beginnings of mathematics?
Read about great men who helped create our mathematical
systems of today: Euclid, Archimedes, Aryabhatta, Al-
Khivarisma, Descartes, Newton, Lagrange, Gauss, Galois,
von Neumann, Wiener.

Sy 167   Teaching children mathematics through games, rhythms
and stunts. Freeport, N.Y.: Education Activities, n.d.
(records)

Teaches mathematic skills and concepts to children.
The records contain 21 selections composed of games,
rhythms and stunts in which various mathematical skills
and concepts are inherent. During the process of parti-
cipating in these motivating and enjoyable physical activities,
the learning of the mathematics skills and concepts becomes a part of the child's physical reality.

Sy 168   Using modern math. Chicago: Society for Visual Educa-
          tion, 1964. (filmstrip)
          A complete step-by-step progressive sequence of instruc-
          tion, based on the principles of the new math. This set
          develops concepts of using and understanding numbers 1-
          12, introduces sets, number symbols and names, and pre-
          sents comparison of increasing and decreasing numbers.

Sy 169   Why study mathematics. San Francisco: Gateway Produc-
          tions, 1964. (16mm)
          Pictures common situations in which a knowledge of
          mathematical fundamentals is useful. Shows events in the
          day of an upper elementary boy in which time keeping,
          measure of distribution, and costs of products are encoun-
          tered. Enumerates other situations in which mathematical
          concepts and skills are necessary to satisfactory perform-
          ance.

Sy 170   Williams, Jay and Raymond Abrashkin. Danny Dunn and
          the homework machine. New York: McGraw-Hill, 1961.
          Danny and his friends find a way to get their homework
          done on Professor Bulfinch's computer. Their trouble be-
          gins when a tattletale discovers their secret.

LANGUAGE ARTS

Sy 171   Adelson, Leone. Dandelions don't bite. New York: Pan-
          theon, 1972.
          An etymology book for young readers. It has an over-
          view with specific word histories and discussion of prob-
          able beginnings of speech, onomatopoeia, related words,
          etc.

Sy 172   Applegate, Mauree. The first book of language and how
          to use it. New York: Watts, 1962.
          Discusses use of each of eight parts of speech of the
          English language, sentence structure, punctuation, para-
          graph writing and choice of words which will express mean-
          ing exactly.

Sy 173   Basic elementary English skills. New York: Educational
          Record Sales, n. d. (phonodisc)
          Presents concepts important to good language usage:
          Making a sentence; opposites; making rhymes; words that

mean about the same; two kinds of sentences.

Sy 174   Bouchard, Lois. The boy who wouldn't talk. New York:
              Doubleday, 1969.
                  Carlos, a Puerto Rican who moved to New York City,
              simply gave up talking because the boys and girls in his
              new community did not understand his language and he did
              not understand theirs. He tried pointing, nodding, making
              faces and signs, and drawing pictures. He is finally able
              to make friends with a boy who is blind; and as the two
              boys try to communicate, Carlos gives up the silence game
              and gradually begins to develop skills in speaking the local
              language.

Sy 175   Brandt, Sue. How to write a report. New York: Watts,
              1968.
                  A book editor and teacher outlines very clearly and
              simply what a report is, how to gather information for it,
              and how to organize it. Uses a different approach by first
              starting with three reports by children, then explains how
              to find the information, make bibliographies, and how to
              make an outline.

Sy 176   Cain, Margaret B. David discovers the dictionary. Chi-
              cago: Coronet, 1963.
                  Programmed text with basic instruction in use of the
              dictionary, divided into 10 sets, with 26-32 frames per set.
              Can be used independently of any dictionary. Concealed
              answers at right of questions are revealed by pulling tab
              sliding device. Slight story line adds interest for younger
              reader. Review questions conclude each set.

Sy 177   Conlon, Eileen. Studying made easy. Metuchen, N. J.:
              Scarecrow, 1967.
                  A work-and-exercise book designed to help individuals
              develop better work and study habits. Covers such library-
              related skills as parts of a textbook, using card catalogs
              and finding books in libraries but also examines how to
              identify the main idea, summarize, select a topic and nar-
              row it. Answers to be written on student's own paper;
              teacher workbook provided free to teachers.

Sy 178   Constructing reports. Chicago: Britannica Educational
              Corporation, 1954.
                  A sequential story showing how one class learns to
              translate ideas into words and finally into finished reports.
              Includes outlines, finding facts, selecting and limiting sub-
              jects.

Sy 179   Epstein, Sam. The first book of words: their family his-
              tories. New York: Watts, 1954.
                  Introduction to the study of words which presents inter-
              esting facts about their origin, how they have become part

of the English language and how their spellings and meanings have changed through the years.

Sy 180   Evans, Bergen. Word craft. Wilton, Conn.: Vocab, Inc.,
        1969. (3 phonodiscs, 2 jigsaw puzzles, 1 player; game
        --20-60 minutes)
        The records describe amusing situations using words and
their related synonyms. In response to hearing a word, the
player places the piece with correct printed word into its
proper position on the puzzle board. A clue to the piece's
position on the board is given by the word's synonyms
which are printed above and below the word's designated
area. Word Craft helps to increase vocabulary and understanding of words.

Sy 181   Give your child a headstart. New York: RCA Records,
        n.d. (record)
        Includes understanding how we read and the sounds of
letters, following directions, speaking, enlarging vocabulary, developing memory.

Sy 182   Greet, W. Cabell. My first picture dictionary. West
        Caldwell, N.J.: Lothrop, 1970.
        Defines eight hundred words by means of easy-to-understand sentences. Each word is accompanied by a picture.
Parts of speech are explained through usage only. The
words are arranged alphabetically within seven categories:
People, Animals, Story-book characters, What we do,
Things, Places and Words that help.

Sy 183   Jacobson, Helen. The first book of letter writing. New
        York: Watts, 1957.
        A how-to-do-it book for friendly letters, thank-you notes,
invitations, business letters, stationery, postage.

Sy 184   Kirkland, Elizabeth. Write it right: a handbook of homo-
        nyms. New York: Golden Press, 1968.
        A dictionary of words which sound alike but have different meanings and are not spelled alike. Words are arranged alphabetically and crossed referenced by insertion
of a dagger after homonym under which definitions are
given. The aim of this book is to help students who confuse words and misspell them.

Sy 185   Longman, Harold. Would you put your money in a sand
        bank? Fun with words. Chicago: Rand McNally, 1968.
        Why did the groceryman sue the pelican? You will find
the answer to this question in this collection which presents many riddles, silly questions, nonsense conversations,
silly poems, puns and jokes. A brief explanation of homonyms is included.

Sy 186   Nurnberg, Maxwell. Wonders in words. Englewood Cliffs,

N. J. :   Prentice-Hall, 1968.
An entertaining and enlightening discussion of the origin
and meaning of words.   In each of ten chapters the author
discusses words which have evolved from specific sources
such as: words with a geographic connection and words
connected with the names of animals, flowers, events, and
people and with ancient superstitions and prejudices.

Sy 187   Punctuation for beginners.   Chicago: Coronet, 1962.
              (16mm, 11 minutes)
          Teaches pupils why to use periods, commas and ques-
          tion marks in sentences.   Gives the use of the period in
          abbreviations and the use of the comma in dates and places.

Sy 188   Reading and language development skills.   (series) Bing-
              hamton, N. Y. :   United Transparencies, Inc. , n. d.
              (overhead transparencies)
          Contains sets geared toward developing reading and lan-
          guage skills.

Sy 189   The Study series.   Hollywood, Cal. :   Charles Cahill and
              Associates, Inc. , 1969.   (filmstrip)
          Contents: How we learn; How we study; How to take
          notes; How to find out.   This series explains that the higher
          order of animals are more capable of learning, that man
          is the only animal with the gifts of speech and the ability
          for complex abstract reasoning.

Sy 190   Using punctuation and capital letters. Holyoke, Mass. : Jam
              Handy, 1968.   (filmstrip--set of 6 filmstrips with an
              average of 22 color frames each.)
          Humorous cartoon treatments illustrate and explain the
          correct usage of punctuation and capital letters.   Contains
          numerous opportunities for class participation for practice
          and drill.   Contents: End punctuation; Capital letters; The
          comma, The apostrophe, The colon; and Italics.

Sy 191   Word magic.   (series) Lincoln, Neb. :   University of Ne-
              braska, Great Plains Instructional TV Library, n. d.
              (videotapes)
          This is an enrichment program utilizing many of the
          communicative arts.   It covers such themes as pantomime,
          good speech habits, imagination, creative writing, poetry,
          use of the dictionary, manners, vocabulary, oral reading,
          facial expressions and letter writing.

Chapter 6

DEVELOPING PEER RELATIONS

ENEMIES

Pr 1   The Bully. New York: McGraw-Hill, 1952. (black and
        white, 11 minutes, sound)
            Shows how Chick Allen, big for his age, bullies smaller
        boys into being on his side. When Chick's class has a pic-
        nic, he brings his gang, intending to spoil the picnic. Ends
        with questions as to what he and the class will do.

Pr 2   Fitzhugh, Louise. Bang bang you're dead. New York:
        Harper, 1969.
            Two episodes in which a gang of small boys occupies a
        hill and plays war but celebrates the end of the war by eat-
        ing ice cream together. Then another gang declares "real
        war" and there are "yells, screams, blood and pain." An
        interesting lesson is taught, mainly in pictures.

Pr 3   Massie, Diane Redfield. Dazzle. New York: Parents Mag-
        azine Press, 1969.
            The old adage "pride goeth before a fall" is learned the
        hard way by Dazzle, a proud peacock. This happens when
        he declares he is king of the jungle.

Pr 4   Stolz, Mary. A dog on Barkham Street. New York: Harp-
        er, 1960.
            A contemporary neighborhood story about poor Edward
        Frost who suffers because his mother won't let him have a
        dog (like the other fellows) and because he is frequently tor-
        mented by a bully, "Fatso" Martin, who lives next door.
        Uncle Josh comes to visit and brings his dog. Edward and
        the dog soon learn to love each other. Edward's friend,
        Argess, also soon learns to love the dog. Suddenly, Uncle
        Josh leaves, taking his dog with him. Sadness prevails.
        Uncle Josh appears again to tell the family how strange his
        dog acts when away from Edward and Argess. He gives the
        dog to Edward. Edward, with the help of Argess and his
        dog, soon gains status on the street.

Pr 5   Udry, Janice M. Let's be enemies. New York: Harper,
        1961.

John, annoyed because James is entirely too bossy, decides that he no longer wants him for a friend and goes to
tell him so. Instead of becoming enemies, they agree that
it would be more fun to go skating. A little treatise on
childhood friendships with illustrations that exactly suit the
story.

Pr 6   _____. Let's be enemies. Weston, Conn.: Weston
        Woods Studio, 1970. (Available as a captioned filmstrip
        or in a set of 4 filmstrips and a recording--filmstrip in
        color, 29 frs., and 33 rpm phonodisc. Correlated with
        cassette tape, 1-7/8 ips.)
        Story of two little boys who become enemies because one
        is too bossy. Then skating becomes the basis of renewed
        friendship. Based on the book of the same title.

HELPING FRIENDS

Pr 7   Adelman, Bob. On and off the street. New York: Viking,
        1970.
        The camera and the tape recorder follow two boys, Vin-
        cent and Danny, as they play, quarrel, and make up in the
        streets of their neighborhood west of Central Park, New
        York. This is the way it really happened and the imagina-
        tive dialogue is the boys' own. The impact of the book can
        best be realized if it is thoughtfully discussed with readers
        and viewers.

Pr 8   Anglund, Joan Walsh. Cowboy and his friend. New York:
        Harcourt, 1961.
        The story of a small boy cowboy and his imaginary
        friend, Bear. Whatever the small cowboy did, wherever
        he went, Bear was always with him. If the cowboy took a
        bath, Bear took one, too. If the cowboy played football,
        Bear played, too. Whatever happened, Bear was always
        there.

Pr 9   _____. Love is a special way of feeling. New York:
        Harcourt, 1960.
        The author-illustrator expresses love as "the happiness
        we feel in helping someone who needs us, the joy of being
        understood--even without words sometimes."

Pr 10   Buckley, Helen E. Michael is brave. West Caldwell, N.J.:
        Lothrop, 1971.
        Timid young Michael is afraid to go down a high slide in
        the playground. But when the teacher asks Michael to help
        a little girl who has climbed to the top of the slide and is
        too frightened to move, Michael comes to the rescue and
        forgets his own fear.

Pr 11   Cohen, Miriam. Will I have a friend? Riverside, N.J.:

Macmillan, 1967.

As Jim approaches school, his chief concern is whether he will have a friend there. For most of his first day he moves around on the edge of things until someone speaks to him and they play together.

Pr 12 Courtesy at school. Chicago: Coronet, 1956. (color--11 minutes)

Uses Jerry's misbehavior at school to illustrate that courtesy means thinking of others. Shows how being courteous helps children enjoy their work and play in the classroom, cafeteria, auditorium, hallways, and on the playground. Pictures Jerry's class working together in the creation of drawings expressing ideas of courteous behavior.

Pr 13 DeRegniers, Beatrice Schenk. May I bring a friend? New York: Atheneum, 1964.

When the king and queen invite a boy to a party, he always asks if he can bring a friend.

Pr 14 Du Blis, William Pene. Bear party. New York: Viking, 1963.

Wise Koala Bear gives a party so that friendship may be restored among the bears.

Pr 15 Flora, James. My friend Charlie. New York: Harcourt, 1964.

There are twelve short stories here all about a boy and his special friend who does funny things.

Pr 16 Hoban, Russell C. A bargain for Frances. New York: Harper, 1970.

"Be careful," Mother warns as Frances goes off to play with her friend, Thelma. Frances remembers the times that she somehow got the worst of it and she agrees to be careful. But it happens again: Frances has been yearning for a new tea set and is duped into buying an old one from Thelma, who uses the money to buy the very set Frances had wanted. But Frances uses her head and by the end of the story she has the new set as well as Thelma's agreement that it is better to be friends than to have to be careful.

Pr 17 _____. Tom and the two handles. New York: Harper, 1965.

Two boys who are best friends always have fist fights when they meet but advice from Tom's father helps to solve the problem.

Pr 18 Hutchins, Pat. Tom and Sam. Riverside, N. J.: Macmillan, 1968.

Humor abounds in this picture book story of two friends who try to outshine each other until friendship overcomes competitiveness in an unusual fashion.

Pr 19   Kantrowitz, Mildred. I wonder if Herbie's home yet. New
         York: Parents Magazine Press, 1971.
         The first-person narration is terse and authentically child-
         like. Each page of text is followed by a page of illustra-
         tions, in most cases a cartoon-type sequence of from two
         to eight pictures, depicting the immediately preceding text.
         The appealing, big-hearted little boys underline this low-
         keyed but so true story about the seriousness with which
         children take their friendships.

Pr 20   Miles, Miska. Rabbit's garden. Boston: Little, Brown,
         1967.
         Fleeing from the terror of a great earthquake, a young
         rabbit finds refuge in a garden. Here, the birds, mice,
         snails, and other small creatures become his friends. To-
         gether they face the dangers of weather, a sly yellow cat,
         and a big yelping brown dog.

Pr 21   Molloy, Anne. Girl from two miles high. New York:
         Hastings House, 1967.
         This story centers around the adjustments a thirteen-year-
         old Phoebe must make to living in Maine with her stern
         grandmother after living with her father in Peru. How Phoe-
         be successfully endures and treats the tempting offer to re-
         turn to Peru to a foster father provides not only character
         development but also a good story. This book would be use-
         ful with a child having social adjustment problems.

Pr 22   Piper, Watty. The little engine that could. Bronx, N.Y.:
         Platt, 1954.
         When the little red engine broke down, it needed help to
         get its cargo for boys and girls over the mountain. Only
         the Little Blue Engine offered its service, and doubtful at
         first, but finally with determined and confident effort pulled
         the cargo over the mountain. A simple cheerful story with
         a repetitive text that conveys the impression of a train in
         motion.

Pr 23   Powers, Virginia. Getting to know me. Burbank, Cal.:
         Cathedral Films, 1969. (filmstrips)
         A set of four filmstrips with recordings designed to il-
         lustrate through specific incidents the fine points of happy
         personal relationships: how a few words can sometimes
         clear up misunderstandings; that the way to win respect is
         by doing rather than talking, how different and similar peo-
         ple make up the world; and the importance of recognizing
         varying abilities.

Pr 24   Shy Molly joins the fun. Ann Arbor, Mich.: University of
         Michigan Audio Visual Educational Center, 1969. (16mm
         film, 15 minutes)

Molly has a social problem--she is too shy to make
friends. The classroom teacher and her peers decide to
help Molly lose some of her shyness.

Pr 25   Thayer, Jane. Andy wouldn't talk. New York: Morrow,
          1958.
        Andy can talk but is too shy until he has an exciting ad-
venture--he just has to tell about it.

Pr 26   Udry, Janice May. The moon jumpers. New York: Harper,
          1959.
        The pleasure of four children as they jump, climb, and
play in the moonlight just before bedtime. Poetic words,
luminous pictures.

Pr 27   Waber, Bernard. Nobody is perfeck. Boston: Houghton,
          1971.
        Eight brief episodes show that even best friends and sun-
ny days can have some shortcomings.

Pr 28   What do you think? Los Angeles: Churchill Films, 1969.
          (6 filmstrips, avg. 34 frs. , color)
        Presents actual photographs of situations that illustrate
childhood conflicts. Uses open-ended captioning technique
to encourage critical thinking about the differing situations
and the viewer's values. Includes the following: What do
you think about finders keepers?; What do you think about
tattling?; What do you think about lying?; What do you think
about promises?; What do you think about helping your family?; What do you think about helping your community?;
Useful for group or individual study in guidance or language
arts.

Pr 29   William, Andy, and Ramon and five friends at school.
          (series) Santa Monica, Cal.: BFA Educational Media,
          1967. (filmstrip)
        Stories of three children from different racial backgrounds
and their friends which describe their families, their neighborhoods, the community, their school, and their recreation.
Based on the book by Peter Buckley and Hortense Jones.

Pr 30   Wilson, Christopher. Hobnob. New York: Viking Press,
          1968.
        Two stubborn brothers, Hob and Nob, deprive themselves
of muffins and friendship until a wise old man teaches them
how to "give and take. "

Pr 31   Zolotow, Charlotte. My friend John. New York: Harper,
          1968.
        A picture book of two small boys who are best friends
carrying on their routine activities. Particularly interesting is the author's implication that the minor differences
which exist between the two are not a deterrent to the forma-
tion of a valid friendship.

MAKING FRIENDS

Pr 32   Anglund, Joan Walsh. A friend is someone who likes you.
        New York: Harcourt, 1958.
        This book shows how a friend can be anybody or anything.
        It talks about how to recognize or find a friend and ends on
        the comforting note that everyone in the whole world has at
        least one friend.

Pr 33   Beim, Jerrold. The smallest boy in the class. New York:
        Morrow, 1949.
        Story of a boy who proved that stature is not always
        measured in feet and inches. He was called Tiny because
        of his size until the day it was proved that he had the big-
        gest heart in the class.

Pr 34   Belpré, Pura. Santiago. New York: Warne, 1969.
        Santiago is uprooted from his home in Puerto Rico and
        taken to New York. Worse still, he had to leave behind his
        beloved pet hen, Selina. And Ernie, whom he wants to im-
        press, won't believe what he tells him. A beautiful picture-
        story of a boy torn between two worlds.

Pr 35   Bonsall, Crosby. It's mine! a greedy book. New York:
        Harper, 1964.
        Mabel Ann and Patrick are good friends until the subject
        of sharing comes up. Then each thinks "what's yours is
        mine." Each wants all the toys, but they finally learn the
        social benefits of sharing and each grows up a little. Good
        illustrations help tell the story.

Pr 36   Cameron, Eleanor. Room made of windows. Boston: Lit-
        tle, Brown, 1971.
        This story is about Julia who centers her world around
        herself and her small intense world. Julia's ambition is to
        be a writer and this story shows how she matures and gets
        a bit of understanding and wisdom.

Pr 37   Carle, Eric. Do you want to be my friend? New York:
        Crowell, 1971.
        The only text is the title question at the start and a shy
        "yes" at the close. The pictures do the rest as the helpful
        mouse overtakes one large creature after another. With
        each encounter, the mouse sees an interesting tail; turn the
        page and there is a huge lion, or a malevolent fox, or a
        peacock, and then, at last, another wee mouse.

Pr 38   Cohen, Miriam. Will I have a friend? Riverside, N. J. :
        Macmillan, 1967.
        Jim is very apprehensive about his first day in school and
        asks his father, "Will I have a friend." The other children
        are busy playing when Jim gets to school. All the children
        seem to be friends and no one pays any attention to Jim.

But at rest time, Paul notices Jim and soon they are friends.

Pr 39   Cornish, Sam. Your hand in mine. New York: Harcourt,
             1970.
             Sam is a likable, lovable little boy living in a black
         neighborhood. He scribbles poems on sidewalks and fences
         --secrets between himself and whoever may see them. A
         crisis in his classroom shows that someone does like him
         and he gets to walk home, hand-in-hand with that someone.

Pr 40   De Leeuw, Adele. Donny. New York: Golden Press, 1961.
             A boy forgets his shyness and makes some friends while
         caring for stray animals.

Pr 41   Ets, Marie Hall. Play with me. New York: Viking, 1955.
             A little girl is looking for a playmate and tries to catch
         woodland animals, but they all run away. When she sat
         down and was quiet, they all came to her.

Pr 42   Friends and neighbors. New York: Sterling Educational
             Films, 1970. (16mm film, 10 minutes)
             Depicts that parents and teachers are not always present
         to encourage good behavior and children must independently
         learn how to treat friends and neighbors, learning to live
         together--to act on more than mere courtesy is the subject
         of this film.

Pr 43   Hecate, Jennifer MacBeth. William McKinley and me,
             Elizabeth. New York: Atheneum, 1967.
             Take two lonely, sensitive children. Make one a witch
         and the other an apprentice. Stir in a mean little girl
         named Cynthia, a pair of great relatives and a toad named
         Hilary Ezra, and you have a brew that makes a beautiful
         tale of friendship.

Pr 44   Hoban, Russell. Best friends for Frances. New York:
             Harper, 1969.
             Frances won't play with her younger sister, Gloria, be-
         cause she's too little and "not much good except for crying."
         Albert won't play with Frances because she is a girl. In
         retaliation, Frances plans an elaborate "No Boys" picnic
         with Gloria, but soon all three become friends. They are
         all three badgers.

Pr 45   How do you feel? Los Angeles: Churchill Films, 1969.
             (6 filmstrips, average 36 frs. each, color)
             Presents live photography showing both positive and nega-
         tive actions in different situations, and captions that are
         thought provoking questions for viewer discussion to help
         him gain a better understanding of himself and others. In-
         cludes the following filmstrips: How do you feel about your
         community?; How do you feel about your home and family?;
         How do you feel about other children?; How do you feel

about being alone? Useful for group and individual study in guidance and language arts.

Pr 46   How friends are made. Hollywood: Shepherd Menken (see
          Aims...) 1968. (16mm film, 11 minutes, color)
          Describes the experiences of an elementary grade boy as
          he makes a friend. It reveals some of the boy's own wonder
          and reflection on the event.

Pr 47   Is anyone to blame. Chicago: Coronet Films, 1970. (film-
          strip with captions)
          Presents a different point of view in which children can
          see themselves in relation to others and to situations. It
          is from the Two Sides to Every Story Series.

Pr 48   Jaynes, Ruth. Friends, friends, friends. Glendale, Cal.:
          Bowmar, 1967.
          A simple story of multi-ethnic friendships in an urban
          setting.

Pr 49   Kamerman, Sylvia E. Little plays for little players: fifty
          non-royalty plays for children. Boston: Plays, Inc.,
          1969.
          Simple-to-produce plays for the primary grades and often
          intangible ideas such as the importance of relationships,
          etc., can be effectively taught through dramatic means.

Pr 50   Krasilovsky, Phyllis. A shy little girl. Boston: Houghton,
          1970.
          Shy little Anne always did everything by herself until the
          new girl came to school.

Pr 51   Little citizens friendship. (series) Burbank, Cal.: Cathe-
          dral Films, 1966. (6 filmstrips, average 33 frs.; 3
          phonodiscs, 6s., 12 in., 33 rpm)
          Simple short stories for developing good character traits
          and better citizenship habits. Contents: Raggedy Elf
          (friendship); Mighty Hunters (Indian legends and the stars);
          Boy (theme of home based on Lincoln); Bike Behavior (safe-
          ty); How the Birds Got Their Color (theme of honesty);
          Little Star (theme of obedience).

Pr 52   Russell, Solveig Paulson. Motherly Smith and Brother Bim-
          bo. Nashville: Abingdon, 1971.
          The alley cat decides he will fatten up the scrawny mouse
          before he eats him. However, in protecting the mouse from
          his fellow alley cats a strange friendship develops.

Pr 53   Schick, Eleanor. 5A and 7B. Riverside, N.J.: Macmillan,
          1967.
          Although Sandy and Roby live in the same tall apartment
          building, they have never met. At last they meet, play to-
          gether and become very good friends. They even "wish on
          the very same star."

Pr 54   Simon, Shirley. <u>Best friend.</u> West Caldwell, N. J. : Loth-
         rop, 1964.
         The question of whether it is better for a girl to have
one best friend or more good friends is treated realistically
in a family story with considerable humor.

Pr 55   Slobodkin, Louis. <u>One is good, but two are better.</u> New
         York: Vanguard, 1956.
         Uses intriguing examples to give children a sense of the
values of companionship.

Pr 56   Steptoe, John. <u>Stevie.</u> New York: Harper, 1969.
         That old crybaby Stevie is a real pest when he moves in
with Robert's family and tags after him. Robert is lone-
some when Stevie leaves and says maybe he wasn't that bad
after all. "Stevie was a nice little guy. He was kinda like
a little brother. "

Pr 57   <u>That's not fair.</u> Pleasantville, N. Y. : Guidance Associates,
         1972. (2 filmstrips, color; phonodisc, 2s. , 12 in. , 33
         rpm)
         Cartoon characters present two open-ended situations in-
volving fairness and equity, having the views to decide what
is fair.

Pr 58   Thompson, Vivian L. <u>Sad day glad day.</u> New York: Holi-
         day House, 1962.
         It is sad when a child moves away and leaves his old
friends, but it is a glad day when he makes new ones.

Pr 59   Wilson, Christopher B. <u>Hobnob.</u> New York: Viking, 1968.
         Two stubborn brothers, Hob and Nob, deprive themselves
of muffins and friendship until a wise old man teaches them
how to "give and take. "

Pr 60   Woods, Betty. <u>My box and string.</u> New York: Scholastic,
         1970.
         Here a boy is so selfish he has to use all his time guard-
ing his boxes from all the people who want to share them.

Pr 61   Woolley, Catherine. <u>Cathy's little sister.</u> New York: Mor-
         row, 1964.
         Chris learns the value of making friends of her own age
instead of trying to join her older sister's crowd.

Pr 62   <u>You Got Mad--Are You Glad.</u> Pleasantville, N. Y. : Guid-
         ance Associates, 1970. (Part I, 52 frames; Part II, 48
         frames, sound, filmstrip)
         Analyzes the ways in which hostility is expressed in a
group of young children and offers alternatives of dealing
with anger. Pictures children starting a fight over which
ballgame to play and shows how an adult takes pictures and
later shows the children their hostile expressions and ges-

tures.   Concludes with an open-ended invitation for students
to express their feelings.

Pr 63   Zolotow, Charlotte.   New friend.   New York: Abelard-
          Schuman, 1968.
               A little girl loses her best friend to someone else but
          finds ways to overcome her hurt.   This book is easy for
          young children to understand.

Pr 64   _____. A tiger called Thomas.   West Caldwell, N. J. :
          Lothrop, 1963.
               A Halloween costume gives a youngster who is new in a
          neighborhood enough self-confidence to make friends.

Intermediate

ENEMIES

Pr 65   Batcher, Julie Forsyth.   A cap for Mul Chand.   New York:
          Harcourt, 1950.
               This boy, who lives in a mud-walled house in an Indian
          village, works to earn the money for a cap to wear on a
          trip to Bombay.   But he has to cope with the village bully
          before he can go.

Pr 66   Burch, Robert.   D. J. 's worst enemy.   New York: Viking,
          1965.
               D. J. Madison and his sidekick, Nutty, try their best to
          scare Clare May, D. J. 's older syster, with an imitation of
          the old bull from the lower meadow.   The plan backfires
          when D. J. 's younger brother, Renfroe, manages to scare
          them.   Renfroe gets in D. J. 's way once too often, however;
          and when Renfroe ends up in the hospital, D. J. decides to
          reform.   Here is a boy who discovers his worse enemy is
          not family or friends but himself.

Pr 67   _____. Queenie Peavy.   New York: Viking, 1966.
               Queenie, rebel, non-conformist, lives in Georgia in the
          1930's.   Her mother works all day and her father is a
          "jail-bird. "   She is warmhearted, intelligent and fast becom-
          ing the school and community "outlaw. "   She has idealized
          her father out of reality.   She is constantly being teased by
          the children in her community because her father is in
          prison.   She is saved from the reformatory by the school
          principal and the local judge.   Queenie slowly learns that
          she can live outside the shadow of the jail.

Pr 68   Lexau, Joan M.   A kite over Tenth Avenue.   Garden City,
          N. Y. : Doubleday, 1967.
               Tim, his sister, and their mother live on New York's
          Tenth Avenue in 1900.   Tim gets the long awaited Chinese
          kite for his birthday.   When at last it comes, the day is

ruined and then saved by a rough, older boy.

Pr 69   Rich, Louise Dickerson. Three of a kind. Philadelphia: Lippincott, 1970.

Until Sally, an orphan and ward of the state, came under the foster care of the Coopers in Maine, she had never really known a real home. But the arrival of Benjie, the Coopers silent grandson marred her happiness as their attention centered upon him. Gradually as Sally learned to care for Benjie, she and a homeless kitten played important parts in bringing about his emergence into the real world.

Pr 70   Rinkoff, Barbara. The watchers. Westminster, Md.: Knopf, 1972.

"What can you expect from a boy whose parents fight all the time?" the neighbors ask. Chris Blake knows, bitterly, what they mean, and he himself tells the story of his troubles: acrimony at home, censure at school, and no friends except the new kid, Sanford, a real loser. Weak and uncoordinated, Sanford is overprotected by his parents and bullied by other boys, and his loyalty to Chris, who defends him, is unshakable. Little by little, Sanford learns independence and gains courage.

Pr 71   Sachs, Marilyn. Peter and Veronica. New York: Doubleday, 1969.

Peter is twelve--bright, popular and carefully watched over by his mother. Veronica is thirteen--a tomboy and bully, with no real friends besides Peter. Unkempt but sharp, Veronica lives with her little brother, sister, and mother, who is divorced. When Peter is about to be bar mitzvahed, he quarrels bitterly with his mother and defies his father to invite Veronica to the ceremony. But Veronica does not come. Suddenly, the friendship is in trouble. Both Peter and Veronica learn a lot about true friendship.

Pr 72   _____. Veronica Ganz. New York: Doubleday, 1968.

At thirteen, Veronica, the bully of her school in the Bronx, has no friends. Afraid of being made fun of because she is so big, she has long since beaten (boys) or slapped (girls) her classmates into subservience. Then a new boy arrives. Although small, Peter is smart and he side steps Veronica's persistent attempts to pulverize him. At last the big girl and the undersized boy have a confrontation which brings some pleasant surprises for the belligerent Veronica.

Pr 73   Stolz, Mary. The bully of Barkham Street. New York: Harper, 1963.

Martin Hastings, large for his age, unhappy, at odds with his family and peers, and with a quick temper, has the deserved reputation of being the local bully and fat boy of the small town where he lives. He is unable to maintain satisfactory relations with the only boy who tries to be friends

and he bullies the boy next door. After he starts to accept
people as they are and does not always try to make excuses
for his failures, Martin begins to establish friendlier relations with his peers.

HELPING FRIENDS

Pr 74   Beim, Lorraine. Two is a team. New York: Harcourt,
           1945.
           Ted, a Negro boy, and Paul, a white boy, are the same
        age and same size. They play happily together until they
        quarrel over making a scooter. After trying to work alone,
        they run into more trouble and discover that only through
        cooperation in work and play can they clear up their diffi-
        culties.

Pr 75   Being friends. Santa Monica, Cal.: BFA Educational
           Media, 1969. (16mm film, 9 minutes)
           Teaches the meaning of friendship. Shows that people
        may disagree and still remain friends. Emphasizes trust
        and helping each other.

Pr 76   Belpré, Pura. Santiago. New York: Warne, 1969.
           Santiago is uprooted from his home in Puerto Rico and
        taken to New York. Worse still, he had to leave behind
        his beloved pet hen, Selina. And Ernie, whom he wants
        to impress, won't believe him. A beautiful picture-story of
        a boy torn between two worlds.

Pr 77   Bishop, Claire. All alone. New York: Viking, 1953.
           Two boys learn the value of cooperation when facing
        danger.

Pr 78   Brink, Carol Ryrie. Two are better than one. Riverside,
           N.J.: Macmillan, 1968.
           A story within a story! Two little girls in Warsaw, Ida-
        ho in the early 1900s have a wonderful year in the sixth
        grade when one receives a pair of "pocket dolls." The dolls
        bring their own special magic and the girls together write
        a novel about the dolls, "The Romantic Perils of Lester and
        Lynette." And the third story occurs sixty years later!
        Different from the author's work and with special appeal.

Pr 79   Calhoun, Mary. Honestly, Katie John! New York: Viking,
           1960.
           As Katie John begins the sixth grade, everything appears
        to go wrong. She forms a boy haters club but then the
        members desert! She finally learns what she must do in
        order to become a teenager and regain her good friend, Ed-
        win.

Pr 80   Carlson, Natalie Savage. Empty schoolhouse. New York:

Harper, 1965.

Older sister Emma tells the story of the year when Lullah goes to the parochial school with the white children. The ups and downs of her friendship with Oralee, the family outings which Emma arranges, and the menace of the two ominous strangers at the motel where Emma works form the background for this story of life in Louisiana today.

Pr 81   Clymer, Eleanor Lowenton. The latch key club. New York: McKay, 1959.

One of the most serious problems of modern city life is that of "latchkey" children, the theme of this book. The author has managed to present the problem and one neighborhood's solution in a story that is fun to read and should be popular with intermediates.

Pr 82   Cornish, Sam. Your hand is mine. New York: Harcourt, 1970.

Sam is a likable, lovable little boy living in a black neighborhood. He scribbles poems on sidewalks and fences-- secrets between himself and whoever may see them. A crisis in his classroom shows that someone does like him and he gets to walk home, hand-in-hand with that someone.

Pr 83   Curry, Jane Louise. Daybreakers. New York: Harcourt, 1970.

Two black children and a white, in a West Virginia mining town, become "travelers in time." They move back to a primitive era when their land was peopled by an alien tribe, with weird rituals and artifacts. The problems of two worlds meet and the children help to resolve them.

Pr 84   First things first. (series) Pleasantville, N.Y.: Guidance Associates, n.d. (filmstrip)

This seven-part series presents a variety of ways to understand and improve interpersonal relations. The series includes: You Got Mad, Are You Glad: What do you expect of others?; Who do you think you are?; That's no fair!; The Trouble with Truth; What Happens Between People.

Pr 85   Fitzhugh, Louise. Harriet the spy. New York: Harper, 1964.

Harriet is an urban, modern, nonconformist rebel with high potential. She carries a notebook to record her spy activities--classmates and neighbors are regular victims. Her caustic comments are found in her lost notebook by some of her classmates, who become indignant and make her an outcast. Her behavior goes from "bad" to "outrageous." Her rebellion comes to a conclusion that leads to much discussion.

Pr 86   Friedman, Frieda. Ellen and the gang. New York: Morrow, 1963.

Ellen is lonely and insecure and as a result becomes involved with a group of juvenile delinquents. But with her family and younger children on the playground, she pulls herself out of this dilemma.

Pr 87   Friermood, Elisabeth. Whispering willows. New York: Doubleday, 1964.
A beautifully told story of the realistic friendship of two girls of different races.

Pr 88   Garfield, James B. Follow my leader. New York: Viking, 1967.
A boy who has lost his sight once again resumes a normal life with the help of his guide dog and friends. His dog leader and friends develop a secret code in Braille.

Pr 89   Greene, Constance C. A girl called Al. New York: Viking, 1969.
Told in the first person in a disarmingly casual, amusing style, the story deals with a few months in the lives of the two seventh grade girls. The narrator (never actually named) is a forthright, good-humored child whose family life is stable and secure. Her best friend, Al (short for Alexandra), whose parents are divorced, lives in an apartment down the hall with her busy distracted working mother. Al--a bright, overfat girl--proudly tries to be a "nonconformist" to hide the hurt and loneliness.

Pr 90   Inyard, Gene. Orange October. New York: Watts, 1968.
Jenny is happy to show her new friend and neighbor the school. Perhaps that is why she rushes through the building the first day. Jenny gets off to a bad start with the new teacher but things grow even worse. The next day Jenny spills ink, the non-washable kind! An everyday story for those who enjoy here-and-now.

Pr 91   Jackson, Jesse. Call me Charley. New York: Harper, 1945.
Charley, twelve, was the only Negro boy in the community of Arlington Heights. This is the story of the ups and downs in Charley's friendship with young Tom Hamilton and his family, of his progress in school, and of the adventures the boys share. The author takes no soapbox, does no preaching. But the hurt and bewilderment of a boy who is treated differently because of the color of his skin gets across to the reader with an impact he is not likely to forget.

Pr 92   Jard, Philip. Tony's steamer. Boston: Little, Brown, 1960.
Tony finds an abandoned steamer, explores it, and makes it his "secret place." Eventually three boys invade his private world and slowly wreck the steamer. Fire breaks out

on the steamer and all the boys work together to put it out.
Good portrayal of boys from mixed races learning to work
and play together.

Pr 93   Keats, Ezra Jack. A letter to Amy. New York: Harper,
          1968.
          Peter has invited not only boys to his party but also a
girl named Amy. But will she come when he has accidentally knocked her down?

Pr 94   Lenski, Lois. Texas tomboy. Philadelphia: Lippincott,
          1950.
          Charlotte Clarissa (better known as Charlie Boy) lived in
Texas at the turn of the century. She was a real tomboy
and, at that time of the story, going through a state of
thoughtlessness and selfishness that is often typical of nine-
year-olds. As the year progresses and she helps keep the
ranch going in spite of a drought, she comes to a realization of the needs and rights of others and begins to grow up.

Pr 95   Let's share with others. Chicago: Coronet, n. d. (color,
          11 minutes, sound)
          Follows Jimmy as he learns how and when to share.
When he tries to operate a lemonade stand without any form
of sharing, he learns that sharing is frequently necessary.
The postman points out other instances of sharing.

Pr 96   Mathis, Sharon Bell. Sidewalk story. New York: Viking,
          1971.
          An affecting easy-to-read story of a persistent little black
girl to whom friendship means caring and helping a friend
in trouble. Upset because her best friend, Tanya, and her
family are being evicted and their belongings piled on the
sidewalk, and frustrated by her own mother's unwillingness
to become involved, Lilly Etta phones first the police and
then the newspaper for help, and in the night creeps out to
cover the things with sheets and blankets--and herself--to
protect them from the wind and rain. Enhanced by several
sensitive double-spread paintings in black and white.

Pr 97   Neville, Emily. Berries Goodman. New York: Harper,
          1965.
          The Goodman family move to the suburbs and nine-year-
old Berries finds his nearest playmate a girl, Sandra. She
is a year older than Berries, feels superior in many ways,
and undertakes to teach him prejudices against Jews. Fortu-
nately, with the help of his older brother, Berries resists.

Pr 98   Orgel, Doris. Next door to Xanadu. New York: Harper,
          1969.
          Patricia admits it--she's fat. The boys call her "fatsy
Patsy" and she has no close friends. What she wants more
than anything in the world is a bosom pal. And along comes

Dorothy Rapport, just her age and right across the hall!
The progress of their friendship is rapid, and Patricia is
smitten with anguish when she learns that Dorothy is going
to move away. But friendship has brought a measure of
self-confidence: Patricia pulls herself together and makes
their last few days cheerful.

Pr 99   Rinkoff, Barbara. Member of the gang. New York: Crown,
         1968.
              Thirteen-year-old Woodie wants to be a member of the
         Scorpions. This gang of five would-be toughs steal and bat-
         tle the Tops, a rival group. During a rumble between the
         gangs, Woodie sees his friend Sonny stabbed. When all the
         other flee, Woodie remains with his friend.

Pr 100   Robinson, Veronica. David in silence. Philadelphia: Lip-
         pincott, 1965.
              When twelve-year-old David moves into a small English
         town, he encounters varied reactions among the neighborhood
         children. Some are friendly but others are downright cruel
         --for David is totally deaf. One of the boys, Michael, takes
         a special interest and learns sign language. The other chil-
         dren are won over, too, and admire David for his courage
         when he tackles something no one else dared do.

Pr 101   Rugh, Belle Dorman. Lost waters. Boston: Houghton,
         1967.
              Carol and her cousins, Mark and Andy, are vacationing
         with her parents in a village in the Lebanese mountains
         where they make friends with several native children. They
         all get along so well that the Americans cannot understand
         why there is such long-standing enmity between two neigh-
         boring villages--until they at last discover a clue to the
         mystery and resolve it.

Pr 102   Shura, Mary Francis. Runaway home. Westminster, Md.:
         Knopf, 1965.
              Eleven-year-old Mike has much difficulty adjusting when
         his family is forced to move to Colorado from Kansas but
         all ends well for him. The behavior of each character and
         most of the situations are realistic enough to permit the
         reader's identification.

Pr 103   Stolz, Mary. Wonderful, terrible time. New York: Harp-
         er, 1967.
              Mady and Sue Ellen live in the same apartment house in
         a city in a neighborhood of which Sue Ellen's father says,
         "You name it and we got it." The two girls spend two weeks
         at a summer camp which they find both wonderful and ter-
         rible. This book deals with the topic of racial understand-
         ing.

Pr 104   When to be a leader, when to be a follower. Mahwah, N. J.:

Troll Associates, n. d.   (filmstrip)
Shows the importance of working with others as both a
leader and a follower.

Pr 105   Who cares. New York: McGraw-Hill, 1968.   (film)
Dramatizes a story about a little boy who would rarely
smile and was always grouchy because he felt he was not
liked.   His classmates discovered that he was a fine mu-
sician and helped him to realize that others did care for
him after all.

Pr 106   Zolotow, Charlotte. The hating book. New York: Harper,
1969.
A story about a girl who hated her friend because she
was ignoring her.   She was afraid and too proud to ask
her why.   She finally did ask her and found out it was a
misunderstanding, which having been left unattended was
interfering with their friendship.

MAKING FRIENDS

Pr 107   Alcock, Gudrun. Turn the next corner. West Caldwell,
N. J.: Lothrop, 1969.
"My dad won't be found guilty of embezzlement, he just
made a mistake," figures twelve-year-old Ritchie Osborne;
but Mr. Osborne is guilty and goes to prison.   Then
Ritchie and his mother sell everything to repay the stolen
money and move to a less exclusive neighborhood.   There
Ritchie learns that race isn't important in friendship for
there are good and bad among all people, and Slugger
Slater, a black boy, becomes his best friend.

Pr 108   Anderson, C. W. A pony for Linda. Riverside, N. J.:
Macmillan, 1951.
Linda loves ponies and when she was seven she was
given Daisy for her very own.   This is the story how she
cared for Daisy and how she learned to ride.   At a local
horse show she shared top honors with another Linda and
found a new friend.

Pr 109   Barnes, Nancy. The wonderful year. New York: Messner, 1946.
Frightened and forlorn when her family moves from
Kansas to Colorado, Ellen has an expectedly happy, wonderful year.   In the gay, natural story, she finds she
loves living in a tent in the strange new country, helping
around the ranch, making friends with an English boy,
learning to ride a long coveted bicycle and becoming "one
of the crowd" when she goes to school in Mesa.

Pr 110   Beim, Jerrold. Swimming hole. New York: Morrow,
1951.

The new boy who doesn't want to swim with anyone who is colored has no fun until he learns that color does not matter. A small picture book that humorously ridicules "color prejudice" in such a way that the youngest child can understand its point.

Pr 111   Bishop, Claire Huchet. <u>All alone.</u> New York: Viking, 1953.
           Marcel and his friend, Pierre, herd their family's cows high on the slope of a mountain in the French Alps. Their experiences illustrate the fact that "there is a better way of life than each man for himself."

Pr 112   Bishop, Curtis. <u>Little league heroes.</u> Philadelphia: Lippincott, 1960.
           Joel, the first Negro boy to win a place on the little league team in West Austin, Texas, is encouraged by his father, coached by the officials and finally earns acceptance by the team.

Pr 113   Bouchare, Lois K. <u>Boy who wouldn't talk.</u> New York: Doubleday, 1969.
           Carlos learns rapidly and understands the English he hears, but is so homesick for Puerto Rico that he refuses to speak. Instead, he uses sign language and pictures to communicate. This changes when he meets Ricky, a blind boy. Unlike the other children, who question a boy who doesn't talk, Ricky becomes Carlos' friend. Carlos does talk to Ricky.

Pr 114   Bradbury, Bianca. <u>The loner.</u> Boston: Houghton, 1970.
           His older brother, Mal, got along with everybody, always was sure of himself, seemed to be a natural at any sport he tried. No wonder twelve-year-old Jay resented Mal. Jay didn't really need money, but he was delighted when he got a job as a dockboy at the summer resort. Nobody missed him since he was always alone anyway, and Jay kept his work a secret. As he gained confidence and made new friends through his job at the marina, Jay began to realize that Mal wasn't so bad.

Pr 115   Brown, Margaret. <u>That Ruby.</u> Chicago: Reilly and Lee, 1969.
           The first day of school in Newark everyone says Ruby looks nice. Bonnie, caught staring at her, is challenged by Ruby. Finally everyone learns to like Ruby except Bonnie, who continues to consider her a troublemaker. After Ruby proves she is a brave girl and one who really wishes people well, Bonnie gives her a chance. A well done story of rivalry between girls in a public school sixth grade.

Pr 116   Carlson, Natalie Savage. <u>Ann Aurelia and Dorothy.</u> New York: Harper, 1968.

Ann Aurelia thinks Mrs. Hicken is the best mother she
has had since her own went away. She and Dorothy become friends on the playground, make a wondrous mixture
of lemonade, get involved in a mix-up at the supermarket
and even get Mrs. Hicken to join the P. T. A. A touching
story of friendship and restored family life.

Pr 117   Chastain, Mayde. Bright days. New York: Harcourt,
         1952.
         A girl learns to accept others without being unduly in-
         fluenced by them.

Pr 118   Cleary, Beverly. Beezus and Ramona. New York: Mor-
         row, 1955.
         Nine-year-old Beatrice Quimby, known as Beezus, finds
         her four-year-old sister, Ramona, a major problem in her
         life. Ramona makes herself the center of attention and is
         constantly praised by other people for her "cute" ways and
         her imagination. On her tenth birthday, after Ramona has
         ruined two birthday cakes, Beezus tells her mother and
         Aunt Beatrice her problem. This leads the two to disclose
         that when they were children they had similar problems.
         With the knowledge that she need not always feel love for
         Ramona, Beezus becomes more relaxed and adopts a new
         attitude toward her. Relationships between sisters are
         rarely smooth and many girls are faced with similar situa-
         tions.

Pr 119   _____. Ellen Tebbits. New York: Morrow, 1951.
         An eight-year-old girl struggles to build a friendship.

Pr 120   Cretan, Gladys Y. Sunday for Sona. West Caldwell,
         N. J.: Lothrop, 1973.
         A lovely, simple story of a young girl who is torn be-
         tween loyalty to her traditional family Sundays and her
         desire to go sailing with her newfound friends.

Pr 121   Finding a friend. Hollywood, Cal.: Charles Cahill and
         Associates, 1970. (16mm film, color, 11 minutes)
         A ten-year-old moves to a new neighborhood and seeks
         new friends.

Pr 122   Fitzhugh, Louise. Harriet the spy. New York: Harper,
         1964.
         This is the story of an eleven-year-old girl's alienation
         from friends and classmates.

Pr 123   Friends. Los Angeles: Churchill Films, 1972. (16mm,
         color, 18 minutes)
         A story about the friendship between Nancy, an extro-
         verted, impatient girl, and her vulnerable best friend.
         Illustrates what happens to feelings when Nancy goes off
         to play with another girl.

Pr 124   Good sportsmanship. Chicago: Coronet, 1950. (16mm,
          11 minutes, color)
          Joe and Bill learn the rules for good sportsmanship while
          they are on the basketball floor, at home, in the classroom,
          and with friends on the street.

Pr 125   Greene, Constance C. A girl called Al. New York: Vik-
          ing, 1969.
          Told in the first person in a disarmingly casual, amus-
          ing style, the story deals with a few months in the lives
          of the two seventh-grade girls. The narrator (never actu-
          ally named) is a forthright, good-humored child whose fam-
          ily life is stable and secure. Her best friend, Al (short
          for Alexandra), whose parents are divorced, lives with
          her busy, distracted working mother. Al--a bright, over-
          fat girl--proudly tries to be a nonconformist to hide the
          hurt and loneliness. Their unconventional friendship with
          Mr. Richards, who works as assistant superintendent of
          the building, draws the girls together.

Pr 126   Hall, Marjory. Bright red ribbon. New York: Funk and
          Wagnalls, 1961.
          When a boy takes an interest in Beverly, she learns the
          importance of neatness.

Pr 127   Jones, Adrienne. Sail Calypso. Boston: Little, Brown,
          1968.
          Two boys, Clay and Paul, are forced to come to terms
          with each other over a sailboat they have found. Each
          thinks of the boat as being his boat and identifies himself
          with it in a special way. But the boat has to be worked
          on before it can sail and the boys soon discover that they
          have to cooperate.

Pr 128   Keeton, Elizabeth B. Friday nights and Robert. Boston:
          Little, Brown, 1973.
          A story of Esmeralda, her trials and tribulations at
          school, her efforts to be friends with the town girls and
          especially with Robert, the boy from the next farm who
          comes to visit every Friday night. When she finally gets
          an invitation to spend the night at the home of one of the
          girls, it turns into a bitter-sweet triumph.

Pr 129   Kloperman, Libby M. Different girl. New York: Lion,
          1969.
          Long the only girl of her age on her street, Betty Lou
          Bowers looks forward to the new neighbors who will live
          next door and hopefully have a daughter. Betty's dream
          comes true but her new neighbor is black! This picture
          of race relations in a small college town shows that care-
          less expressions and hidden feelings can create fertile
          ground for problems to grow in.

Pr 130   Lattimore, Eleanor F.   A smiling face.   New York: Mor-
          row, 1973.
          The arrival of a new family is an exciting event for
          children on most any street.   But when a Negro family
          moves into an all-white housing development on the edge
          of Freedom, Kentucky, eight-year-old Grace and her
          friend, Beth Ann, are disturbed by the hostility directed
          toward the new neighbors.

Pr 131   Little, Jean.   Look through my window.   New York: Harp-
          er, 1970.
          Emily's very predictable life as an only child suddenly
          changes when her family moves into an 18-room house and
          her cousins--those wild Southerland kids--come to stay with
          them.   She discovers that life in a big family can be re-
          warding if sometimes exasperating, and after meeting Kate,
          she discovers both the hurts and joys of true friendship.

Pr 132   _____.   One to grow on.   Boston: Little, Brown, 1969.
          Janie Chisholm is trying to grow up but she attempts
          to get attention by lying and exaggerating.   Then she meets
          Lisa Daniels and thinks she has found a friend, but Lisa is
          only using Janie to get to know her brother, Rob.   When
          Janie's godmother takes her to a beautiful island camp for
          the summer, Janie begins to grow up and to find real
          friends.

Pr 133   _____.   Spring begins in March.   Boston: Little, Brown,
          1966.
          The story of Sally's sister, Meg, who cannot get along
          with anyone but her best friend.   When Meg's teacher gives
          her a warning about her poor grades, she must accept help
          from the people she has resented most.

Pr 134   Lovelace, Maud Hart.   Valentine's day.   New York:
          Crowell, 1966.
          The author gives an excellent portrayal of how a little
          girl feels in a new neighborhood and a new school when
          she has not been there long enough to get acquainted be-
          fore Valentine's Day.   The fact that Janie is a Negro (only
          in the realistic pencil illustrations is the reader so in-
          formed) is beside the point.   At school there is a Valen-
          tine Box, and Janie wonders if she will receive any cards.
          It is a snowy day, and on the way back to school after
          lunch Janie helps a classmate rescue her Valentines from
          a gusty wind.   This makes for a happy and natural ending.

Pr 135   Making friends.   Santa Monica: BFA Educational Media,
          1950.   (three filmstrips, 30 frs. each)
          Discusses desirable personality and behavior traits.   Il-
          lustrates important aspects of human relationships and
          shows the value of friends in the home school.

Pr 136   Neville, Emily. It's like this, Cat. New York: Harper,
                 1963.
                 Fourteen-year-old Dave Mitchell, growing up in New
            York City, tells of his affection for a tomcat and his first
            friendship with a girl.

Pr 137   _____ . Seventeenth Street gang. New York: Harper,
                 1966.
                 When Hollis moves to their block, the Seventeenth Street
            gang makes it difficult for him to get acquainted. Minnow,
            the imaginative one, leads the others in a practical joke on
            Hollis which backfires on her so that she instead of he is
            the one left out. The shifting of friendships among this
            mixed group of city boys and girls provides a plot that
            will hold the reader's interest.

Pr 138   Nordstrom, Ursula. Secret language. New York: Harper,
                 n. d.
                 In this story of life at boarding school, Vicky overcomes
            her shyness when she makes friends with Martha and they
            share a "secret language. "

Pr 139   Orgel, Doris. Next door to Xanadu. New York: Harper,
                 1969.
                 Patricia needs a friend and hopes a girl will move in
            next door and become her friend. The boys in her apart-
            ment house call her "fatsy Patsy. " When Dorothy moves
            in, they do become friends and Patricia also learns how
            to be a friend.

Pr 140   Panetta, George. Shoeshine boys. New York: Grosset
                 and Dunlap, 1971.
                 MacDougal Thompson and Tony Boccaccio develop a firm
            friendship and even form a partnership. They enter the
            shoeshine business. MacDougal has been in business for
            some time. Tony learns from MacDougal but still gets
            polish on stockings when he tries to shine shoes. Tony is
            able to offer MacDougal little until they learn to share
            each job. Each boy shines one shoe for each customer.

Pr 141   Rich, Elaine Sommers. Hannah Elizabeth. New York:
                 Harper, 1964.
                 Because she is only ten years old and the only one of
            that age in the community, Hannah Elizabeth must play
            with the boys, even if she is called Hanny Lizard, or play
            alone.

Pr 142   Reynolds, Pamela. Different kind of sister. West Cald-
                 well, N. J. : Lothrop, 1968.
                 Debbie is Sally's retarded sister. After several years
            in an institution, Debbie is returned to her family, but
            Sally is deeply concerned because she does not want her
            friends to learn of Debbie. In fact, Sally has never men-

tioned having a sister at all. A worthwhile title on the
theme of learning to accept and live with one's own family.

Pr 143   Robinson, Veronica. David in silence. Philadelphia: Lip-
         pincott, 1965.
              When twelve-year-old David moves into a small English
         town, he encounters varied reactions among neighborhood
         children. Some are friendly but others are downright cruel,
         for David is totally deaf. One of the boys, Michael, takes
         a special interest and learns sign language. They soon
         communicate easily and become best friends. The other
         children are won over, too, and admire David for his cour-
         age when he tackles something no one else dared do.

Pr 144   Rose, Karen. Single trail. Chicago: Follett, 1969.
              Two boys go to the same school in a Los Angeles neigh-
         borhood. Rick has learned to make friends quickly in
         spite of his family's moving nine times in twelve years.
         Earl does not care whether people like him or not--espe-
         cially white people. An effective tale with high identifica-
         tion value.

Pr 145   Sachs, Marilyn. Peter and Veronica. New York: Double-
         day, 1969.
              This book takes up where Mrs. Sachs' last book, Veron-
         ica Ganz, left off. The Bronx in 1941 serves as back-
         ground for this story about the fun and also the pain of a
         friendship which is looked at with a hostile eye of two sets
         of families. Smart, pint-sized Jewish Peter Wedemeyer
         and big, clumsy, anti-social (and Lutheran) Veronica stand
         first together against the world, then against each other,
         and at last side by side again in closer understanding.
         The problem and the dialogue are handled extremely well,
         as is the ensuing breach between the friends, a breach
         healed in a most natural way.

Pr 146   Scott, Sally. Jenny and the wonderful jeep. New York:
         Harcourt, 1963.
              A girl learns that she should be willing to give others
         the same treatment she wishes to receive.

Pr 147   Shotwell, Louise R. Magdalena. New York: Viking, 1971.
              Magdalena hated her long braids but her grandmother,
         Nani, thought that braids were the proper way for a Puerto
         Rican girl to wear her hair, even in Brooklyn. Magdalena
         develops a warm and close friendship with Spook Gonzalez,
         the school's problem child.

Pr 148   Shura, Mary Frances. Seven stone. New York: Holiday
         House, 1972.
              Maggie finds that it's her turn to be the outsider when
         Tibbie, a strange new girl, enters school and is assigned
         to Maggie to show around. Trouble really begins when a

jealous classmate loses the spelling bee to the new girl
and Maggie is caught in the middle. In her developing
friendship with Tibbie, she learns the true secret of the
"seven stone."

Pr 149   Simon, Shirley. Best friends. West Caldwell, N. J.:
          Lothrop, 1964.
          Sixth grader Jenny Jason is deserted by her best friend
          but gradually finds new friends and new interests in the
          class marionnette play. Her grandmother saves the day
          for her in spite of unorthodox ways and Jenny learns that
          many friends are better than one.

Pr 150   Smaridge, Norah. Looking at you. Nashville: Abingdon,
          1962.
          Practical advice on getting along with your family, mak-
          ing friends, becoming more mature. Recommended for
          sixth-grade girls.

Pr 151   Urmston, Mary. New boy. New York: Doubleday, 1950.
          The story of Jack Corwin who came from California to
          start fifth grade in a Connecticut school. Jack's problems,
          of going from one school where he was top boy to another
          where he is a stranger forced to endure the humiliation of
          teasing, are finally solved through common adventures and
          increased understanding.

Pr 152   What will Kathy do--friendship versus ability. New York:
          Doubleday, n. d. (16mm film)
          A dramatization about friendship versus ability, a dilem-
          ma encountered by many children everyday. School-con-
          nected situations.

Pr 153   Wooley, Catherine. Cathy's little sister. New York:
          Morrow, 1964.
          At nine Chris has made no friends independently but
          constantly trails her older sister, Cathy, and her friends.
          She even finds an excuse to stay home from school when
          Cathy is sick, and thus misses out on being in a class
          play. When Cathy has a slumber party and excludes Chris
          from the activities, she is crushed. On a subsequent
          overnight trip to Detroit with her father, Chris visits a
          home where she has a wonderful time with girls her own
          age. She also meets a little girl who trails her sister,
          even as she does, and begins to see herself as she is.
          Chris returns with plans for a slumber party of her own
          to which she will invite school classmates and she is
          launched on a program of making friends of her own.

Pr 154   _____. Ginnie and Geneva. New York: Morrow,
          1948.
          Ginnie's first difficult experience of school is in the
          fourth grade when she has quite a time learning how to

take teasing.   In the process, Geneva becomes her best
friend.

Pr 155   _____.   Ginnie and the new girl.   New York: Morrow,
           1954.
     Ginnie resented the attention Geneva was paying the new
girl, Marcia, but soon found other fourth-grade friends and
interests to replace her dependence on one friend.

Chapter 7

LEARNING ONE'S SOCIAL ROLE

<u>Primary</u>

ROLE MODELS

Sr 1   Babbitt, Natalie. <u>Phoebe's revolt</u>. New York: Farrar, 1968.
    Phoebe Euphemia Brandon Brown, who hates the bows and ruffles and fluff and frills and curls that rich little girls are expected to wear in 1904, decides to rebel. On the day of her party Phoebe refuses to get out of the bath-tub until she can wear her father's clothes.

Sr 2   Bonsall, Crosby. <u>The day I had to play with my sister</u>. New York: Harper, 1972.
    This story tells of an impatient boy who tries to teach his younger sister to play hide and seek. The extremely simple text, written from the boy's point of view, is one with which children can readily identify. Pastel illustra-tions on every page add touches of humor to the text, which is divided into chapters. The realistic atmosphere makes Bonsall's book an excellent addition to the very early read-ing shelves.

Sr 3   Carlson, Natalie Savage. <u>Ann Aurelia and Dorothy</u>. New York: Harper, 1968.
    Ann thinks Mrs. Hicken is the best mother she has had since her own went away. She and Dorothy become friends on the playground and make lemonade and go to the super-market. They even get Mrs. Hicken to join the P.T.A.

Sr 4   Caudill, Rebecca. <u>Did you carry the flag today?</u> New York: Holt, 1966.
    A young mountain boy, filled with curiosity and enthusi-asm, finally achieves the honor of carrying the school flag --a reward for good behavior.

Sr 5   Cretan, Gladys Yessayan. <u>All except Sammy</u>. Boston: Little, Brown, 1966.
    All except Sammy Agabashian are musicians in his fam-ily, and he longs to be included in newspaper pictures of the "Musical Agabashians." Though he plays championship

baseball, he is hopeless as a musician--he has absolutely
no rhythm and is tone-deaf besides. But at last, in school,
he discovers another talent and is finally recognized as one
of the "Artistic Agabashian Family."

Sr 6   Greene, Carla. I want to be a homemaker. Chicago: Chil-
        dren's Press, 1961.
        A little girl plays house and learns that to be a good
homemaker one must be a cook, cleaner, nurse, teacher
and artist.

Sr 7   Johnson, Elizabeth. The little knight. Boston: Little,
        Brown, 1957.
        Amusing tale of a rebel princess who wants to be a
knight, not marry one, and of a rebel prince who objects
to namby-pamby princesses. The two get together with the
princess disguised as a stable boy and between them, perform the three tasks which the princess's father has set for
her suitors. Their identities are then disclosed and they
live happily ever after.

Sr 8   Keats, Ezra Jack. A letter to Amy. New York: Harper,
        1968.
        Peter, the hero of The Snowy Day, Whistle for Willie,
and Peter's Chair, is growing up. He even wants to invite
a girl to his birthday party. As he goes out in a storm to
mail the invitation, a burst of wind blows the letter away.
Rushing to retrieve the note, he bumps into Amy, knocks
her down and makes her cry. Now Peter is sure that she'll
never come to his party.

Sr 9   _____. Peter's chair. New York: Harper, 1967.
        Peter's cradle, crib and high chair are taken over by a
new baby sister. He even has to give up noisy games because of the new arrival. Before his special little blue
chair can be painted that sissyish pink for Susie, he and
his dog Willie pack up their prize possessions and run away
--but not too far.

Sr 10   Klagsbrun, Francine. Free to be ... you and me. New
        York: McGraw-Hill, 1974.
        A collection of activities and stories for children illus-
trating the expanding social roles in contemporary society.
Although fictional, the stories are an interesting combination
of humor and realism.

Sr 11   Krasilovsky, Phyllis. Very little boy. New York: Double-
        day, 1962.
        He was smaller than all the other little boys on his
street but he grows and grows until he is no longer a "very
little boy."

Sr 12   _____. The very little girl. New York: Doubleday,

1953.
A tiny little girl grows and grows until she is big enough
to be the big sister for a new brother.

Sr 13   Lexau, Joan M. The rooftop mystery. New York: Harper,
         1968.
         On his family's moving day, Sam and his friend Albert
         are very helpful. But while trying to move Iris' big doll
         without being seen by their friends, they run into a few
         problems and the doll disappears. It takes some clever de-
         tective work to solve the mystery and return the doll to
         Iris.

Sr 14   The man who wanted to fly (a Japanese tale). Chicago:
         Coronet, 1969. (film, color, 11 minutes)
         The animated puppet story of a man who wanted to fly,
         to be free to choose his life style. He flies away with
         some ducks.

Sr 15   Mizumna, Kazue. If I were a mother. New York: Crowell,
         1968.
         The maternal characteristics of twelve different animals
         show loving ways of being a mother. But most of all, "if
         I were a mother I would like to be just like my mother,"
         thinks a little girl as she plays with her doll.

Sr 16   Parsons, Ellen. Rainy days together. New York: Harper,
         1971.
         A simple tender account of how a little girl spends a
         satisfying rainy day at home with her mother. Cosily
         dressed, in long, warm dresses and fuzzy slippers, they
         happily share meals, stories, and quiet games. At dinner
         time they light a fire and expectantly await Daddy, who like
         many picture book daddies, is a solidly built, bearded young
         man whose arrival completes the loving family circle.

Sr 17   Radlauer, Ruth. Father is big. Glendale, Cal.: Bowmar,
         1967.
         A little Negro boy and his father enjoy life together as
         the little boy wonders if he will ever be as big as his fath-
         er. Brief text opposite appealing full-page color photographs,
         which show love and strength in the everyday life of this
         Negro family.

Sr 18   Roth, Mary Jane. The pretender princess. New York:
         Morrow, 1967.
         Clara Dobbs, a regular little girl, decides that she is
         wearing an imaginary crown and robe. But do princesses
         really have more fun?

Sr 19   Watson, Nancy. Jimmy. Westminster, Md.: Knopf, 1965.
         Jimmy, a five-year-old boy, is ridiculed by his sisters
         for he likes to play house with them. He soon meets a

new boy in the neighborhood, who brings his fire truck over
to Jimmy's, and Jimmy develops a new interest.

OCCUPATIONS

Sr 20   At work ... city. Chicago: Encyclopaedia Britannica Edu-
        cational Corp. , 1969.   (37 frames, color)
        Captioned frames of actual photographs illustrate the
        variety of occupations found in a large metropolitan area and
        the fact that a city requires many interdependent occupations
        in order to function.

Sr 21   Basic concepts in social studies. New York: Learning Cor-
        poration of America, 1970. (4 sound filmstrips, average
        66 frames, color; 2 phonodiscs, 12 inches, 33 rpm)
        This set of four filmstrips and two records is based on
        four books by Marie Winn. The cartoon-type visuals which
        are in full color are not the same illustrations which appear
        in the books. Contents: Why people have special jobs; The
        man who made spinning tops; Why we use money; The fisher-
        man who needed a knife; Why we have taxes; The town that
        had no policeman; Why we have laws; Shiver, gobble, and
        snore.

Sr 22   Beim, Jerrold. Tim and the tool chest. New York: Mor-
        row, 1951.
        When a boy begins to be interested in building things, his
        father helps him.

Sr 23   Childcraft. Vol. 8. What people do. Chicago: Field En-
        terprises, 1972.
        Even very young children want to begin to learn about the
        world of work and to plan for their role in it. Sections on
        "People who work in special clothes, " "People who work
        with special tools, " and "People who work together" provide
        opportunities to describe a wide range of occupations.

Sr 24   Flora, James. Fishing with dad. New York: Harcourt,
        1967.
        Daniel goes out on his father's commercial fishing boat
        and learns what it is like to be a deep-sea fisherman.

Sr 25   Gray, Genevieve. I know a bus driver. New York: Put-
        nam, 1972.
        When Bobby leaves his pet turtle on the bus, it is re-
        turned to him by the driver who is a neighbor. The driver
        offers to take Bobby on his first run the next day, so the
        boy can learn more about how the bus driver helps his com-
        munity.

Sr 26   Merriam, Eve. Mommies at work. New York: Knopf,
        1962.

At home, "Mommies make cookies to munch" and "Kiss places that hurt and places that don't. " But mommies do all kinds of work in many other places. They work in tall office buildings, on ranches, in stores, banks, hospitals, theaters, schools, and in many other places. Some build bridges, split atoms, assemble cars, and walk tight ropes. Detailed illustrations show mothers working in many different occupations.

Sr 27   Powell, Meredith. What do do? Chicago: Children's Press, 1972.
         Verses relate to many occupations that a girl can choose.

Sr 28   Wilkinson, Jean. Come to work with us in a hospital. Chicago: Children's Press, 1970.
         One in a series of nine books intended to develop vocational awareness in the primary grades by providing accurate career information. Colored pictures portray a variety of occupations in the adult world. Specific tasks include: the admitting clerk, laundry manager, maintenance engineer, housekeeper, medical records, librarian, dietition, pharmacists, x-ray technician, etc.

Sr 29   Wonderful world of work. Jamaica, N.Y.: Eye Gate House, 1970. (filmstrip)
         Helps children explore the world of work and many occupations open to them. Basic theme is that we should ignite early interest in occupational interest and choices as a means of successful learning and guidance. Open-endedness promotes classroom discussion and individual thought.

MANNERS

Sr 30   Considering others. Tujunga, Cal.: Herbert M. Elkins, 1968. (30 frames, color)
         Presents basic manners for social behavior by contrasting the behavior of a small donkey with what children should do.

Sr 31   DeSantis, Helen. Bubble baths with hair bows, a little girl's guide to grooming. New York: Doubleday, 1963.
         Little girls will wish to emulate the routines and simple techniques of cleanliness and good grooming.

Sr 32   Home manners. Mahwah, N.J.: Troll Associates, 1970. (42 frames)
         Features helpful hints for getting along with brothers and sisters, parents and pets. Shows children manners can be pleasing to one's self as well as to others.

Sr 33   Joslin, Sesyle. What do you say, dear? New York: Young Scott Books, 1958.
         A guide to appropriate social behavior for young ladies and gentlemen.

Sr 34   Leaf, Munro. Manners can be fun. Philadelphia: Lippin-
             cott, 1958.
             Funny pictures illustrate simple advice on how to act
when introduced to people, how to behave at home and at
school and when playing with other boys and girls.

Sr 35   Parish, Peggy. My golden book of manners. New York:
             Golden Press, 1962.
             Animals join children to show them the polite thing to do
in a variety of social situations. Especially appropriate for
a late maturing child.

Intermediate

ROLE MODELS

Sr 36   Barrett, Anne. Midway. New York: Coward-McCann, 1967.
             Mark is dull and ordinary in comparison with members of
his brilliant family. He is the middle of the five Mundy
children, which makes matters worse. Still, at school, he
seems to be the one called on to defend the peculiarities of
the family. Then one day while he's sitting on a tree limb,
Midway comes to visit. Midway, with his green eyes, steers
Mark away from dullness into success and confidence, and
into being as brilliant as the rest of the family.

Sr 37   Beatty, Patricia. Hail Columbia. New York: Morrow,
             1970.
             Oregon in 1893 is the setting for this story. Louisa
Baines, thirteen years old, tells what happened the year her
(active suffragette) aunt came to visit her sedate family.
Taking her niece in tow (Aunt) Columbia embarked on one
cause after another right in Astoria. There were Finns and
Chinese to be helped, corrupt politicians to be battled. By
the end of her stay, Louisa knew that the town would never
forget Columbia Baines.

Sr 38   Beim, Lorraine. Alice's family. New York: Harcourt,
             1948.
             When mother broke her foot, Alice tried to perform the
household duties and boss her brother and sister.

Sr 39   Blassingame, Wyatt. Story of the Boy Scouts. Scarsdale,
             N.Y.: Garrard, 1968.
             Here is a book which should interest most young boys
and certainly their scoutmasters. Mr. Blassingame successfully traces the beginnings of scouting in several nations,
showing how various similar groups were eventually merged
into the present-day Boy Scout organization. Several true
stories of rescues, hiking, and even an Antarctic exploration
are included, while helping others, attending jamborees, and
working on conservation projects are portrayed as those

activities of scouting which lead to international understanding and friendship.

Sr 40   Boy Scout's handbook.   North Brunswick, N. J.:   Boy Scouts
         of America, 1965.
         Handbook which deals with scouting and the responsibilities.   It presents information needed to pass tests and
         meet requirements for progress from Tenderfoot to Eagle
         Scout.

Sr 41   Bragdon, Elspeth.   That Jud!   New York: Viking, 1957.
         Jud's frustrations, his loneliness, and sometimes his
         temper lead him into troubles such as truancy and window-
         breaking.   In the course of his struggles to find satisfaction,
         Jud proves his worth to the community and gains self-re-
         spect when he risks his life to put out a dangerous fire.

Sr 42   Brenner, Anita.   A hero by mistake.   New York: Scott,
         1953.
         A frightened Indian overcomes his fears and finally be-
         comes a hero.

Sr 43   Cleaver, Vera and Bill.   Lady Ellen Grae.   Philadelphia:
         Lippincott, 1968.
         A very funny story about Ellen Grae, eleven-year-old
         tomboy and exuberant tall-story specialist, who tries to be-
         come a lady to please her father and to get out of going to
         live with her aunt and cousin in Seattle.

Sr 44   Crocker, Betty.   New boys' and girls' cookbook.   New York:
         Golden Press, 1965.
         A picture cookbook with easy step-by-step recipes for
         cookies, cakes, party treats, sandwiches.   Well illustrated.
         Promotes the idea that cooking is for both sexes.

Sr 45   Darrow, Whitney.   I'm glad I'm a boy!   I'm glad I'm a
         girl!   New York: Simon and Schuster, 1970.
         A boy and a girl tell each other why each is glad of
         what they are.

Sr 46   Daugherty, Sonia.   Ten brave men; makers of the American
         way.   Philadelphia: Lippincott, 1951.
         Dramatic accounts of ten men who believed in the princi-
         ples upon which this country was built: William Bradford;
         Roger Williams; Patrick Henry; Samuel Adams; Thomas
         Jefferson; George Washington; Benjamin Franklin; John Paul
         Jones; Andrew Jackson; Abraham Lincoln.

Sr 47   _____.   Ten brave women.   Philadelphia: Lippincott,
         1953.
         Dramatic incidents in the lives of ten women from Anne
         Hutchinson to Eleanor Roosevelt, which focus on their brav-
         ery, wisdom, and service to humanity: Anne Hutchinson;

Abigail Adams; Dolly Madison; Narcissa Whitman; Julia
Ward Howe; Susan B. Anthony; Dorothea Lynde Dix; Mary
Lyon; Ida M. Tarball; Eleanor Roosevelt.

Sr 48   De Angeli, Marguerite. Bright April. New York: Double-
         day, 1946.
         Because of her happy home, enjoyment of school and de-
         light in being a Brownie Scout little brown April is mostly
         "Bright April," but occasionally is "dark April" as is the
         month for which she is named.

Sr 49   DeLeeuw, Adele. The Girl Scout story. Scarsdale, N.Y.:
         Garrard, 1965.
         A simply written history of the Girl Scout movement,
         stressing its importance in promoting international good will.

Sr 50   Del Rey, Lester. Cave of spears. New York: Knopf,
         1957.
         A stone age boy longs to receive his tribe's rites of man-
         hood but must wait until the tribe solves its food problem.

Sr 51   Faulknor, Cliff. The in-betweener. Boston: Little, Brown,
         1967.
         Chad Streeter is at the "awkward age"--no matter what
         he does for fun, it always seems to end in disaster for all
         concerned. He is sure there is absolutely no hope that his
         father will ever understand or compromise with him. His
         mother tries to smooth things out between Chad and his fath-
         er. Things do not really begin to improve until after the
         mine collapses.

Sr 52   Fitzhugh, Louise. Long street. New York: Harper, 1965.
         Beth Allen, her family, and a new family from Mississip-
         pi explore some of the attitudes of the past that shaped fam-
         ily life and social roles. Some of the attitudes were based
         on "old wives' tales," some on superstition, some on ig-
         norance.

Sr 53   Fritz, Jean. Brady. New York: Coward-McCann, 1960.
         How Brady Minton's father came to write in the family
         Bible in 1836 the record that on the day the barn burned
         Brady worked right along with the adults. An exciting ac-
         count, set in Washington County, Pennsylvania, in the pre-
         Civil War anti-slavery debate.

Sr 54   Gag, Wanda. Gone is gone. New York: Coward-McCann,
         1935.
         The story of a man who wanted to do housework. But
         after a few hours of misery filled with one disaster after
         another, he decided to return to his job happily.

Sr 55   Gage, Wilson. Big blue island. Cleveland: World, 1964.
         Darrell goes to live with his great-uncle on an island and

discovers he has a place in the world.

Sr 56   Gee, M. H. Chicano, amigo. New York: Morrow, 1972.
         Kiki, an eight-year-old Chicano, considers eleven-year-
old Marc Conley his special scout hero. Marc had pro-
tected Kiki from husky Erv Tatum, a cub scout about Kiki's
age. Kiki loves the boy scouts and dreams of becoming a
cub. He is so persistent in his attentions to Marc that
Marc is almost ready to fight him. Then comes the earth-
quake and Kiki is buried in an old house. Ironically, this
turns out to be a really funny story useful in discussions of
human relations.

Sr 57   George, Jean. My side of the mountain. New York: Dut-
         ton, 1959.
         Sam Gribley does what many boys and girls dream of
doing--spends a winter alone on a mountain in the Catskills.

Sr 58   Gowdy, George. Young buffalo bill. New York: Lothrop,
         1955.
         This story emphasizes young Buffalo's reaction to the re-
sponsibility forced on him at the death of his father. He
assumes the position of "man of the house."

Sr 59   Hall, Elizabeth. Stand up, Lucy. Boston: Houghton, 1971.
         Lucy's Aunt Letitia, hitherto unknown to her, suddenly
announces she is coming for a visit. She arrives for a
week with three heavy trunks. At the same time the town
is greatly excited by two events: a speech in the park by
a "suffragist" and a visit by Senator Throckmorten, Theodore Roosevelt's running mate. Both Lucy and her Aunt
are staunch fighters for women's rights in this tale of the
year 1904.

Sr 60   Hays, Wilma P. Mary's Star. Williamsburg, Va.: Colon-
         ial Williamsburg, 1968.
         Mary Breckenridge wishes very much to be a boy. She
rides, plays, and sometimes dresses like a boy. Her fif-
teen-year-old brother has recently returned from England
and is very much the gentleman. He feels they must be
grown up since their mother is dead and their father is at
war. Then the children learn of their father's death and
that they are penniless. Mary learns that she must grow
up and that she has an important role in the family life.

Sr 61   Hodges, Margaret. Hatching of Joshua Cobb. New York:
         Farrar, 1967.
         Joshua Cobb's mother takes him to camp and reluctantly
leaves him. It is his first time away from home. He is
assigned to cabin 13 and a counselor who calls him "Corn
Cobb." The counselor underfeeds and, in general, makes
camp unpleasant for the boys. However, Joshua sticks it
out and discovers he is more of a person than he had thought.

Sr 62   Hopkins, Lee Bennett. Girls can too. New York: Watts,
         1972.
         Poems with many moods: exuberant, rough and tumble,
         tender and funny--all showing that when it comes to being
         "first and best and brave and smart," girls can too.

Sr 63   Howath, Betty. Be nice to Josephine. New York: Watts,
         1970.
         Charley was perfectly willing to be late to the Saturday
         baseball game to help his mother. But to spend the whole
         day with a girl? Yes, his mother said firmly, little Jose-
         phine and her mother were coming for the day, they were
         cousins and blood is thicker than water. Disgruntled, Char-
         ley planned a day that a girl would hate--fishing. But Jose-
         phine volunteered as worm digger (actually she preferred
         snakes) and knew about fishing. She was so interesting that
         Charley found himself enjoying the day.

Sr 64   Hoyt, Mary Finch. American women of the space age. New
         York: Atheneum, 1966.
         Brief biographies of some women who have made signifi-
         cant contributions to U.S. space program through research
         in medicine, nutrition, math, etc.

Sr 65   Kielty, Bernadino. Jenny Lind. Boston: Houghton, 1959.
         A warm human story of an unwanted child's choice of
         what to do with her life and the gift of an excellent voice.
         Her choice brings her phenomenal success through many
         years of hard work and frequent periods of loneliness.

Sr 66   Kingman, Lee. The year of the raccoon. Boston: Houghton,
         1966.
         Joey, fourteen, the middle son of a successful father,
         feels that he is a misfit. Already Jerry, his older brother,
         is an accomplished pianist; and Jack, at nine, has a decided
         scientific bent. Joey's projects either don't interest the
         family, or they come out badly--until Bertie, an infant rac-
         coon, comes into Joey's life. In helping Bertie grow up,
         Joey matures and discovers that he is an important member
         of his own family.

Sr 67   Klein, Norma. Girls can be anything. New York: Dutton,
         1973.
         The book begins with a boy telling a little girl that girls
         cannot be doctors. Episode by episode the distressed girl
         finds cheer from her parents who relate that females can
         indeed be doctors, pilots, presidents, and anything.

Sr 68   Krumgold, Joseph. ...And now Miguel. New York:
         Crowell, 1973.
         A picture of life on a New Mexico sheep ranch presented
         with charm and simplicity, through the story of twelve-year-
         old Miguel, whose dearest wish is to be accepted as a man
         in his family.

Sr 69   Langton, Jane. The boyhood of Grace Jones. New York:
         Harper, 1972.
         Wrapped up in dreams of adventure and success inspired
         by the boy hero of her favorite book, junior high school stu-
         dent, Grace Jones, pays little heed to the admonitions of
         concerned adults or friends about her tomboyish ways. She
         meets life with zest and neither the inevitable instances of
         defeat and disillusionment nor the increasing awareness of
         her feminity, which brings about changes in attitude, keep
         her from developing her own personality in her own way.

Sr 70   Lathrop, Dorothy P. Tomboy. Westminster, Md.: Knopf,
         1965.
         Janie plays sports with the boys and is called a tomboy
         by the other girls but she soon takes a liking for a boy on
         her team and develops other interests.

Sr 71   Lovelace, Maud H. Betsy in spite of herself. New York:
         Crowell, 1946.
         Betsy experiments with a new spelling of her name, new
         styles of clothes, and a pose of sophistication.

Sr 72   Mirsky, Reba Paeff. Thirty-one brothers and sisters. Chi-
         cago: Follett, 1952.
         Ten-year-old Nomusa is one of the thirty-one children of
         the six wives of a Zulu chief. It is a very happy life in the
         kraal on the South African veld with brothers and sisters
         sharing responsibilities and pleasures, and especially their
         great pride in their father. Nomusa dislikes the duties of
         a girl and wants to do the things the boys do. More than
         anything else, she yearns to go with the men on the annual
         elephant hunt, but she knows that is impossible. The story
         shows not only the satisfaction that may be part of member-
         ship in a tribal family but also that deviation from traditional
         masculine and feminine roles may be more severely dealt
         with in a more primitive culture than our own.

Sr 73   Nathan, Dorothy. Women of courage. New York: Random,
         1964.
         Five outstanding women and their stories: Susan B. An-
         thony, Jane Adams, Mary McLeod Bethune, Amelia Earhart,
         and Margaret Mead.

Sr 74   O'Neill, Mary. Ali. New York: Atheneum, 1968.
         Ali is entranced with the new machines sent to his Bed-
         ouin settlement by the government in Tunis. But he is
         shocked and ashamed when he learns that his father and the
         tribal elders have decided that he must attend the school
         that the machines have built. For he considered himself a
         man! His friendship with Limjid, his capture of a gazelle
         fawn and his own freedom to choose make this an unusual
         story.

Sr 75   Penny, Grace Jackson. <u>Moki.</u> Boston: Houghton, 1960.
          Moki is the story of a little Cheyenne girl who envied
the boys and men in her tribe the freedom and activity which
were denied the women. It wasn't enough for her to learn
how to make a clay pot from her grandmother or to feed
her beloved pet, Rabbit Person. But, when one of her
friends is bitten by a poisonous snake, she learns that an
Indian girl can be as brave as an Indian boy.

Sr 76   Pierik, Robert. <u>Archy's dream world.</u> New York: Mor-
          row, 1972.
          Archy Oglesby in daydreams is a brave hunter, a daring
businessman, a genius neuro-surgeon. In real life though,
Archy's world revolves around a conflict with his ex-All
American basketball-playing father who expects his same
abilities in his son. Humor lightens the conflict in this
tale. Nicely resolved.

Sr 77   Potter, Bronson. <u>Isfendiar and the wild donkeys</u>. New
          York: Atheneum, 1967.
          It was at the kilns that Isfendiar, an Iranian charcoal
burner's son, heard the legends that fired his imagination
and told him of wild donkeys, the noblest beasts in the
world. The day Isfendiar set out across the desert to find
those donkeys he was not so much a man as he was on the
day he returned.

Sr 78   Sachs, Marilyn. <u>Veronica Ganz.</u> New York: Doubleday,
          1968.
          Veronica is tall for thirteen, a nuisance to her teacher,
and she bullies the little children. Peter, who is smaller
than she, taunts and teases her until it becomes a problem.
Gaining insight into her behavior, Veronica changes in very
natural and believable ways.

Sr 79   Sankey, Alice. <u>Judo Yell.</u> Racine, Wis.: Whitman, 1972.
          To hold his own against a bully, young Jim Brandon takes
up judo. He than finds that the joy of the sport and its
philosophy make it meaningful in its own right and that it
solves more kinds of problems than he ever thought possible.

Sr 80   Smaridge, Norah. <u>Looking at you.</u> New York: Atheneum,
          1962.
          Recommended for sixth-grade girls. Advice on getting
along with your family, making friends, and being more
mature. To be a girl is important.

Sr 81   Sneve, Virginia. <u>Driving hawk.</u> New York: Holiday, 1972.
          Little Jimmy had a great deal of growing to do before
his father would call him "my son Jimmy." The excitement
of a rodeo, being sent to find a lost mare in a storm, and
other experiences lead to Jimmy's growing up and earning
his father's respect.

Sr 82   Spykman, E. C. Edie on the warpath. New York: Har-
         court, 1966.
             Eleven-year-old Edie embarks on a bitter battle to vindi-
         cate her sex. Scathing remarks by her worldly eldest broth-
         er, Theodore, as to the obvious inferiority of all girls, are
         emphasized by the new public spectacle of lady suffragettes
         in a struggle for their rights. Edie wages ingenious and
         dedicated warfare, resentful of all males. Then the under-
         standing of her stepmother, the wise sympathetic words of
         a father, who is not always sympathetic, and her own prized,
         dramatic, and utterly unnecessary display of courage restore
         Edie to a sense of proportion and a knowledge of happiness.

Sr 83   Stamm, Claus. Three strong women: a tall tale from
         Japan. New York: Viking, 1962.
             Forever Mountain, a champion wrestler, meets three
         women, a daughter, her mother, and grandmother. These
         three women carry cows and uproot trees with greater ease
         than he.

Sr 84   Sterling, Dorothy. Lucretia Mott: gentle warrior. New
         York: Doubleday, 1964.
             Nineteenth-century American women were supposed to stay
         home and keep quiet about world events, but this admired
         Quaker mother of six spent her 87 years traveling and talk-
         ing about Negro and women's rights.

Sr 85   Stevenson, Janet. Women's rights. New York: Watts,
         1972.
             Including brief biographies of famous suffragists, the
         author follows the struggle for women's rights in America,
         beginning with Lucretia Mott and the forming of the Declara-
         tion of Women's Rights, and continuing through 1920 with the
         ratification of the 19th Amendment. The photographs are
         interesting, the writings measured, objective, and clear, and
         the text particularly valuable for its discussion of the nature
         of forces marshalled against sufferage.

Sr 86   Taves, Isabella. Not bad for a girl. Philadelphia: Lip-
         pincott, 1972.
             Sharon Lee is pretty, small, and she can play baseball.
         That a 12-year-old girl can perform on the baseball dia-
         mond better than the average boy is too much for most of
         the men in Whittier and definitely more than a majority of
         the Little League coaches can handle. But Sharon gets a
         chance to play on the Cubs team and performs well. Though
         Sharon isn't the first girl to play in the League, her pres-
         ence catches the attention of the press and finally TV. The
         publicity and hostility do not please Sharon, but she is able
         to stand it all because the Cubs' manager is fair and most
         of her teammates are regular guys.

Sr 87   Tibbets, Albert. Boys are boys; stories from around the

world.   Boston: Little, Brown, 1969.
A dozen tales about boys living in as many countries.
The subjects range from a supposed sissy who is really a
motorcycle champion to a Mexican lad who would be a silversmith.

Sr 88   Ullman, James Ramsey.   Banner in the sky.   Philadelphia:
           Lippincott, 1954.
           A particularly effective dramatization of the conflict be-
           tween Rudi and his desire to climb the great mountain and
           his mother's fears for his safety.   His experiences with the
           great climber Captain Winter, the avalanche on the mountain,
           and the surprising climax tell the story of Rudi's growth
           from boyhood to manhood.

Sr 89   Vierick, Phillip.   The summer I was lost.   New York: Day,
           1965.
           Boys lacking in physical stamina and those who have felt
           lost amid life's struggles will identify with Paul's story.
           They may be encouraged by Paul's experience to recognize
           and develop their own talents.

Sr 90   Walden, Amelia Elizabeth.   A girl called Hank.   New York:
           Morrow, 1951.
           Clothes and grooming become important to tomboy Hank
           when she becomes interested in the friendship of a certain
           boy.

Sr 91   Wallace, Barbara.   Claudia.   Chicago: Follett, 1969.
           A fast-paced, well written story with a high degree of
           interest and appeal for pre-teen girls.   Claudia has lots of
           problems.   She thinks her family doesn't like her, because
           she is a real tomboy.   Janice and her friend, Polly, are
           "icky."

Sr 92   Wier, Ester.   The loner.   New York: McKay, 1963.
           Boys will enjoy David's experiences in a growing aware-
           ness of his worth, his adventure in an abandoned mine, and
           his face-to-face encounter with a bear.   They will agree
           with the deeper message of the book that people need love
           and a feeling of worth.

Sr 93   Withers, Carl.   A rocket in my pocket: the rhymes and
           chants of young Americans.   New York: Holt, 1948.
           Over four hundred rhymes, chants, game songs, tongue
           twisters and ear teasers frequently used by children while
           processing each other for appropriate social roles.   This
           collection may be of special interest to adults who are con-
           cerned with social growth and development.

Sr 94   Wojciechowska, Maia.   Shadow of the bull.   New York:
           Atheneum, 1964.
           Manolo is expected to fight the bull as his father, a great

toreador, did, but he meets the test in his own way. Reminiscent of Krumgold's stories but simpler and easier.

Sr 95   Yates, Elizabeth. Carolina's courage. New York: Dutton, 1964.
         Carolina's family makes the long journey by ox drawn wagon from New Hampshire to Nebraska. The last stage of the trip is made in safety, because Carolina is brave enough to play with an Indian child and exchange dolls with her.

Sr 96   Zolotow, Charlotte. William's doll. New York: Harper, 1972.
         William's desire for a doll is finally satisfied by his grandmother despite his father's and brother's insistence that "dolls are sissy." However, William is not a sissy. He is very good at shooting baskets and maneuvering electric trains, but he still wants a doll. The grandmother's understanding and explanation of William's desire should make sense to young children and to any adults who may read this story.

OCCUPATIONS

Sr 97   Careers... Pleasantville, N.Y.: Guidance Associates, n.d. (filmstrips)
         Contents: Allied health services, business and office occupations, communication, industry, machine trades, personal service, sales, skilled workers, building trade, transportation. Discusses kinds of occupations, qualifications, future in career.

Sr 98   City is many things. Los Angeles: Churchill Films, 1968. (5 filmstrips, 37 frames each, color)
         Presents through photographs in communities across the country an overall picture of what makes up a city--includes multi-ethnic groups. Contents: A city is people at work; A city is people at leisure; A city is services; A city is transportation; A city is buildings.

Sr 99   Community helpers. Chicago: Society for Visual Education, 1965. (6 sets of 8 photographs, 13 x 18 inches, color)
         Each set in the series illustrates some important aspects of the subject being studied with unusually large and clear color photographs accompanied by supplementary information, questions, and references on reverse of pictures. Contents: Fire department helpers, postal helpers; dairy helpers; supermarket helpers; hospital helpers; police department helpers.

Sr 100   Fathers--what they do. Hollywood, Cal.: Aims Instructional Media Services, 1968. (16mm film, 10 minutes)

Shows fathers working in order to provide for their
families. Includes the self-employed man.

Sr 101   Fathers work. Los Angeles: Churchill Films, 1968.
          (filmstrip)
          Beginning and ending with father at home, each film-
strip follows him through his day's work in the community
and shows the skills, responsibilities, and personal relationships on the job. Interspersed among the captions on
the frames are questions that lead the viewer to think about
how work is done. Contents: My dad is a carpenter; My
dad is a moving man; My dad works in a shoe store; My
dad works in a factory; My dad works in a service station;
My dad works in a supermarket.

Sr 102   Hall, Natalie. The world in a city block. New York:
          Viking, 1960.
          The story of nine-year-old Nick who wanted to go with
his older brother and see the world with the merchant
marines. Instead, he took over the family bakery route--
delivering the delicious smelling fresh loaves of Italian
bread.

Sr 103   Mothers--what they do. Los Angeles: Films/West, Inc.,
          n. d. (16mm film, 11 minutes, color)
          Portrays three kinds of mothers: the full-time house-
keeper, the full-time worker, and the part-time worker.
Gives examples of responsibilities three such mothers
might have.

Sr 104   Mothers work too. Los Angeles: Churchill Films, 1968.
          (6 filmstrips, average of 39 frames each, color)
          Each filmstrip follows a mother through her working
day performing a needed service in the community. She
is shown meeting the needs of her family as well as ful-
filling the responsibilities of her job. Interspersed among
the captions on the frames are questions that lead the
viewer to think about how work is done. Multi-ethnic in
background. Contents: My mother is a dental assistant;
My mother is a waitress; My mother works in a bank; My
mother works in an office; My mother works in a drug
store; My mother works at home.

Sr 105   Rossomando, Frederic, Florence Leventhal, and Marilyn
          Szymaszek. Earning money. New York: Watts, 1967.
          People everywhere work to earn money to pay for food
to eat, clothes to wear and a place to live. This book
tells how Mr. Carter, who works for the telephone company, earns money to buy the things his family needs. It
explains overtime pay, income taxes and social security
tax.

Sr 106   Rowe, Jeanne. City workers. New York: Watts, 1969.

Firemen, policemen, postmen, nurses, doctors, file
clerks, and waitresses are just a few of the many different types of city workers whose service jobs are described
in this book.

MANNERS

Sr 107   Allen, B. Mind your manners. rev. ed. Philadelphia:
           Lippincott, 1964.
           Pointers on good manners at home and as a house guest,
           how to introduce people, proper table etiquette, how to ac-
           cept or decline an invitation.

Sr 108   Beery, Mary. Manners made easy. 3rd ed. New York:
           McGraw-Hill, 1966.
           Comprehensive handbook includes information on good
           grooming, personal cleanliness, clothing, as well as how
           to show consideration for others at home, school, on dates,
           in restaurants, and other public places.

Sr 109   Being boys--being girls. Carmel Valley, Cal.: Discovery
           Teaching Films, Inc., n.d. (16mm film, color, 10
           minutes)
           Considers the part played by physical development in
           growing up. Explains that new responsibilities at school,
           at home and to one's self require social growth.

Sr 110   Clark, Mary Elizabeth. Etiquette Jr. New York: Double-
           day, 1965.
           Discusses the social convention, formal and informal,
           boys and girls are likely to be puzzled by--home, theater,
           teas, dances, conversation, etc.

Sr 111   Good manners. (series) Chicago: Encyclopaedia Britan-
           nica Education Corporation, 1955. (filmstrips)
           Depicts boys and girls in everyday situations and in
           their relationships with each other and with adults around
           them. Emphasizes consideration for the feelings and com-
           fort of others. (Manners at School, 48 frames; Manners
           at Play, 48 frames)

Sr 112   Growing up--boys. Holbrook, N.Y.: View Lex, 1971.
           (43 frames, sound, color)
           Describes how a boy grows and changes as he pro-
           gresses from boyhood to manhood. Male pubertal and
           adolescent development is described and explained. Shows
           why there is a particular need at this time for good health
           practices. Relates mature adulthood to the ability to as-
           sume responsibilities.

Sr 113   Growing up--girls. Holbrook, N.Y.: View Lex, 1971.
           (45 frames, sound, color)

Describes the growth patterns of girls compared to boys and the factors which influence them. Prepubertal and pubertal changes, including menstruation, are simply and clearly explained. The need for good health practices is emphasized. Shows that physical growth, particularly during adolescence, is accompanied by changes in feelings, behavior, and ways of thinking.

Sr 114   Hoke, Helen. Etiquette: your ticket to good times. New York: Watts, 1970.
Discusses basic rules of etiquette for introducing people, dining out, visiting at a friend's house for a week-end, giving a party, being a good guest, writing acceptances, invitations and thank-you notes, and talking on the telephone. The last chapter deals with the rules of etiquette which apply especially to boys.

Sr 115   Leaf, Munro. Manners can be fun. rev. ed. Philadelphia: Lippincott, 1958.
Funny pictures illustrate simple advice on how to act when introduced to people, how to behave at home and at school, and when playing with other boys and girls.

Sr 116   Learning about manners. (series) Los Angeles: Family Films, 1970. (filmstrip)
Features a group of students who make some important discoveries about kindness, respect and consideration for other people in a variety of everyday situations.

Sr 117   Lee, Tina. Manners to grow on; a how-to-do-book for boys and girls. New York: Doubleday, 1955.
A guide to good manners in home, social, school, church, and other public situations.

Sr 118   Loeb, Robert. Manners for minors. New York: Association Press, 1964.
Discusses personal appearance, behavior at home and in public, good sportsmanship and prejudice, attitudes toward school and homework, reasons for writing and speaking correctly.

Sr 119   Magic with manners. (series) Austin, Tex.: Visual Instruction Bureau, University of Texas, 1961. (tapes, average 15 minutes each)
Thirteen audio-tapes presents solutions to a variety of problems which young people encounter in the process of growing up. Contents: Brother and sister trouble; The gift came back; Flubs with clubs; It's a date; Letter perfect; The locked door; The new kind of party; School can be fun; Small talk; The sound of the way you look; Story of a house party; Table talk; The way people see you.

Sr 120   Post, Emily. The Emily Post book of etiquette for young

people. New York: Funk & Wagnalls, 1967.
Etiquette is good common sense linked to thoughtfulness
for others, and its purpose is to make you more attractive
and easy to get along with.   This book discusses basic
principles of consideration and unselfishness which make
for pleasant family relations, the right thing to do in a
restaurant, in a theater or at a sports event, how to choose
clothes that are becoming and appropriate, how to write
invitations and thank-you notes, and what to do when visiting and entertaining.

Sr 121   Saunders, Rubie.   The Franklin Watts concise guide to
                good grooming for boys.   New York: Watts, 1972.
                A clearly written basic guide to grooming for boys which
            offers sensible advice on personal cleanliness, hair and
            skin care, diet, exercise, clothing and good manners.   Ap-
            pended are "A good grooming checklist" and two detailed
            diets for losing and gaining weight.   Humorous, cartoon-
            like, black-and-white line drawings help clarify the text
            and add appeal.

Sr 122   Young, Marjabelle.   Stand up, shake hands, say "How do
                you do?"   New York: McKay, 1969.
                A simple and practical guide to everyday good manners
            for boys.   Tells what a boy needs to know about being a
            good member of his own family, attending dances, making
            introductions, table manners, being a guest, giving parties,
            writing letters, being well-groomed and being a good sport.

Chapter 8

ESTABLISHING RELATIONS WITH SOCIAL
GROUPS AND INSTITUTIONS

<u>Primary</u>

COMMUNITY

Sg 1   Bendick, Jeanne. <u>A place to live.</u> New York: Parents
        Magazine Press, <u>1970.</u>
        A discussion of community life and the interdependence
of the life within the community. Has real application to
the child's world.

Sg 2   <u>Community health.</u> New York: McGraw-Hill, n. d. (set of
        6 filmstrips with an average of 48 color frames each)
        Poses typical health problems which affect the community
and explains how a community meets and solves these problems. Contents: Safety in the community; Maintaining community health; The water we drink; Safeguarding our food;
Community sanitation; Communicable disease.

Sg 3   De Regniers, Beatrice S. <u>A little house of your own.</u>
        New York: Harcourt, <u>1954.</u>
        The importance of a secret house of one's own as well
as suggestions as to where it may be found. Stresses the
right of privacy.

Sg 4   <u>Discovering the inner city.</u> Jamaica, N. Y. : Eye Gate
        House, 1971. (6 color filmstrips with record)
        Describes the aspects of the inner-city (New York) that
primary children would know and understand. Black racial
groups are represented.

Sg 5   Hoff, Syd. <u>Stanley.</u> New York: Harper, 1962.
        Stanley is a caveman sport who wishes to live at peace
with his neighbors in the old-fashioned way, writing on cave
walls and cultivating his own food. This is a problem un-
acceptable to his fellows until he decides to live in a house
and behave as they do.

Sg 6   <u>I have an egg.</u> New York: Celebrity Holdings, Inc. , 1969.
        (16mm film, optical sound, 14 minutes)
        Shows blind children learning what an egg is and feeling

it in various forms--yolk, white, hard-boiled, and the new
chick. Helps children understand and feel helpful toward
blind people.

Sg 7   Let's be good citizens at play. Tucson, Ariz. : Gateway
        Prod. , 1953. (10 minutes, black and white, 16mm)
        Shows a group of elementary school children in play ac-
tivities that illustrate good citizenship practices. Exempli-
fies such practices as friendliness, consideration of others,
cooperation, sharing, being good losers and winners, re-
specting how others live, and taking responsibility for one's
acts.

Sg 8   Rockwell, Harlow. My doctor. Riverside, N. J. : Macmil-
        lan, 1973.
        In a simple, almost sparse style, some of the mysteries
of the doctor's office routine and equipment are explained.
The tone is warm and reassuring as the reader learns of
bandages, stethoscopes, eye charts, and what procedures
comprise a routine physical examination. An excellent book
for parents of doctor-shy apprehensive children, and a must
for every pediatrician's waiting room.

Sg 9   Rowe, Jeanne. City workers. New York: Watts, 1969.
        Firemen, policemen, postmen, nurses, doctors, file
clerks, waitresses are just a few of the many different types
of city workers whose service jobs are described in this
book.

Sg 10   Rowland, Florence W. Let's go to the hospital. New York:
        Putnam, 1968.
        What happens to a boy when he goes to the hospital to
have his tonsils out? In the Admissions Office, he and his
mother answer many questions for the hospital records!
Then he goes to the laboratory for tests. In his room, the
nurse helps him to get ready for the operation。 While he
recovers from his tonsillectomy, he learns about all the
many people who staff the hospital.

Sg 11   Schools and sharing - let's share a see-saw. New York:
        McGraw-Hill, n. d. (16mm, 10 minutes)
        Examines the value of sharing and the value of arriving
at a decision to share in a democratic manner.

Sg 12   Shay, Arthur. What happens when you go to the hospital.
        Chicago: Reilly and Lee, 1969.
        In this record of Karen's trip to the hospital, she learns
the admitting routine, giggles at the hospital gown, quails at
the X-ray machine, parts tearfully from her parents and
wakes the next morning to the fact that the operation is over.

Sg 13   Who helps us. Washington, D. C. : Educational Media,
        1969.

Excellent photographs tell what happens behind the scenes of different community services. Contents: Fire department; Police department; Supermarket; Bakery; Laundry; Service station; Dentist; Dairy; Library; Post office.

Sg 14   Winn, Marie. Shiver, gooble, and snore. New York: Simon and Schuster, 1971.
Shiver, Gobble and Snore learn that life is not fun at all when there are no laws. A few simple games emphasize this point.

ETHNIC GROUPS

Sg 15   Beim, Jerrold. Swimming hole. New York: Morrow, 1951.
The new boy who doesn't want to swim with anyone who is colored has no fun until he learns that color doesn't matter. A small picture book that humorously ridicules color prejudice in such a way that the youngest child can understand its point. Louis Darling's excellent drawings, printed in full color, accent the theme. If we must have books for younger children that present social problems, this is a good example.

Sg 16   Brandon, Brumsic. Luther, from inner city. New York: Eriksson, 1969.
Luther, a little black city boy, is seen as he talks with his friends and roams the city streets. Without trying to make a joke he brings out funny statements.

Sg 17   Brown, Marcia. Stone soup. New York: Scribner, 1947.
When the French villagers heard that soldiers were coming, they hid all their food; but when they saw them making soup from stones, they added vegetables to it.

Sg 18   De Angeli, Marguerite. Bright April. New York: Doubleday, 1946.
April, a little Negro girl, has a happy middle-class home, school, and social life. She is unaware of social prejudice and encounters it for the first time at a Brownie party when a girl refuses to sit next to her. April accepts this girl's intolerance and wins her over as a friend. With the aid of her family and scout leader, April is able to cope with and understand racial discrimination.

Sg 19   Ets, Marie Hall. Bad boy, good boy. New York: Crowell, 1967.
Illustrated by the author, this story about a Mexican family in California centers on small Roberto, a troublemaker. When mother leaves home more problems arise for the family. Then Father lets Roberto attend the Children's Center where he learns to play with the other children and to speak English.

Sg 20   _____ . Nine days to Christmas. New York: Viking,
               1959.
               This is the story of Ceci, a little girl of Mexico City,
               just five and now old enough to have her own posada, the gay
               parties held on the nine days preceding Christmas. She may
               also choose her own piñata. The picture captures all the
               gaiety, excitement and anticipation preparatory to the Christ-
               mas season. With simple lines, a few colors, and a soft
               gray background that deepens in intensity as the day comes
               to a close, Marie Ets has caught the brilliant richness of
               color, the movement and vibrant life that are so much a
               part of this handsome city.

Sg 21   Galbraith, Clarke K. Victor. Boston: Little, Brown, 1971.
               Victor lives in two worlds, the English speaking world at
               school and the Spanish speaking world of his home, and he
               is having trouble in both until Parents' Night at school when
               his worlds come together.

Sg 22   Glendinning, Sally. Jimmy and Joe catch an elephant.
               Scarsdale, N.Y.: Garrard, 1969.
               A black and a white boy have an adventure with an es-
               caped circus elephant.

Sg 23   Grossman, Barney. Black means. New York: Hill and
               Wang, 1970.
               A principal and a teacher and students of PS 150 in the
               Bronx, New York collaborated to produce these short state-
               ments giving positive values to the word "Black." Each
               phrase is illustrated by a full-page figure or scene.

Sg 24   Hautzig, Esther. At home, a visit in four languages.
               Riverside, N.J.: Macmillan, 1968.
               This brightly illustrated book shows an American family
               in Chicago, a French family in Marseilles, a Spanish fam-
               ily in Barcelona and a Russian family in Leningrad engaged
               in the same everyday activities, getting ready for company
               and serving and entertaining their guests. The names of
               the people and objects pictured are given in each of the
               four languages, with pronunciation guide below each word.

Sg 25   Keats, Ezra Jack. Whistle for Willie. New York: Viking,
               1964.
               That the little boy is a Negro is evident only from the
               illustrations. That is very likely a profound lesson for a
               young white child--that a human being can be a Negro with-
               out having anyone remark on the fact. Adventures of a lit-
               tle boy who tries to whistle for his dog the way big boys
               do.

Sg 26   Korshak, Jack. The strange story of Oliver Jones. New
               York: Doubleday, 1966.
               Oliver Jones was very proud of the whiteness of his skin

until the morning he woke up and looked in the mirror to
find he was black! This short illustrated story-verse describes the change in Oliver's attitude toward people when
he discovered that "goodness and badness--just grow from
within--but never depend--on the color of skin."

Sg 27   Lionni, Leo. Little blue and little yellow. New York:
             Astor-Honor, 1959.
             Simple blots of color are the title characters in this book.
         Their parents are bigger blots, their homes still bigger
         blots and their playmates are blots of different colors. Lit-
         tle Blue and Little Yellow hug each other and turn green.

Sg 28   May, Julian. Why people are different colors. New York:
             Holiday, 1971.
             Major races are examined in this book for young readers
         and listeners. The book describes many kinds of differen-
         tiation, but makes it clear that all appearances are only
         superficial distinctions.

Sg 29   What about other people? Jamaica, N.Y.: Eye Gate House,
             1969. (filmstrip)
             Studies the person in relationship to others and discusses
         the different types of social groups.

Sg 30   What do you expect of others? Pleasantville, N.Y.: Guid-
             ance Associates, 1970. (3 color filmstrips with record)
             Shows how a child's expectations influence his actions
         and how prejudgments of others can be avoided.

                                NATION

Sg 31   Godden, Rumer. The mousewife. New York: Viking, 1951.
             A compassionate little mouse frees a captive dove. This
         book deals subtly with the concept of freedom.

Sg 32   Holiday for us. New York: Educational Record Sales, n.d.
             (phonodisc)
             Frank Luther tells about the United States' holidays in
         song and story.

Sg 33   Leaf, Munro. Fair play. Philadelphia: Lippincott, 1939.
             Explains why we have rules, laws, and government, and
         tells how each of us can make our country a better and hap-
         pier place for everyone.

Sg 34   Little citizens. (series) Burbank, Cal.: Cathedral Films,
             1966. (filmstrips)
             Simple stories for developing good character traits and
         better citizenship habits.

Sg 35   Miller, Natalie. The story of the liberty bell. Chicago:

Children's Press, 1965.
How a bell which was cast for the State House in Philadelphia becomes a symbol of freedom during the revolution
and later in the United States.

Sg 36   What is a Congressman?   Mahwah, N. J.:   Troll Associates,
          1969.   (filmstrip)
          Full-color drawings explain what being a Congressman of
          the United States means and shows what a Congressman does.

                              SCHOOL

Sg 37   Bambote, Pierre.   Daba's travels from Ouadda to Bangui.
          New York: Pantheon, 1970.
          There is little money to send a boy to school when one
          must harvest beeswax and honey in the wild as the chief
          cash crop.   Nevertheless, Daba becomes a schoolboy.
          Mourou, his father, has a good year with the wax and his
          small cotton patch.   This makes it possible for him to send
          Daba to Bangui where he can go to school.   Daba is studi-
          ous and bright; he passes the National State Examine in first
          place and is awarded a scholarship to study in France.   The
          small boy of six who left home to learn reading and writing
          takes a long, long journey which requires many years of
          separation from his much loved family in the Central Afri-
          can Republic.

Sg 38   Bulla, Clyde Robert.   Eagle Feather.   New York: Crowell,
          1953.
          Eagle Feather dislikes the idea of school until he visits
          the trading post with his father, meets a boy his own age,
          and learns what school would mean to him in companionship
          and knowledge.   Now that he is eager to go, a moment's
          careless tinkering with Cousin Crook Nose's truck robs him
          of an immediate chance.   He must now pay for damages
          done in service.   Unhappy, the greedy cousin does not re-
          lease him when his term of work expires; so Eagle Feather
          runs away.   Finally, rescued by his father, Eagle Feather
          is assured that he can now live at home again, and go to
          school at the same time.

Sg 39   Cohen, Miriam.   Will I have a friend?   Riverside, N. J.:
          Macmillan, 1967.
          Jim is very apprehensive about his first day in school
          and asks his father, "Will I have a friend?"   The other
          children are busily playing.   All seem to be friends and
          pay no attention to Jim.   However, at rest time, Paul no-
          tices Jim and afterward they too play together.

Sg 40   Leaf, Munro.   The boy who would not go to school.   New
          York: Scholastic, 1971.
          Robert Francis refuses to go to school until he is grown.

He gets bigger but he can't do anything because he didn't go
to school.   He then gives in and comes to find out that
school is fun.

Sg 41   School and family relations.   (series) New York: Educa-
             tional Projections, Inc. , n. d.   (transparencies)
         Suggests ways to improve school and family relations and
the nature of interpersonal relations.   Contents: Cooperat-
is fun; Did you ask permission?; Do it the right way; Fun
with the family; I help at home; Riding the bus; Did you
call?

Sg 42   Yashima, Taro.   Crow boy.   New York: Viking, 1955.
         The story of a strange, shy little boy in a Japanese vil-
lage school who was ignored by his classmates until suddenly and almost too late, a new teacher showed them that
Crow Boy has much to offer.   It tells of how he outgrew
the derisive name of "Chibi or Tiny Boy," and instead became "Crow Boy."   He comes to be accepted by his classmates.   This book helps children understand themselves and
others; shows what it means to be an outsider--to be different.

Intermediate

COMMUNITY

Sg 43   Blassingame, W.   Story of the boy scouts.   Scarsdale, N. Y. :
             Garrard, 1968.
         Here is a book which interests most young boys and cer-
tainly their scoutmasters.   Mr. Blassingame successfully
traces the beginning of scouting in several nations, showing
how various similar groups were eventually Scouts organiza-
tions.   Several true stories of rescue, hiking, and even an
Antarctic exploration are included, while helping others, attending jamborees, and working on conservation projects are
portrayed as the activities of scouting which lead to international understanding.

Sg 44   Cities and government.   New York: McGraw-Hill, 1967.
             (sound, color, 9 minutes, 16mm)
         Shows how boys who need a place to play baseball learn
about city government.   Explains the selection and function
of the city council.   Describes teamwork in city government
world.

Sg 45   Clyner, Eleanor.   Big pile of dirt.   New York: Holt, 1968.
         On our street there was an empty lot.   It was small but
it was full of junk.   Mike tells the story of his efforts to
find a space in his neighborhood where he and his friends
and the little kids could play ball.   Then the mayor and
some ladies decided to have the lot cleared out, the children

sent away. The frustrations of children trying to find a
place to play in a big city are poignantly pictured here.
The story ends surprisingly when the neighbors rally behind
the children.

Sg 46   Community helpers. Glendale, Cal.: Bowmar, n.d. (rec-
            ord, 33-1/3 rpm, 12-inch)
         Presents a complete picture of community living by plac-
         ing emphasis on the individual workers. Gives the listener
         an understanding of the community, develops the understand-
         ing of individual responsibility, and the need for rules and
         regulations.

Sg 47   De Leeuw, Adele. The Girl Scout Story. Scarsdale,
            N.Y.: Garrard, 1965.
         A simply written history of the Girl Scout movement,
         stressing its importance in promoting good will.

Sg 48   Footnotes to community helpers. Vol. 2. Bronx, N.Y.:
            Wilson, n.d.
         Goes beyond the usual policeman, fireman, postman con-
         cept of "community helpers." Explains that the division of
         labor means that every neighbor in his own way is a com-
         munity helper. Presents the community in a perspective
         which show that what is going on now is part of a long pat-
         tern of change and growth.

Sg 49   Good sportsmanship. Chicago: Coronet, 1950. (sound,
            color, 11 minutes, 16mm)
         Joe and Bill learn the rules for good sportsmanship while
         they are on the basketball floor, at home, in the classroom,
         and with friends on the street.

Sg 50   Living in our community. Chicago: Encyclopaedia Britan-
            nica, 1969. (31 frames, color, filmstrip)
         Captioned frames of actual locations and people explain
         what a community is, illustrate the division of labor neces-
         sary to the functioning of a community, and indicate that,
         although not all communities are alike, they have certain
         characteristics in common.

Sg 51   More to talk about. Irving on Hudson, N.Y.: Hudson
            Photographic Industries, Inc., n.d. (study prints)
         Presents photographs of familiar city scenes which will
         motivate discussion about urban life and build vocabulary,
         concepts and positive social attitudes.

Sg 52   The neighborhood community. Chicago: Encyclopaedia Bri-
            tannica Films, 1956. (6 filmstrips, color)
         Photographic study of a neighborhood in terms of the in-
         terdependence of the individuals and families in achieving a
         safe, convenient, pleasant way of life. Touches on various
         financial, social, and economic aspects and dramatizes daily

give-and-take in school, home and playtime situations.

Sg 53   Neighborhoods series.   Chicago: Coronet, 1967.   (6 film-
           strips and records)
           This series depicts the family, social, school and busi-
           ness life in many kinds of neighborhoods as seen through the
           eyes of youngsters in these areas.   It shows how neighbor-
           hoods change and how those living in them can help to im-
           prove them.   Contents: Neighborhoods of many kinds; Neigh-
           borhoods in the city; Neighborhoods in the suburbs; Neighbor-
           hoods in small towns; Neighborhoods in the country; Neigh-
           borhoods change.

Sg 54   Oppenheim, Joanne.   On the other side of the river.   New
           York: Watts, 1972.
           The east and west portions of the town of Wynlock are
           connected only by a bridge and the people on either side of
           the river cannot tolerate each other.   But after the bridge
           collapses, they all learn a lesson in living and working to-
           gether.

Sg 55   Radlauer, Edward.   What is a community.   Encino, Cal.:
           Elk Grove Press, 1967.
           This discussion of how communities grow, change, and
           help each other, deals briefly with the need for laws, taxes,
           community helpers, schools, playgrounds, roads and streets.
           It also discusses what each member of the family can do to
           serve his community.

Sg 56   Robinson, Barry.   On the beat; policemen at work.   New
           York: Harcourt, 1968.
           Photographs and brief text about two New York police-
           men show them as devoted public servants looking out for
           the welfare of all citizens, even when off duty.

Sg 57   Turner, Mina.   What a town meeting means to me.   Boston:
           Houghton, 1951.
           Using a new England town with a population of 3,000 as
           an example, author and artist explain how the town meeting
           works, defines the function of town government and the re-
           sponsibility of the individual.

Sg 58   Vogel, Ray.   The other city.   Canfield, Ohio: White, 1969.
           In their own words and in their own photographs, four
           teenage boys explore the city close to them.   The boys roam
           their urban wasteland photographing the derelict houses, the
           abandoned cars left lying in the streets, their homes, their
           school, families and friends--and their glimpses of the out-
           side world of zoos and ferry boat rides.   Their photographs
           (of New York) and their words and observations as compiled
           by Mr. Vogel make up this book.

Sg 59   Why we have laws.   New York: Learning Corporation of

America, 1970. (film)
An animated story introducing the basic concept of laws.
It concludes that no one can live peacefully without rules and
that if people help make their own laws, they will usually
make fair ones.

Sg 60   Why we have taxes--the town that had no policeman.   New
         York: Learning Corporation of America, 1970.   (film)
         Explains how due to the need of a policeman, everyone
gives some money and the idea of taxation is born.

ETHNIC GROUPS

Sg 61   Agle, Nan Hayden.   Maple Street.   New York: Seabury,
         1970.
         Margaret is nine, black, and sad because her best
friend has moved.   The neighborhood is black, but a poor
white family from Virginia moves in next door and it is
clear from the start that Ellie, who is the same age, will
have nothing to do with Negroes.   But she is forced to.
Her father is absent, her mother hospitalized, and Ellie
seethes while black neighbors care for the small children
left alone.   Margaret has been gathering signatures for a
playground petition, her vision of green grass and trees instead of concrete.   A wary friendship is achieved between
Margaret and Ellie.

Sg 62   American families.   Chicago: Coronet, 1971.   (6 filmstrips,
         color; phonodisc, 6s., 12-in., 33 rpm)
         Describes normal family life of six families of different
ethnic backgrounds--Puerto Rican, Black, Jewish, Italian,
Chinese, and English.

Sg 63   Americans before Columbus.   Mahwah, N. J.: Troll Asso-
         ciates, 1968.   (filmstrip, 40 frames, color)
         The customs, rituals, methods of farming and hunting
and homes of various tribes of American Indians are presented in colorful drawings.

Sg 64   Armer, Laura Adams.   Waterless mountain.   New York:
         Longmans, 1931.
         This is an unusual story of Navaho Indian life as seen
through the eyes of Younger Brother, who learns the songs
of the medicine men and makes new songs for himself.   The
customs and tribal beliefs are skillfully woven into the narrative.   The author is noted for her copies of sand paintings.   Written with sympathy and understanding, it reveals
the mysticism and love of beauty which is innate in the Indian of the highest type.   All children who like poetry and
who care for the Indian will enjoy it.   The illustrations in
aquatone by the author and Sidney Armer reflect the beauty
of the story and its setting in the deserts and canyons of
northern Arizona.

Sg 65   Baker, Elizabeth. Stronger than hate. Boston: Houghton,
         1969.
         There aren't any Afro-Americans in Wharton but the lo-
         cal people hold an annual celebration honoring a 200-years
         deceased black Whartonite.   Wharton has its chance to find
         out its true feelings about blacks when several families seek
         homes in Wharton.   They are middle class families with em-
         ployment nearby.   The town divides over the presence of
         these blacks.   High school-aged Francie Ferris, a real es-
         tate agent's daughter, and Brew Marshall, both first family
         offspring, are forced to take swift action when the black
         families are terrorized, and the entire town faces itself
         when one of the black children dies.

Sg 66   Ball, Dorothy Whitney. Don't drive up a dirt road. New
         York: Lion, 1970.
         Nineteen-year-old Dicky boy Lewis believes he is bound
         for trouble if he remains in his Mississippi home.   His
         good job with a humanitarian white man is impossible after
         he learns of the lynching of an innocent man.   When Mr.
         Robbins is shot and his home burned, Dicky feels he has
         caused his death.   He participates in the walk through Mis-
         sissippi which Martin Luther King leads as a protest against
         the Goodman, Schwerner, and Chaney deaths.   These things
         plus the destruction of their church cause his family to
         move north.   There, in substandard housing, Dicky and his
         folks strive to maintain family ties.   Unique in its account
         of the Mississippi Civil Rights program from the point of
         view of a local black.

Sg 67   Baum, Betty. Patricia crosses town. Westminster, Md. :
         Knopf, 1965.
         Twelve-year-old Patricia is one of the first New York
         children to be bused across town to integrate an all-white
         school.   Impulsive and mischievous, she is suspicious of
         all white children and afraid of being rejected.   Her teacher
         in the new school uses her interests in puppetry and acting
         to help her gain confidence; these interests also lead to her
         friendship with Sarah, who overcomes Pat's distrust.   Sarah
         and another white girl later come across town to show their
         affection for Pat and put on their interracial puppet show to
         celebrate Pat's father's return from the hospital.

Sg 67a   Beim, Jerrold. Swimming hole. New York: Morrow, 1968.
         The new boy who doesn't want to swim with anyone who
         is colored has no fun until he learns that color does not
         matter.

Sg 68   Benchley, Nathaniel. Small wolf. New York: Harper,
         1972.
         A sad and simple story set on the island of Manhattan
         about the Indians displaced from their homes and hunting
         grounds by the white man.

Sg 69   Black, Algernon. The first book of ethics. New York:
          Watts, 1965.
          An explanation and introduction to the problems of how
          men should behave toward men, presented from Ethical cul-
          ture viewpoint and therefore not based on the idea of ethics
          as absolute standard.

Sg 70   Brodsky, Mimi. The house at 12 Rose Street. New York:
          Abelard-Schuman, 1966.
          The problems of a twelve-year-old Negro boy whose fam-
          ily has moved into a white neighborhood are not easily solved,
          but they are probed deeply in this skillfully written and time-
          ly story. The characterizations are well rounded and the
          conflicts perceptively presented.

Sg 71   Burchardt, Nellie. Reggie's no-good bird. New York:
          Watts, 1967.
          Reggie's brutality to a bird imperils his relationships
          with his multi-ethnic peers.

Sg 72   Carlson, Natalie Savage. Marchers for the dream. New
          York: Harper, 1969.
          Bethany is eleven and black and finds it hard to under-
          stand why her family can't find a decent home for the $60
          a month they can afford. When her grandmother decides to
          go to Washington to share in the Poor People's March,
          Bethany goes along to take care of her and when she re-
          turns, she finds the courage to work for justice in her own
          way.

Sg 73   Christopher, Matt. Baseball flyhawk. Boston: Little,
          Brown, 1963.
          Chico, when he moves from Puerto Rico to New York,
          finally becomes a member of the baseball team and a fast
          friend of the most popular boy on the team.

Sg 74   Clark, Ann Nolan. Little Navajo bluebird. New York:
          Viking, 1943.
          The story of Doli, a charming Navajo songstress, whose
          heart carries the burden of her people and who does her
          best to further the old customs and ways. Through the sym-
          pathy and wisdom of her brother's wife, she comes to see
          that the Red Man's Trail and the White Man's Trail may
          meet.

Sg 75   Clifford, Eth. The year of the three-legged deer. Boston:
          Houghton, 1972.
          Callous and inhumane acts by white men against the Del-
          aware Indians in Indiana during the early 19th Century bring
          anguish and separation to Jesse Benton and his Indian wife
          and their two children. Authentic in background and com-
          pelling despite its awkward flashback techniques--a thought-
          provoking dramatization of the evils of prejudice.

Sg 76   Colman, Hila. End of the game. Cleveland: World, 1971.
         When black Donny visits white Timmy's home for three
         weeks, he is expected to carry a good behavior pattern with
         him. Instead, Donny allows Timmy's sisters to blame him
         for all the bad things that happen. Their mother then ac-
         cepts the bad things because "an underprivileged ghetto child
         doesn't know any better." When the boys are lost, Donny's
         mother comes to the Stevens home to wait out the search.
         The boys are found and Timmy's mother discovers the truth,
         but Donny and Timmy have been honest with each other and
         part friends.

Sg 77   Craig, John. Zach. New York: Coward, 1972.
         After the death of his family, an uncle and aunt, in a
         fire on the Canadian Ojibway reservation, Zach Kenebec
         finds an unwelcome identity as the last of the Agawas. His
         search to find others of the tribe and his odyssey over Can-
         ada and the U.S. West involve him with every situation and
         type of person. In relationships that ultimately prove mean-
         ingful, Zach finds the ties that bind people together are not
         blood, age, sex, or race, but common values.

Sg 78   De Angelo, Marguerite. Thee, Hannah. New York: Double-
         day, 1940.
         Her parents' scolding always started "Thee, Hannah!" be-
         cause she tried to brighten up her plain Quaker clothes.
         She rescues a Negro slave because her clothes identified
         her as a friend. Thus, Hannah learns to be proud of her
         heritage.

Sg 79   Dignity: invitation to new experiences. Cincinnati, Ohio:
         Friendship Press, 1969. (Game--board, cards, 4 play-
         ers, 30 minutes)
         The object of the game, which depicts many socio-eco-
         nomic areas, is for the player to move from the lowest
         stratum of society through to a designated successful ending.
         The players' moves are blocked by penalties forcing them to
         move back. Dignity has been used effectively by fourth
         graders in giving them an understanding of some of the hard-
         ships that people face as they try to move out of the poverty
         levels of society.

Sg 80   Douglass, Frederick. Life and times of Frederick Douglass.
         New York: Crowell, 1966.
         A book that was and is exciting and a remarkable record
         of a man who was born a slave and died a national figure of
         esteem described with modesty and candidly. He speaks
         with objectivity about personal matters and with passion
         about public affairs.

Sg 81   Durham, John. Me and Arch and the pest. New York:
         Four Winds Press, 1970.
         Bit and his folks move from Georgia to Los Angeles.

There they live in South Los Angeles, close to Watts in a
mostly black neighborhood.   Arch, a black boy, becomes
Bit's best friend--which doesn't please Bit's folks, nor
Arch's either.   The boys remain friends, however, become
joint owners of a pedigreed dog, apprehend some criminals,
and save a blue ribbon champion.   An action-packed story
of friendship.

Sg 82   Eddie, American Indian boy.   Chicago: Society for Visual
             Education, Inc., n.d.   (film)
         Presents the unique position of the American Indian in
society, his economic and social problems on the reservation and his cultural alienation in the city as evidenced by
Eddie, who moved from a reservation.

Sg 83   Erwin, Betty K.   Behind the magic line.   Boston: Little,
             Brown, 1969.
         Dozie was born in the ghetto and she helps Mama by
cleaning and caring for the younger children.   When she
meets Uncle Samuel Dan at her playhouse in the vacant lot,
magic enters her life.   He finds money enough for a huge
steak that feeds the entire family, he knows a remedy that
helps the baby's teething, and he saves Whitney from trouble
and helps Papa get the family out of the city.   A realistic
tale of inner-city life today.

Sg 84   Evans, Eva Knox.   All about us.   New York: Western
             Publishing, 1947.
         Expounds the scientific and common sense lessons that
neither race nor skin color nor blood type affect the basic
dignity of all men.

Sg 85   _____.   People are important.   New York: Golden Press,
             1951.
         The people, not their customs, are the important thing.
The differences among people in language, dress, food,
types of dwelling and ways of doing things are explained.
To understand that our ways may seem strange to others is
the first step in getting along with the world's two billion
people.

Sg 86   Garden, Nancy.   What happened in Marston.   New York:
             Four Winds Press, 1971.
         Dave Bellinger's eighth grade is integrated when Joel
Garth is enrolled.   The teachers and whole school were
prepared for the movement of the one black into the school
but the most carefully prepared were the eighth graders.
The teachers' pep talks about treating Joel "nice" build a
wall of unnaturalness between the boy and the white students.
A very real problem in sound relationship is described in
this story.

Sg 87   Graham, Lorenz B.   North Town.   New York: Crowell,

1965.
After race trouble in the South, sixteen-year-old David Williams and his family move to North Town, only to find that they have not escaped discrimination. David's experiences in an integrated high school, his brush with the juvenile court, and the family's housing problem are handled with unemotional sympathy and a note of optimism.

Sg 88   Harris, Janet. The long freedom road. New York: McGraw-Hill, 1967.
Presents the history of the Negro's struggle for first class citizenship. Included are discussions of the Supreme Court decision that "separate but equal" schools are unconstitutional, the Montgomery bus boycott, sit-ins, freedom riders, the "March on Washington," the Mississippi project gains made by Negroes, and problems which still remain unsolved.

Sg 89   Harris, Marilyn. Peppersalt land. New York: Four Winds Press, 1970.
Tollie and Slocum are like a blue and white morning glory on one vine. Slocum visits her Grandmother English every summer, while Tollie, a black orphan from babyhood has known no other parent save "The Grandmother." But the summer of their twelfth year, both girls lose their enchantment over Budding Grove, Georgia. Mr. Cicero, the storekeeper, begins to look at the two girls differently. And, too, there is angry, talented black Howard Jackson. The conflict between these two causes Tollie and Slocum to flee into the dangerous viper-infested swamp called Peppersalt Land. And everyone involved is forced to examine themselves and take a stand.

Sg 90   Hough, Elizabeth. It's time for brotherhood. Philadelphia: Macrae Smith, 1962.
After a brief comment on the concept of "Love thy neighbor" as it appears in many religions, there are stories of individuals and groups whose lives and work have been shining examples of this principle of brotherhood put into action.

Sg 91   Hull, Eleanor. Trainful of strangers. New York: Atheneum, 1968.
Eight children from many different backgrounds are on their way to attend a television show on quasars. When the lights go out and the subway train stalls, they begin to get acquainted. What happens to their families afterwards--and the next Saturday's TV show--makes an unusually interesting character study of young people in the big city.

Sg 92   I wonder why. New York: Rosenthal Productions, 1964.
(16mm film, black and white)
A photographic essay describing the feelings of a child as he ponders the injustices with which he has to live be-

cause of the color of his skin.

Sg 93   Jackson, Jesse. Call me Charley. New York: Harper,
         1945.
         Charley proves that he can meet the challenge of being
         the only Negro boy in his school. But this happens only
         after he learns that there are people hoping he can live up
         to the demands of daily life.

Sg 94   [No entry]

Sg 95   Justus, May. New boy in school. New York: Hastings,
         1963.
         Simply told story of a small black boy's adjustment in
         an all white school. Not only is he a new boy but he is
         also black.

Sg 96   Kesselman, Wendy Ann. Angelita. New York: Hill and
         Wang, 1970.
         Angelita is sad and lonely in her new home in New York
         City. She misses the fields and trees of her Puerto Rican
         home and thinks the city is like a big cage until she makes
         some friends in her class at school. Will be useful with
         Puerto Rican immigrants and their children and with other
         children who have moved to a city from a small town.

Sg 97   Korshak, Jack. The strange story of Oliver Jones. Chi-
         cago: Mid-American Publishing Company, 1966.
         Oliver Jones was very proud of the whiteness of his skin
         until the morning he woke up and looked in his mirror to
         find he was black! This short illustrated story-verse de-
         scribes the change in Oliver's attitude toward people when
         he discovered that "goodness--badness--just grow from with-
         in--but never depend--on the color of skin."

Sg 98   Lampman, Evelyn. The year of Small Shadow. New York:
         Harcourt, 1971.
         This is the story of an eleven-year-old Indian boy who
         spends a year living in town with a white lawyer while his
         father is in prison for horse-"borrowing." Small Shadow
         learns much about the strange customs and characteristics
         of whites and eventually overcomes the prejudice of the
         townspeople toward him, but when at the end of the year he
         realizes that the people of the community are trying to make
         him turn his back on his own people, he returns with his
         father to the reservation. Told with gentle humor, the
         story gives a perceptive, believable picture of Indian-white
         relationships in the Pacific Northwest in the 1880s.

Sg 99   Martin, Patricia Miles. Chicanos. New York: Parents
         Magazine, 1971.
         The history, way of life, and contributions of Mexican-
         Americans told simply for young readers.

Sg 100   Mathis, Sharon Bell. Sidewalk story. New York: Viking,
           1971.
           The world of Lily Etta and her friend Tanya is thrown
           into chaos when the men come to evict Tanya's mother and
           her seven children from their Harlem flat. Lily Etta is
           determined to get help. How she does secure help makes
           a heart-warming story of true friendship between two lit-
           tle girls. Winner in 1970 of the Council on Interracial
           Books for Children contest.

Sg 101   Neville, Emily Cheney. Berries Goodman. New York:
           Harper, 1965.
           Berries Goodman and his family move from their
           cramped apartment in New York City to the suburbs so
           that they can have a backyard and a place for a dog. In-
           stead of finding openness, Berries becomes enclosed by
           the walls of prejudice because of his relationship with Sid-
           ney Fine, a Jewish boy. They become good friends and
           enjoy bike riding, playing football, and just being together.
           Berries' next-door neighbor, Sandra, has acquired a pre-
           judice against Jews from her mother and resents the rela-
           tionship of the boys. An accident in which Sidney is in-
           jured forces his parents to insist he not play with Berries.
           Believing this to be unfair, the boys defy their parents and
           meet secretly until discovered. Years later, when they
           are in high school and both have moved closer to New York,
           the boys renew their friendship to the surprise of their
           parents.

Sg 102   Politi, Leo. Moy Moy. New York: Scribner, 1960.
           It is from the viewpoint of Moy Moy, a young girl, that
           we feel the unique excitement of New York festivities in a
           Los Angeles Chinese-American community. This book does
           a good job of portraying the Chinese as an ethnic group in
           the United States.

Sg 103   Riementz, Jill. Sweet Pea. New York: Harcourt, 1969.
           Sweet Pea is a little black girl who lives deep in the
           Alabama countryside, but she's like other little girls every-
           where: "If I had three wishes, I would go to New York,
           be an airline stewardess, and be in the twelfth grade."
           Her life is shown in simple text and skillful photography in
           all its harsh poverty but with a joyous quality many may
           enjoy.

Sg 104   Rose, Karen. Single trail. Chicago: Follett, 1969.
           Two boys go to the same school in a Los Angeles neigh-
           borhood. Ricky has learned how to make friends quickly
           in spite of his family's moving nine times in twelve years.
           Earl does not care whether people like him or not, espe-
           cially white people.

Sg 105   Sachs, Marilyn. Peter and Veronica. New York: Doubleday, 1969.

Peter is twelve--bright, popular and carefully watched over by his mother. Veronica is thirteen--a tomboy and bully, with no real friends besides Peter. Unkempt, sharp, she lives with her little brother, sister, and mother who is divorced. When Peter is about to be barmitzvahed, he quarrels bitterly with his mother and defies his father to invite Veronica to the ceremony. But Veronica does not come. Suddenly, the friendship is in trouble. Both learn a lot about true friendship.

Sg 106   Shotwell, Louisa A. Roosevelt Grady. Cleveland: World, 1963.

Roosevelt Grady illuminates a social problem in American life that is often forgotten--the lot of the impoverished migrant worker. Although the Grady's have few material possessions, the family displays an inner strength built on bonds of love and integrity which help them to endure and finally overcome their problems.

Sg 107   Sorensen, Virginia. Around the corner. New York: Harcourt, 1971.

Eleven-year-old black Junie Johnson's mother warned him not to associate with the newcomers in their rapidly changing neighborhood in Alexandria, a suburb of Washington, D. C. She said they were poor, white squatters, were dirty, and lived with animals. But Junie, lured by their hillbilly music, met the Hinkles and his acquaintance with them gradually blossomed into friendship between the black and white families.

Sg 108   Walter, Mildred Pitts. Lillie of Watts: A birthday discovery. Los Angeles: Ward Ritchie Press, 1969.

The story of a few days in the life of an eleven-year-old girl has interest because it is set in Watts and because it puts into perspective the problems of a ghetto child.

Sg 109   What about other people? Jamaica, N.Y.: Eye Gate House, 1969. (filmstrip)

Studies the person in relationship to others and discusses the different types of social groups.

Sg 110   Weiner, Sandra. It's wings that make birds fly: the story of a boy. New York: Pantheon, 1968.

Based on taped conversations with Harlem children, primarily with one child (Otis Bennett), the author has given us a most moving picture of a young boy, a picture beautifully augmented by photographs. It is Otis himself who gives the book warmth and dignity, expressing in his candor all the need for love, the tender heart, and the acceptance of his broken and shifting home life. His comments are sometimes poignant and sometimes funny and always genuine.

Sg 111   Wier, Ester. Easy does it. New York: Vanguard, 1965.
          The Reeses, the first Negroes to move into an all-
          white neighborhood, are boycotted. Chip Woodman likes
          the Reese boy, who is his age. Problems arise but all
          works out in the end.

Sg 112   Will. Four leaf clover. New York: Harcourt, 1959.
          Mark and Peter need some luck so they look for a 4-
          leaf clover. A bull charges, they land in a tree, the
          branch breaks, they fall on a horse, etc. They finally
          relax and admire the "lucky" clover leaf.

Sg 113   William, Andy and Ramon and five friends at school.
          Santa Monica, Cal.: BFA Educational Media, 1967.
          (filmstrip)
          Stories of three children from different racial back-
          grounds and their friends which describe their families,
          their neighborhood, the community, their school and their
          recreation.

Sg 114   Yates, Elizabeth. Amos Fortune, free man. New York:
          Dutton, 1950.
          Tells the story of a Negro man and his struggles to
          freedom. It tells of his sympathy and courage to do the
          right thing. Shows respect for others is important even
          in achieving a personal goal.

Sg 115   Young, Margaret. The first book of American Negroes.
          New York: Watts, 1966.
          The American Negro and his history; where the Negro
          lives; education; employment; cultural contributions; the civil
          rights movement. Gives account of the struggles and accom-
          plishments of the American Negro from 1619 to the present.

                              NATION

Sg 116   Are you a good citizen? Chicago: Coronet, 1949. (16mm
          film, 11 minutes)
          Points out basic qualifications of a good citizen. Shows
          the role of a good citizen in a democracy. Stimulates in-
          dividuals to check on their own citizenship qualifications.

Sg 117   Bradley, Duane. The newspaper, its place in a democracy.
          New York: Van Nostrand, 1965.
          An experienced reporter analyzes the place of the news-
          paper in the United States today, with many timely as
          well as historical illustrations. Includes discussion of the
          work of a newsman, problems of freedom of press, uses
          of propaganda.

Sg 118   Brown, Harriet M. America is my country. Boston:
          Houghton, 1955.

Brings together symbols, documents, quotations, songs,
and landmarks which help young people to understand what
it means to be an American and to accept their responsibilities as citizens of a democracy.   Valuable material for
social studies and for the celebration of patriotic holidays.

Sg 119   Cavanah, Frances. Our Country's Freedom.   Chicago:
         Rand McNally, 1966.
         This history traces the development of freedom from
         Colonial times to the present, stressing the idea that
         liberty is a hard won blessing requiring continual vigilance
         in its defense.

Sg 120   Children of America.   Elgin, Ill.: Child's World, 1969.
         (8 study prints)
         Drawings illustrate the different children that make up
         America.   Indians, Blacks, Jews, Anglos, Chinese, Mexi-
         cans, Italians, and Puerto Ricans.   It shows their clothing
         and their features as they are involved in activities.
         Helps children understand and appreciate other people.

Sg 121   Commager, Henry Steele.   The great constitution, a book
         for young Americans.   Indianapolis: Bobbs, 1961.
         Describes the Constitution and tells of the ideals of the
         founding fathers who were a part of the creation of the
         Constitution.   It describes the difficulties involved in pre-
         paring a document which would provide a better govern-
         ment.

Sg 122   De Leeuw, Cateau.   Determined to be free.   Nashville:
         Thomas Nelson, 1963.
         A young patriot who spied for the American troops
         while passing as a Tory is rejected by his friends and
         neighbors.

Sg 123   Democracy: What you should know about it and why.
         New York: McGraw-Hill, 1964.   (kit)
         Contents: Why study democracy; Democracy in America;
         Basic ideas of a democracy; Democratic society; Economics
         and government; Meeting the challenge to democracy.

Sg 124   Five families.   New York: Scholastic Book Service, 1972.
         (filmstrip)
         Designed to make young children aware of different cul-
         tural patterns in American society.   Describes rather
         average and typical family activities of a Chinese family
         in San Francisco's Chinatown, a reservation Navajo family
         in Arizona, a Mexican-American bilingual family in Ari-
         zona, a black family in New York City, and a Caucasian
         family with an unusual occupation.

Sg 125   Forbes, Esther.   Johnny Tremain.   New York: Newbery
         Award Records, 1970.   (Phonotape cassette, 2s, 1-7/8

ips, 21 minutes)
Dramatization of this story of the American Revolution
opens with the trial of Johnny for stealing a valuable silver cup. Johnny's tale was that his mother had given it
to him and claimed relationship with a rich Boston merchant. A stirring story with authentic background sounds
and music.

Sg 126   Goldman, Peter. Civil rights, the challenge of the four-
          teenth amendment. New York: Coward-McCann, 1965.
          Account of Negroes' struggles to achieve quality as
          American citizens. Presents leaders, freedom marches,
          rides, and sit-ins. Stresses individual responsibility in
          making these efforts successful.

Sg 127   Hall, Elvajean. Pilgrim stories. Chicago: Rand, 1964.
          A simple narrative describing the troubles and adven-
          tures of the Pilgrims, from their persecution in England
          to their first difficult years in the colonies at Plymouth
          Rock.

Sg 128   Hoffman, Edwin D. Pathways to freedom: nine dramatic
          episodes in the evolution of the American democratic
          tradition. Boston: Houghton, 1964.
          Nine exciting episodes in our history illustrating how
          we secured our present freedoms.

Sg 129   Johnston, Johanna. Together in America. New York:
          Dodd, 1965.
          The book is an attempt to show that people of both
          European and African descent have contributed to America's
          discovery, growth and strength from the beginning--that
          the contributions of some who have labored under brutal
          disadvantages have been remarkable; and that the needs
          and pressures of the times have played a part in what hap-
          pened and what was accomplished in every era.

Sg 130   Leaf, Munro. Fair play. Philadelphia: Lippincott, 1967.
          Explains why we have rules, laws, and government.
          This book tells how each of us can make our country a
          better and happier place for everyone to live.

Sg 131   Lens, Sidney. Working men: the story of labor. New
          York: Putnam, 1960.
          Detailed history of American labor which presents
          growth of unions, their past successes, challenge of the
          future and brief biographies of leaders of labor movements.

Sg 132   Lindop, Edmund. The first book of elections. New York:
          Watts, 1968.
          This book explains clearly how elections work. Writ-
          ten by a teacher of government and history, it discusses
          many phases of elections in the U. S. including voter quali-

fications, voting machines, electioneering, campaigns, national conventions, nominations, and the electoral college.

Sg 133   McNeer, May. Give me freedom. Nashville: Abingdon,
          1964.
          Biographies of seven men and women: Penn, Paine,
          Lovejoy, Stanton, Markham, Anderson, and Einstein, whose
          lives and actions were dedicated to a Freedom cause.

Sg 134   Michaelis, John U. Social studies for children in a de-
          mocracy: recent trends and developments. Englewood
          Cliffs, N. J. : Prentice-Hall, 1963.
          One of the best and most up-to-date source on content,
          principles, and methods in the important area of social
          studies.

Sg 135   Miers, Earl Shenck. Freedom. New York: Grosset,
          1965.
          The author discusses the history and meaning of Ameri-
          can freedom and rights, as found in the United States Con-
          stitution.

Sg 136   Miller, Natalie. The story of the Liberty Bell. Chicago:
          Children's Press, 1965.
          In 1752 the Liberty Bell was first cast for the Pennsyl-
          vania State House in Philadelphia. Gradually the bell be-
          came a symbol of America's fight for independence. The
          author tells how Philadelphia's inhabitants gathered when
          the bell rang to discuss tax laws and freedom.

Sg 137   Our Country's Flag. New York: McGraw-Hill Films,
          1960. (film)
          Traces the history of the American Flag showing how
          it was selected and how the stars were added to its de-
          sign as new states came into being.

Sg 138   Our heritage of freedom. (series) Jamaica, N. Y. : Eye
          Gate House, 1959. (color, 43 frames)
          Discusses the American heritage of freedom, the people,
          and the future of America. Presents the American dream
          of freedom as it was kindled by valiant men and women
          who lifted democracy into a living example in a workable
          way of life.

Sg 139   Wagner, Ruth. Put democracy to work. New York:
          Abelard-Schuman, 1961.
          Presents the facts and meaning of democracy as a way
          of life, and prepared boys and girls to put democracy to
          work at home and on a worldwide basis.

Sg 140   What do you do about rules? Pleasantville, N. Y. : Guid-
          ance Associates, n. d. (filmstrip/record)
          A two-part presentation of the unresolved dilemma of

where to divide personal independence for group needs and
allegiance.

Sg 141   What liberty and justice means.   Los Angeles: Dimension
          Films, 1964.   (16mm, 10 minutes)
          Uses examples from everyday life to depict liberty as
          the freedom to choose, and justice as fairness and mutual
          respect for the beliefs and ideals of others.

                              SCHOOL

Sg 142   Arora, Shirley L.   Left-handed Chank.   Chicago: Follett,
          1966.
          Kumaran, twelve, who lives in India, is very proud of
          his father, head of the fishermen.   It is a poor season
          and the men blame it on their leader who is influenced by
          the new ideals of the Inspector of Fisheries.   Slowly, after
          near death at sea when they are rescued because of the
          inspector, the men realize that it isn't luck (like finding a
          left-handed shell) but information they need, and the boy
          goes to school.

Sg 143   Brown, Margery W.   That Ruby.   New York: Viking,
          1962.
          The first day of school in Newark everyone, except
          Ruby, looks nice.   Bonnie, caught staring at her is
          challenged by Ruby.   Finally, everyone learns to like
          Ruby, except Bonnie, who continues to consider her a
          troublemaker.   After Ruby proves that she is a brave girl
          and one who really wishes people well, Bonnie gives her
          a chance.   A well done story of rivalry between girls in
          a public school.

Sg 144   Carlson, Natalie.   School bell in the valley.   New York:
          Viking, 1963.
          Belle learns that the problems of not having an educa-
          tion are greater than those faced in acquiring proper
          training.

Sg 145   Clark, Ann Nolan.   Little Navajo Bluebird.   New York:
          Viking, 1943.
          Little Bluebird, a Navajo girl, who has seen how Big
          Brother returned from school with only scorn for the life
          of his mother's hogan, is determined that she will never
          let them send her to school.   But from Uncle's young wife
          and Sister Hobah, she learns that school may have much
          to teach her that will make life healthier and happier with-
          out taking away any of the old customs that she loves.

Sg 146   Clarke, John.   High school drop out.   New York: Double-
          day, 1964.
          Fed up with school, convinced he can do something

bigger and better, Joe Bancroft quits. His parents, especially his father, go along with his plans to work and
earn good money because their lives have been tuned to
work young. Only Joe's girlfriend, Carla, tries to change
his mind. After several bad experiences, Joe returns to
school. When Joe mutters, "School is such a drag!" many
boys will agree; but when he vows after repeated failures,
"I am going to make it!," his real life counterparts may
give returning to school a second thought.

Sg 147   Coles, Robert. Dead end school. Boston: Little, Brown,
                1968.
                Jimmy isn't too pleased when his mother decides against
          letting him be shifted to another crowded run-down school.
          When the other parents in the neighborhood join his mother
          in protest, Jimmy and his classmates discover a whole new
          world in a good school across town.

Sg 148   De Jong, Meindert. Wheel on the school. New York:
                Newbery Award Records, n.d. (Phonodisc--2s, 12 in,
                33 rpm--also available in cassette--based on book of
                the same title)
                Dramatization of the experience of a small group of
          Dutch school children who decide to entice the storks back
          to their hometown.

Sg 149   Finlayson, Ann. Runaway teen. New York: Doubleday,
                1963.
                Libby Canfield runs away to Chicago when she feels she
          is slighted by her mother and stepfather on her 16th birth-
          day. Because she lacks a high school diploma, she is un-
          able to get a decent and enjoyable job. For recreation,
          she goes with a local gang, is looked upon as a member
          of it, and almost gets into serious trouble. She finally
          is aware of what she is becoming and she makes peace
          with her family.

Sg 150   How do you feel? Los Angeles: Churchill Films, 1969.
                (6 filmstrips, average 36 fr each, color)
                Presents live photography showing both positive and
          negative actions in different situations, and captions that
          are thought-provoking questions for viewer discussion to
          help him gain a better understanding of himself and others.
          Includes the following filmstrips: How do you feel about
          your community?; How do you feel about your home and
          family?; How do you feel about other children?; How do
          you feel about being alone? Useful for group and individual
          study in guidance and language arts.

Sg 151   Lampman, Evelyn. Go up the road. New York: Athene-
                um, 1972.
                Once again twelve-year-old Mexican-American Yolanda
          had to leave school before the end of the term, thus failing

to pass into fifth grade. In telling Yolanda's story and
how she achieved her goal of reaching fifth grade, the
author demonstrates the plight of the migrant worker as
well.

Sg 152   Lenski, Lois. Prairie school. Philadelphia: Lippincott,
            1951.
            The great blizzard of 1949 is the setting for this story
            which is valuable in showing boys and girls the problems
            of going to school in the wheat growing prairie country.

Sg 153   Lewiton, Mina. Faces looking up. New York: Harper,
            1960.
            An account of school children of twelve different coun-
            tries, their similarities and differences, what they learn,
            and their influence on the future of their countries.

Sg 154   Muehl, Lois. The hidden year of Devlin Bates. New
            York: Holiday, 1967.
            A very convincing portrait of a loner whose non-con-
            formity and poor achievement at school cause friction and
            conflict between him and his parents. His gradual accep-
            tance of responsibility and decision to make the first move
            toward mutual understanding is believable and satisfying.

Sg 155   Rose, Karen. Single trail. Chicago: Follett, 1969.
            Two boys go to the same school in a Los Angeles neigh-
            borhood. Ricky has learned how to make friends quickly,
            in spite of his family's moving nine times in twelve years.
            Earl doesn't care whether people like him or not--especial-
            ly white people.

Sg 156   Scarry, Patsy. Schools around the world. Morristown,
            N.J.: Silver, 1965.
            What is it like to go to school in the United States,
            Canada, Europe, Africa, the East and Australia--how stu-
            dents get there, what activities are carried on and what is
            studied.

Sg 157   School rules: how they help us. Chicago: Coronet, 1953.
            (16mm, color, 11 minutes)
            Shows everyday scenes in which rules influence our be-
            havior, and emphasizes that exceptions can't be granted.
            Shows some ways a new student can learn rules and the
            rules to work cooperatively to improve them.

Sg 158   Schools and learning: learning is my job. New York:
            McGraw-Hill, 1968. (16mm, color, 10 minutes)
            Presents a child as he explains to his grandmother how
            he is taught and given the responsibility to learn. Reviews
            the methods employed--reading, experiments, solving prob-
            lems, and reconstructing what has already been done.
            Shows brain learning by viewing and listening to audio-

visual tools, by inquiring and by doing.

Sg 159   Speiser, Jean. Schools are where you find them. New
           York: Day, 1971.
           Many photographs from the countries of the United
           Nations and simple text describe the schools of today--
           where they are, how children get to school, how they
           learn, what the schools and teachers are like.

Sg 160   Ways to settle disputes. Chicago: Coronet, 1950. (16mm
           11 minutes)
           Alice, Jerry and Eddie learn everyday incidents at play
           and school, how disputes can be settled by compromise,
           by obeying the rules, by finding the facts or finding opin-
           ions according to what is involved.

                              WORLD

Sg 161   Dobler, Lavinia. Arrow book of the United Nations. New
           York: Four Winds Press, 1963.
           Answers specific questions about the United Nations sub-
           mitted by children; covers how it began, the Charter, the
           members, how it works, and the U.N. headquarters.

Sg 162   Donan, Rozella. People around the world. Encino, Cal. :
           Elk Grove Press, 1968.
           Explains to the young reader or listener very simply
           why people are alike the world over. Needs for shelter,
           water, food, clothing, work and communication are dis-
           cussed.

Sg 163   Doss, Helen. All the children of the world. Nashville:
           Abingdon, 1958.
           In simple text and colorful illustrations, children are
           taught to appreciate the individual differences that make
           each person special and the world an interesting place to
           live in.

Sg 164   French, Harry. The lance of Kanana. West Caldwell,
           N. J. : Lothrop, 1932.

Sg 165   Kelen, Emery. Peace is an adventure. Des Moines:
           Meredith, 1967.
           Peace is transmitted in numerous ways. This book is
           an interesting one--sharing stories about the people and
           the agencies that work for the United Nations.

Sg 166   Kenworthy, Leonard. Three billion neighbors. Boston:
           Ginn, 1965.
           Photographs and captions present different ways of life
           for people around the world; helps children understand
           their neighbors and people in general better.

Sg 167   Larsen, Peter. United Nations at work throughout the
              world. West Caldwell, N.J.: Lothrop, 1971.
              Shows how the various agencies of the U.N. Develop-
          ment Program are improving the life of children in the
          world's developing countries. Each chapter tells how a
          child's life has been affected by a particular agency work-
          ing in the village.

Sg 168   Lobsenz, Norman M. The Peace Corps. New York:
              Watts, 1968.
              This survey traces the formation and progress of the
          Peace Corps with stories about its volunteers and their
          work.

Sg 169   Our world neighbors: India. Lakewood, Fla.: Imperial
              Film, 1969. (4 filmstrips, color, and 4 phonodiscs:
              8s, 12in, 33rpm)
              Four filmstrips make up the series: Water blesses In-
          dia; The face of India; Village life in India; and India's
          people.   The variety of people, occupations, religions,
          and geographical terrain found in India are captured in
          these filmstrips.

Sg 170   Sasek, M. This is the United Nations. Riverside, N.J.:
              Macmillan, 1968.
              An interesting guide to the United Nations, the organiza-
          tion of which is briefly explained. The various rooms,
          art objects, and items of interest are pictured and stories
          told about them. A chart shows the flags of the 122 na-
          tions that make up the United Nations; and the specialized
          agencies--UNESCO, UNICEF, WHO, etc., are listed and
          identified.

Sg 171   Schlinling, Paula. The United Nations and what it does.
              West Caldwell, N.J.: Lothrop, 1962.
              The structure and workings of the United Nations--its
          many agencies, councils, and committees.

Sg 172   Schools, families, neighborhoods. Chicago: Field Enter-
              prises, 1969. (3 filmstrips, color; and phonodisc--6s,
              12in, 33rpm; 36 studyprints; 9 shortstrips; 4 charts)
              An entire first grade social studies program with de-
          tailed instructions in an excellent teacher's guide. Stresses
          inquiry approach to inductive learning. Contents: Schools
          around the world, Families around the world, and Neighbor-
          hoods around the world.

Sg 173   Sommerfelt, Aimee. The road to Agra. New York: Cri-
              terion, 1961.
              A thirteen-year-old boy walks almost 300 miles to take
          his little blind sister to an eye hospital. Some of the
          work of UNICEF is brought into this story of modern India.

Sg 174   Villages around the world.   East Providence, R. I. :   Avid
              Training Systems, 1971.   (sound filmstrip)
              Shows how people live in rural and agricultural com-
          munities and why they choose certain areas in which to
          live.

Sg 175   Whittlesey, Susan.   U.S. Peace Corps: the challenge of
              good will.   New York: Coward-McCann, 1963.
              Six volunteers report their experiences in underdeveloped
          countries where they trained people to help themselves.
          Included are suggestions by which readers may assist the
          Peace Corps.

PART III

INDEXES

245

AUTHOR INDEX

247

The courage of Sarah Noble
In 53
Dead end bluff In 79
Every day courage and a common
sense In 54
Hannah's brave year In 81
Henry explores the jungle In
76
House upon a rock In 72
How many miles to Babylon?
In 58
I always wanted to be somebody
In 62
Independent voices In 69
Indian uprising In 59
Island of the blue dolphins In
71
Kristy's courage In 41
The long journey In 52
Luis was lost In 42
Magical Melons In 47
Melindy's Medal In 56
My brother, Stevie In 50
Never try Nathaniel In 57
Night of the wall In 63
On to Oregon In 70
Pappa Pellerin's daughter In
64
Prisoners in the snow In 48
September island In 61
Shadow of a bull In 80
Someplace else In 74
Take wing In 68
Timothy's Hawk In 45
The trail of the hunter's horn
In 49
Two in the wilderness In 77
Wagon Scout In 40
White water, still water In
44
Zeb In 38
Zeb and his family In 39

DECISION MAKING
Primary:
Beginning responsibility -
Being on time In 6
Beginning responsibility -
Getting ready for school
film In 7
The biggest bear In 12
Harold and the purple crayon
In 10

Nothing to do In 9
This for that In 8
Wee Gillis In 11

Intermediate:
Ann Aurelia and Dorothy
In 88
Annie, Annie In 91
The big decision In 87
A fair world for all In 93
Farm boy In 95
Florina and the wild bird In
89
A handful of thieves In 86
The hidden year of Devlin
Bates In 100
Ideas, thoughts and feelings
In 96
Joel spends his money In 92
Old Yeller In 94
A papa like everyone else
In 102
Peter's chair In 98
Swamp chief In 85
That bad Carlos In 99
Trouble after school In 97
The velvet room In 101
The very hot water bottle In
83
Where the lillies bloom In
90
A wish for little sister In
84

EMOTIONS
Primary:
Boy who wouldn't talk Ac 8
Dandelion Ac 10
The fairy doll Ac 13
Feelings about others Ac 11
Getting to know me Ac 12
How do you feel? Ac 14
I feel the same way Ac 18
Laugh and cry: your emotions
and how they work
Ac 7
Mr. Gumpy's outing Ac 9
Moods and Emotions Ac 17
Talking without words Ac 19
Whistle for Willie Ac 16
The year of the raccoon Ac
15

FRIENDSHIP
Primary:

Intermediate:

HONESTY

INDIVIDUAL DIFFERENCES

ROLE MODELS

TITLE INDEX

PUBLISHERS' LIST

Abelard-Schuman, Ltd.
257 Park Ave. S.,
New York, N.Y.   10010

Abingdon Press
201 Eighth Ave. S.,
Nashville, Tenn.   37202

AEVAC Inc.
500 Fifth Ave.
New York, N.Y.   10036

Aims Instructional Media Ser-
  vices, Inc.
P.O. Box 1010
Hollywood, Cal.   90028

American Heritage Publishing Co.
McGraw-Hill, Inc.
1221 Ave. of the Americas
New York, N.Y.   10020

American Library Association
50 East Huron St.
Chicago, Ill.   60611

Associated Film Services
3419 W. Magnolia Blvd.
Burbank, Cal.   91505

Association Press
291 Broadway
New York, N.Y.   10007

Astor-Honor, Inc.
48 East 43rd St.
New York, N.Y.   10016

Atheneum Publishers
122 E. 42nd St.
New York, N.Y.   10017

Athletic Institute
Merchandise Mart, Room 805
Chicago, Ill.   60654

Audio-Visual Ed. Center
University of Michigan
Ann Arbor, Mich.   48104

AVI Associate, Inc.
825 Third Ave.
New York, N.Y.   10022

Avid Training Systems
Division of PH and E Elec-
  tronics
Box 4263, 10 Tripps Land
East Providence, R.I.   02914

Avis Films
1408 W. Olive Ave.
Burbank, Calif.   91506

Beacon Press
25 Beacon St.
Boston, Mass.   02108

BFA Educational Media
2211 Michigan Ave.
Santa Monica, Calif.   90404

Bobbs-Merrill Company, Inc.
4300 West 62nd St.
Indianapolis, Ind.   46268

Bowmar Records
622 Rodier Drive
Glendale, Calif.   91207

Boy Scouts of America
Supply Division
North Brunswick, N.J.   08902

Bradbury Press, Inc.
  2 Overhill Rd.
  Scarsdale, N.Y.   10583

Bristol Myers
  630 Fifth Ave.
  New York, N.Y.   10020

Caddy, John D.
  Box 251
  Canoga Park, Calif.

Charles Cahill & Associates, Inc.
  P. O. Box 1010
  Hollywood, Calif.   90028

Cathedral Films, Inc.
  2921 W. Alameda Ave.
  Burbank, Calif.   91505

Celebrity Holdings, Inc.
  62 W. 45th St.
  New York, N.Y.   10036

Children's Press
  1224 W. Van Buren St.
  Chicago, Ill.   60607

Child's World
  1556 Weatherstone Lane
  Elgin, Ill.   60120

Churchill Films
  662 N. Robertson Blvd.
  Los Angeles, Calif.   90069

Citation Press
  Div. of Scholastic Book Ser-
    vices
  50 W. 44th St.
  New York, N.Y.   10036

Classroom Materials, Inc.
  93 Myrtle Drive
  Great Neck, N.Y.   11021

Cokesbury Service Dept.
  100 Maryland Ave. , NE
  Washington, D.C.   20002

Colonial Williamsburg Foundation
  Merchandising Dept.
  Williamsburg, Va.   23185

Continental Press, Inc.
  (No street)
  Elizabethtown, Pa.   17022

Coronet Instructional Films
  65 E. South Water St.
  Coronet Bldg.
  Chicago, Illinois   60601

Jarvis Couillard Associates
  1300 Esplanade Hollywood
    Riviera
  Redondo Beach, Calif.   90277

Coward, McCann & Geoghegan,
    Inc.
  200 Madison Ave.
  New York, N.Y.   10016

Creative Educational Society, Inc.
  515 N. Front St.
  Mankato, Minn.   56001

Creative Visuals, Inc.
  P.O. Box 1911
  Big Spring, Texas   79720

Criterion Books
  Abelard-Schuman, Ltd.
  257 Park Ave. S.
  New York, N.Y.   10010

Crowell, Thomas Y. , Company
  201 Park Ave. , S.
  New York, N.Y.   10003

Crown Publishers, Inc.
  419 Park Ave. S.
  New York, N.Y.   10016

Curriculum Materials Corp.
  1319 Vine St.
  Philadelphia, Pa.   19107

The John Day Company, Inc.
  257 Park Ave. , S.
  New York, N.Y.   10010

Delacorte Press
  Dist. by Dial Press, Inc. 1
    Dag Hammarskjold Plaza
  245 East 47th St.
  New York, N.Y.   10017

Demco Educational Corporation
2720 Fordem Ave.
Madison, WI.   53704

Dial Press, Inc.
1 Dag Hammarskjold Plaza
245 E. 47th St.
New York, N.Y.   10017

Dimension Films
733 N. La Brea Ave.
L.A., Calif.   90038

Discovery Teaching Films, Inc.
Box 424
Carmel Valley, Calif.   93924

Walt Disney Products
Educational Film Division
500 S. Buena Vista Ave.
Burbank, Calif.   91503

Dodd, Mead & Co.
79 Madison Ave.
New York, N.Y.   10016

Doubleday & Company, Inc.
501 Franklin Ave.
Garden City, N.Y.   11530

Doubleday Multimedia
1370 Reynolds Ave.
Santa Ana, Calif.   92705

Duell, Sloan & Pearce, Inc.
60 E. 42d St.
New York, N.Y.   10017

Dutton, E.P., & Co., Inc.
201 Park Ave. S.
New York, N.Y.   10003

Ealing Corp.
2225 Massachusetts Ave.
Cambridge, Ma.   02140

Edu-Cards Corp.
60 Austin Blvd.
Commack, N.Y.   11725

Education Media, Inc.
106 W. 4th Ave.
Ellenburg, Wash.   98926

Educational Activities Inc.
P.O. Box 392
Treeport, N.Y.   11520

Educational Films Library Assn.
17 W. Goth St.
New York, N.Y.   10023

Educational Games Company
Box 363
Peekskill, N.Y.   10566

Educational Projections Inc.
1319 Vine St.
Philadelphia, Pa.   19107

Educational Reading Services
64 E. Midland Ave.
Paramus, N.J.   07652

Educational Record Sales
157 Chambus St.
New York, N.Y.   10007

Educational Recordings of
      America, Inc.
Box 6062
Bridgeport, CT   06606

Eerdmans, Wm. B., Publishing
      Co.
255 Jefferson Ave., S.E.
Grand Rapids, Mich.   49502

Herbert M. Elkins Co.
10031 Commerce Ave.
Tujunga, Calif.   91042

Encyclopaedia Britannica Educa-
      tional Corp.
425 N. Michigan Ave.
Chicago, Ill.   60611

Enterprise Publications
20 N. Wacker Drive
Chicago, Ill.   60606

Eriksson, Paul S., Inc.
119 West 57th St.
New York, N.Y.   10019

Eye Gate House, Inc.
146-01 Archer Ave.
Jamaica, N.Y.   11435

Family Films Inc.
5823 Santa Monica Blvd.
Los Angeles, Calif. 90038

Farrar, Straus & Giroux, Inc.
19 Union Sq., W.
New York, N.Y. 10003

Field Enterprises Educational
Corp.
510 Merchandise Mart Plaza
Chicago, Ill. 60654

Filmfair, Inc.
10820 Ventura Blvd.
Studio City, Calif. 91604

Films/West Inc.
518 N. La Cieniga Blvd.
Hollywood, CA 90028

Filmstrip-of-the Month Clubs,
Inc.
355 Lexington Ave.
New York, N.Y. 10017

Fleet Press Corporation & Fleet
160 Fifth Ave.
New York, N.Y. 10010

Folkways Records & Service Corp.
165 W. 46th St.
New York, N.Y. 10036

Follett Publishing Company
P. O. Box 5705
Chicago, Ill. 60680

Format Films, Inc.
4741 Laurel Canyon Rd.
No. Hollywood, Calif. 91607

Friendship Press
Distribution Office, Box 37844
Cincinnati, Ohio 45237

Funk & Wagnalls Company
Dist. by Thomas Y. Crowell
Co.
666 5th Ave.
New York, N.Y. 10019

Garrard Publishing Company

2 Overhill Rd.
Scarsdale, N.Y. 10583

Gateway Products, Inc.
Bureau of A-V services
University of Arizona
Tucson, AZ 85721

Ginn & Co.
Statler Bldg.
Boston, MA 02117

Graded Press, Methodist Publishing House
201 8th Ave. S.
Nashville, TN 37203

Great Plains Instructional TV
Library
U. of Nebraska--P.O. Box
80669
Lincoln, NB 68501

Grosset & Dunlap, Inc.
51 Madison Ave.
New York, N.Y. 10010

Hale, E. M., & Company
1201 S. Hastings Way
Eau Claire, Wis. 54701

Jam Handy School Service, Inc.
2781 E. Grand Blvd.
Detroit, MI 48211

Harper & Row Publishers, Inc.
10 E. 53rd St.
New York, N.Y. 10022

Harcourt Brace Jovanovich, Inc.
757 Third Ave.
New York, N.Y. 10017

Harvey House, Inc.
5 S. Buckhout St.
Irvington-on-Hudson, N.Y.
10533

Hastings House Publishers, Inc.
10 E. 40th St.
New York, N.Y. 10016

Hawthorn Books, Inc.

260 Madison Ave.
New York, N. Y.   10016

Hill & Wang, Inc.
19 Union Sq. W.
New York, N. Y.   10003

Holiday House, Inc.
18 E. 56th St.
New York, N. Y.   10022

Holt, Rinehart & Winston, Inc.
383 Madison Ave.
New York, N. Y.   10017

Horizon Publishing
P. O. Box 625
Far Rockaway, N. Y.   11691

Houghton Mifflin Co.
2 Park St.
Boston, Mass.   12107

Hudson Photographic Industries,
   Inc.
Irving-on-Hudson, N. Y.   10533

Imperial Film Co. , Inc.
4404 S. Florida Ave.
Lakewood, Florida   33803

Inside Out Productions, Inc.
Dist. by Scholastic Books
Inquiry Dept.
900 Sylvan Ave.
Englewood Cliffs, N. J.   07632

Journal Films
909 W. Diversey Pkwy.
Chicago, Ill.   60614

Kleinberg Films
3890 Edgenien Drive
Pasadena, Calif.   91107

Knopf, Alfred A. , Inc.
Subs. of Random House, Inc.
Order Dept. , 457 Hahn Rd.
Westminster, Md.   21157

Learning Arts
P. O. Box 917
Wichita, Kansas   67201

Learning Corp. of America
711 Fifth Ave.
New York, N. Y.   10022

Leonard Peck Products
83 Clifford Drive
Wayne, N. J.   07470

Lerner Publications Company
241 First Ave. N.
Minneapolis, Minn.   55401

Lion Press
c/o Sayre Publishing, Inc.
52 Park Ave.
New York, N. Y.   10016

Lippincott, J. B. Company
E. Washington Sq.
Philadelphia, Pa.   19105

Little, Brown & Company
34 Beacon St.
Boston, Mass.   02106

Karl B. Lohmann, Jr.
1006 Sunset Court W.
Lafeyette, In   47906

Long Filmshole Service
7505 Fairmont Ave.
El Cerrito, Calif.   94530

Longman's, Inc.
72 Fifth Ave.
New York, N. Y.   10011

Lothrop, Lee & Shepard Co.
Div. William Morrow & Co.
6 Henderson Drive
West Caldwell, N. J.   07006

McGraw-Hill Book Company
1221 Ave. of the Americas
New York, N. Y.   10020

McGraw-Hill Testfilms
330 W. 42nd St.
New York, N. Y.   10036

McKay, David, Company, Inc.
750 Third Ave.
New York, N. Y.   10017

Macmillan Publishing Company,
  Inc.
  Riverside, N. J.   08075

Macrae Smith Company
  225 Fifteenth St.
  Philadelphia, Pa.   19102

Marsh Film Enterprises
  7900 Rosewood Drive
  Shawnee Mission, Kansas
    66205

Meredith Corp.
  Consumer Book Div.
  1716 Locust
  Des Moines, IA   50336

Messner, Julian, Inc.
  Simon & Schuster, Inc.
  1 W. 39th St.
  New York, N. Y.   10018

Mid-America Publishing Co.
  1511 Grand Ave.
  Des Moines, IA   50309

Miller-Brody Products, Inc.
  342 Madison Ave.
  New York, N. Y.   10017

Minnesota Mining and Manufactur-
    ing
  Medical Film Library
  2501 Hudson Rd.
  St. Paul, Minn.   55119

University of Minnesota
  Audio Visual Education Services
  Room 55 Westbrook Hall
  Minneapolis, Mn.   55455

Modern Learning Aids
  Director of Ward's Natural
    Science
  P. O. Box 302
  Rochester, N. Y.   14003

William Morrow & Company, Inc.
  105 Madison Ave.
  New York, N. Y.   10016

Martin Moyer Productions

900 Federal Ave.
Seattle, Wash.   98102

National Instructural TV Center
  Box A
  Bloomington, IN   47401

Nelson, Thomas, Inc.
  407 Seventh Ave. So.
  Nashville, Tenn.   37203

Newbery Award Records, Inc.
  342 Madison Ave.
  New York, N. Y.   10017

Norton, W. W. & Company, Inc.
  500 Fifth Ave.
  New York, N. Y.   10036

Oak Tree Press, Ltd.
  116 Baker St.
  London, England   W. 1

Obolensky   (See)
  Astor-Honor, Inc.
  48 East 43rd Street
  New York, N. Y.   10016

Oregon School of the Air Radio
    Station
  Box 5175
  Corvalis, Oregon   97331

Oxford Films, Inc.
  1136 N. Las Palmas Ave.
  Hollywood, CA   90038

Oxford University Press, Inc.
  16-00 Pollitt Drive
  Fair Lawn, N. J.   07410

Pantheon Books
  201 E. 50th St.
  New York, N. Y.   10022

Parents Magazine Press
  52 Vanderbilt Ave.
  New York, N. Y.   10017

Parnassus Press
  2721 Parker St.
  Berkeley, Calif.   94704

Phillips, S. G., Inc.
305 W. 86th St.
New York, N.Y.   10024

Platt & Munk Publishers
Division of Questor Education
Products Co., 1055 Bronx
River Ave.
Bronx, N.Y.   10472

Plays, Inc., Pubs.
8 Arlington St.
Boston, Mass.   02116

Popular Science-Outdoor Life
Books
355 Lexington Ave.
New York, N.Y.   10017

Port-A-Films
4180 Dixie Highway
Drayton Plains, Mich.   48020

Prentice-Hall, Inc.
Englewood Cliffs, N. J.   07632

G. P. Putnam's, Sons
200 Madison Ave.
New York, N.Y.   10016

Quist, Harlin, Books
Dial Press, 1 Dag Hammar-
skjold Plaza, 245 East 47th
St.
New York, N.Y.   10017

Rand McNally & Co.
Customer Service Dept.
Box 7600
Chicago, Ill.   60680

Random House, Inc.
Order Dept., 457 Hahn Rd.
Westminster, Md.   21157

RCA Records & Tape Sales
New York, N.Y.

Reader's Digest Press
Dist. by E. P. Dutton & Co.,
Inc.
241 Park Ave. S.
New York, N.Y.   10003

Regional Education TV Advisory
Council
155 W. Washington Blvd.
L. A., Calif.   90015

Reilly & Lee Company
Regnery, Henry, Company
114 West Illinois St.
Chicago, Ill.   60610

Ritchie, Ward, Press
3044 Riverside Drive
Los Angeles, Calif.   90039

Ronald Press Company
79 Madison Ave.
New York, N.Y.   10016

Rosenthal Products
1040 6th Ave.
New York, N.Y.   10018

St. Martin's Press, Inc.
175 Fifth Ave.
New York, N.Y.   10010

Scarecrow Press Inc.
52 Liberty St.
Metuchen, N. J.   08840

Warren Schloat Productions Inc.
Div. of Prentice-Hall, Inc.
115 Tompkins Ave.
Pleasantville, N.Y.   10570

Scholastic Book Services
Div. of Scholastic Magazines
50 West 44th St.
New York, N.Y.   10036

Science House, Inc.
59 4th Ave.
New York, N.Y.   10003

Scott Education Division
104 Lower Westfield Rd.
Holyoke, MA   01040

Scott, W. R., Inc.
33 Ave. of the Americas
New York, N.Y.   10014

Charles Scribner's Sons

597 Fifth Ave.
New York, N.Y.   10017

Seabury Press, Inc.
815 Second Ave.
New York, N.Y.   10017

Silver Burdett Company
Div. of General Learning Co.
250 James St.
Morristown, N.J.   07960

Simon & Schuster, Inc.
630 Fifth Ave.
New York, N.Y.   10020

Society for Visual Education, Inc.
Div. of the Singer Co.
1345 Diversey Parkway
Chicago, Ill.   60614

Steck-Vaughn Company
Box 2028
Austin, Texas   78767

Sterling Educational Films
241 E. 34th St.
New York, N.Y.   10016

Troll Associates
320 Route 17
Mahwah, N.J.   07430

United Transparencies Inc.
P. O. Box 688
Binghamton, N.Y.   13902

United World Films, Inc.
221 Park Ave. S.
New York, N.Y.   10003

University of California Press
2223 Fulton St.
Berkeley, Calif.   94720

Upjohn Co.
700 Portage Rd.
Kalamazoo, Mich.   49002

Urban Media Materials
P. O. Box 133
Fresh Meadows, N.Y.   11365

Vanguard Press, Inc.
424 Madison Ave.
New York, N.Y.   10017

Van Nostrand Reinhold Co.
450 W. 33rd St.
New York, N.Y.   10001

View-Lex, Inc.
Broadway Ave.
Holbrook, N.Y.   11741

Viking Press, Inc.
625 Madison Ave.
New York, N.Y.   10022

Visual Instruction Bureau
University of Texas
Austin, Texas   78712

Vocabulary Inc.
31 Center St.
Wilton, Conn.

Walck, Henry Z., Inc.
19 Union Square West
New York, N.Y.   10003

Warne, Frederick, & Company,
   Inc.
101 Fifth Ave.
New York, N.Y.   10003

Washburn, Ives, Inc.
McKay, David, Co., Inc.
750 Third Ave.
New York, N.Y.   10017

Watts, Franklin, Inc.
845 Third Ave.
New York, N.Y.   10022

Wayne State University
Audio Visual Production Center
680 Putnam
Detroit, MI   48202

Western Publishing Co., Inc.
850 Third Ave.
New York, N.Y.   10022

Weston Woods Studios
   Weston Woods St.
   Weston, CT   06880

Wff'n Proof Pubs.
   1490-UU South Blvd.
   Ann Arbor, MI   48104

White, David, Company
   60 East 55th St.
   New York, N.Y.   10022

White Saddle Books
   9144 Knauf Rd., Route 3
   Canfield, Ohio   44406

Whitman Publishing Company
   Western Publishing Co., Inc.
   1220 Mound Ave.
   Racine, Wis.   53404

H. Wilson Corporation
   555 W. Faft Drive
   South Holland, Ill.   60473

Wilson, H. W., Co.
   950 University Ave.
   Bronx, N.Y.   10452

Windmill Books, Inc.
   c/o Abelard-Schuman
   257 Park Ave. S.
   New York, N.Y.   10010

World Publishing Co.
   2080 W. 117th St.
   Cleveland, Ohio   44111